STEVE EMANUEL'S
BOOTCAMP FOR THE MBE:
EVIDENCE

EMANUEL BAR REVIEW ADVISORS

Steven L. Emanuel
Founder and Editor-in-Chief
Emanuel Bar Review

Joel Wm. Friedman
Jack M. Gordon Professor of Procedural Law and Jurisdiction and
  Director of Tulane ITESM Ph.D. Program
Tulane University Law School

James J. Rigos
Owner and Editor-in-Chief
Rigos Professional Education Programs

STEVE EMANUEL'S
Bootcamp
for the MBE

EVIDENCE

STEVEN L. EMANUEL

Founder & Editor-in-Chief,
Emanuel Bar Review
Member, NY, CT, MD and VA bars

www.aspenlaw.com

Emanuel Bar Review is a division of Aspen Publishers, a Wolters Kluwer company.

Aspen Publishers
Attn: Permissions Department
76 Ninth Avenue, 7th Floor
New York, NY   10011-5201

For information about Emanuel Bar Review, contact:

email: info@emanuelbarprep.com
phone: 1-888-MBE-PREP
fax: 781-207-5815
website: www.emanuelbarprep.com

Printed in the United States of America.

1 2 3 4 5 6 7 8 9 0

ISBN 978-0-7355-9740-2

TABLE OF CONTENTS

PREFACE

Dear *Bootcamp* enrollee:

This book consists mainly of a short outline on Evidence. I hope that you'll read the outline before you watch the online substantive lecture that's part of Steve Emanuel's Bootcamp for the MBE. If you can't read the outline before watching the online lecture, read it by way of review afterwards.

The outline section of this book does not contain any MBE-format questions — that's what we'll be doing in the 2-volume *"Emanuel's Essentials"* set of multi-choice questions and answers in context, which is part of your materials.

I have written the outline in an attempt to cover virtually all the substantive rules of law that the MBE examiners test in their Evidence questions, and to highlight the traps they set. I've tried to omit any topic or rule of law that doesn't seem to pop up on the MBE, no matter how important that topic may have been in your law school Evidence course.

The last part of the book consists of the 33 questions on Evidence extracted from our 200-Question Self-Assessment Test, together with our model answers to those questions. I hope that you will first take the Self-Assessment Test on a stand-alone basis, and that you will only consult the Contracts questions in this book as a means of reviewing after you've taken the Self Assessment Test.

Good luck, and see you online soon!

Steve Emanuel

Larchmont, NY

April 2010

EVIDENCE OUTLINE

TABLE OF CONTENTS
EVIDENCE OUTLINE

Chapter 4

HEARSAY

Chapter 5

HEARSAY EXCEPTIONS AND EXCLUSIONS

Chapter 6
CONFRONTATION AND
COMPULSORY PROCESS

Chapter 7
PRIVILEGES

Chapter 8
REAL AND DEMONSTRATIVE EVIDENCE,
INCLUDING WRITINGS

Chapter 9
OPINIONS, EXPERTS,
AND SCIENTIFIC EVIDENCE

Chapter 10
BURDENS OF PROOF, PRESUMPTIONS,
AND OTHER PROCEDURAL ISSUES

Chapter 11
JUDICIAL NOTICE

EVIDENCE OUTLINE

Like the MBE, this outline assumes that the Federal Rules of Evidence ("FRE") are in force as to all issues. "ACN" refers to "Advisory Committee Notes" to a particular Federal Rule of Evidence. "M&K" refers to Mueller & Kirkpatrick, Evidence hornbook (Aspen, 3d Ed., 2003). "McC" refers to McCormick on Evidence (West, 4th Ed., 1992). "Lilly" refers to Lilly, An Introduction to the Law of Evidence (West, 2d Ed., 1987).

CHAPTER 1
BASIC CONCEPTS

I. KINDS OF EVIDENCE

A. Direct versus circumstantial

1. **Direct evidence:** *Direct* evidence is evidence that, if believed, *automatically resolves* the issue.

    Example: W says, "I saw D strangle V." This is direct evidence on whether D strangled V.

2. **Circumstantial:** *Circumstantial* evidence is evidence which, even if believed, does not resolve the issue unless *additional reasoning* is used.

    Example: W says, "I saw D running from the place where V's body was found strangled, and I found a stocking in D's pocket." This is only circumstantial evidence of whether D strangled V, because it requires *reasoning* to get to the ultimate issue on which it's asserted to be probative. (The reasoning is that a person found running from a strangling, with a stocking in his pocket, is more likely to be the strangler than someone not running and/or without a stocking.)

3. **Probative value:** The probative value of direct evidence is not necessarily higher than circumstantial evidence, but the relevance of a particular item of circumstantial evidence tends to be more heavily *scrutinized* by the judge before being admitted. So on the MBE, you'll want to consider the issue of relevance more aggressively if the evidence is circumstantial.

B. Testimonial versus real and demonstrative:

1. **Testimonial:** *"Testimonial"* evidence arises when a witness, W, makes assertions in court. The fact-finder must *rely on W's interpretation* of W's sensory data, W's memory, etc.

2. **Real and demonstrative:** *"Real"* evidence is a thing *involved in the underlying event* (e.g., a weapon, document, or other tangible item). *"Demonstrative"* evidence is a tangible item that illustrates some material proposition (e.g., a map, chart, summary). The fact-finder may interpret either real or demonstrative evidence by *use of its own senses*, without intervening sensing and interpretation by a witness.

II. CONDITIONS FOR ADMITTING EVIDENCE

A. Relevant: Only *relevant* evidence may be admitted. FRE 402.

1. **Definition:** Evidence is "relevant" if it has "*any tendency* to make the existence of [a material] fact . . . *more probable or less probable than it would be without the evidence.*" FRE 401.

    a. **"A brick is not a wall":** To be relevant, a piece of evidence need not make a material fact more probable than not; it must *merely increase or decrease the probability (even by a small amount)* that the material fact is so. As the idea is often put, "A brick is not a wall." In other words, the piece of evidence merely has to be one brick in the wall establishing a particular fact.

       Example: D is on trial for murdering his wife V. She was unquestionably murdered, but D's defense is that someone else must have done it. The prosecution offers testimony by Wit, who says that 10 months before V's death, he saw D squeeze V's arm hard and say to V, "Don't make me hurt you" in a menacing voice. This evidence is relevant to whether D is the killer — it increases, even if by only a small amount, the likelihood that D is the killer. That is so because a jury could rationally conclude that a man who is known to have threatened his wife with physical harm is more likely to kill her than a man who is not known to have made such a threat to his wife.

    b. **Relevance of circumstantial evidence:** On the MBE as in real life practice, issues of relevance are much more likely in the case of *circumstantial* evidence than direct evidence. If the evidence is circumstantial, the judge will examine the proponent's underlying "hypothesis" about the logical significance of the evidence — that is, the asserted logical inference — in order to determine whether a reasonable jury could find that the evidence makes the point at issue more likely to be true than without the evidence. M&K, §4.1.

       Example: In a murder case in which the prosecution alleges that the victim's wife was the one who hired what the defense concedes was a contract killer, the prosecution offers evidence that the wife was the beneficiary of a large insurance policy on the victim's life. If the defense objects to this evidence on relevance grounds, the court will determine whether a reasonable jury could find that a spouse who is the beneficiary of a large insurance policy on the victim's life is more likely to procure the victim's death than, all other things being equal, a spouse who is not the beneficiary of such a policy.

       In this case, the court will certainly conclude that the answer is "yes" — the fact that the spouse is an insurance beneficiary may not make it very probable that the spouse is the one who hired the killer, but, based on general human experience, the existence of the policy certainly increases by at least some small amount the likelihood that the spouse was the hirer.

2. **Exclusion:** Even relevant evidence may be excluded if its *probative value* is *substantially outweighed* by the danger of: (1) *unfair prejudice*; (2) confusion of the issues; (3) misleading of the jury; or (4) considerations of undue delay, waste of time, or needless presentation of cumulative evidence. FRE 403.

       Example: D is on trial for murder. W testifies that she saw D run out of the house where the murder had just happened. The defense asks, "How do you know it was D you saw?" W answers, "Because I had seen his photo in the paper a few months previously while he was on trial for rape." (Assume that D was acquitted of that rape charge.) The defense objects. A court would likely exclude this answer on the grounds that under FRE 403, its probative value is substantially outweighed by the unfair prejudice to D from having the jury think he was a rapist.

B. **Offering testimonial evidence**

    1. **Lay (i.e., non-expert) witness:** The Federal Rules impose very few restrictions on the *competency* of lay (non-expert) witnesses, only these:

[1] W must take an *oath*, i.e., solemnly promise to testify truthfully. FRE 603.

[2] W must testify from *personal knowledge*. FRE 602.

[3] W should normally state *facts* rather than *opinions*. But under FRE 701, W may give an opinion if it is: (1) rationally based on his own perceptions; (2) helpful to the fact-finder; and (3) not based on scientific, technical or other specialized knowledge. See *infra*, p. 95.

a. **No rules of competence:** Most important for purposes of the MBE, there are *no general rules making any group of persons incompetent.* Under FRE 601, *everyone* is competent (except for judges and jurors in the case at issue, made incompetent by Rules 605 and 606 respectively).

    i. **Young children:** Thus whereas some states limit testimony by *young children,* the FRE contain no provision restricting such testimony. So even a very young child can testify under the FRE, as long as the child can take the oath to testify truthfully, and can speak from personal knowledge.

    ii. **Diversity cases:** But in a civil diversity case, the federal court must generally honor a state rule of competency, such as a rule disabling children from giving the kind of testimony in question.

2. **Experts:** It's easier for an *expert* to give an *opinion* than for a lay person to do so:

a. **Expert testimony:** The expert may give an opinion if:

❏ the opinion relates to "scientific, technical or other *specialized knowledge*";

❏ the opinion will assist the trier to "*understand the evidence* or determine a fact in issue"; and

❏ the testimony is based on *sufficient facts or data* and is the product of "*reliable* principles and methods," and W has *applied* those principles and methods *reliably* to the *facts of the case.*

FRE 702. For more about expert opinion testimony, see *infra*, p. 95.

3. **Ultimate issues:** At common law, opinions on "*ultimate*" issues are usually barred. But under FRE 704, even such opinions are allowed (except when they relate to the mental state of a criminal defendant).

C. **Making and responding to objections:**

1. **Making objections:**

a. **Not automatic:** Evidence will not be excluded unless the opponent makes an *objection.* FRE 103(a)(1).

b. **Timely:** The objection must be *timely* (usually before the witness can answer the question). FRE 103(a)(1).

c. **Specific:** The objection must be *specific* enough to explain to the trial judge and the appeals court the basis for it. *Id.*

d. **Taking of exceptions:** At common law, the opponent whose objection is denied must "*take exception*" in order to preserve the objection for appeal. But under the Federal Rules, exceptions are no longer necessary.

2. **Responding to objection:** If the judge sustains objection, the proponent must usually make an "*offer of proof*" in order to preserve his right to argue on appeal that the evidence should have been admitted. That is, proponent must make it clear to the court (either by the lawyer's

own explanation of what the evidence would be, or by questions and answers to the witness outside the jury's presence) what the evidence would be. FRE 103(a)(2).

D. Sequestration of witnesses: If a witness were permitted to observe the testimony of other witnesses for the same side, he would be able to tailor his testimony (perhaps by perjury) so that it matched this other testimony. To prevent this, the FRE give the trial judge the right (indeed, the obligation, if so requested by a party) to *exclude all other witnesses* from the courtroom while one witness is testifying. This is known as *sequestration of witnesses.*

   1. FRE 615: Sequestration is covered in FRE 615, which begins: "At the *request of a party* the court *shall order witnesses excluded* so that they cannot hear the testimony of other witnesses and it may make the order of its own motion."

      a. Exceptions: The Federal Rules recognize several *exceptions* to this principle of sequestration. Under FRE 615, the court may *not* order the sequestration of: "(1) a *party* who is a *natural person,* or (2) an *officer or employee* of a *party* which is *not a natural person* designated as its representative by its attorney, or (3) a person whose presence is shown by a party to be *essential* to the presentation of the party's cause, or (4) a person authorized by statute to be present."

      b. Mandatory: The most important thing to remember about the issue of sequestration on the MBE is that any party has the *absolute right* to require the judge to exclude all witnesses (other than witnesses covered by the above exceptions) from hearing other witnesses' testimony. So once a party makes the request for sequestration, the *judge does not have discretion to deny the request.*

CHAPTER 2

CIRCUMSTANTIAL PROOF: SPECIAL PROBLEMS

I. RELEVANT EVIDENCE SOMETIMES EXCLUDED

A. Possible exclusion: Normally, all relevant evidence is admissible. FRE 402. But even relevant evidence may be excluded if its probative value is "substantially outweighed by the dangers of unfair prejudice, confusion of the issues, or misleading the jury...." FRE 403. Special rules govern certain types of circumstantial evidence which have been found over the years to be so misleading or so prejudicial that they should be categorically excluded without a case-by-case balancing of probative value against prejudice. We cover these special rules here, especially the one dealing with "character evidence."

II. CHARACTER EVIDENCE

A. General rule: Evidence of person's "*character or a trait of character*" is, in general, *not admissible to prove that he "act[ed] in conformity therewith on a particular occasion."* FRE 404(a). (But there are some exceptions, discussed below, such as the right of a criminal accused to put on evidence of his good character.)

   Example 1: In a civil suit from an auto accident, P cannot show that D has the general character trait of carelessness, or even that D is a generally careless driver, to suggest that D probably acted carelessly in the particular accident under litigation.

   Example 2: In a criminal case, D is charged with robbing the First National Bank while wearing a red mask. As part of the prosecution's case in chief, the government seeks to prove that seven years ago, D was charged with (but never convicted of) embezzling $300 from his employer. The evidence is inadmissible because its only relevance is that it tends (somewhat weakly) to prove that "Because D is a thief, he's more likely to have stolen on the present occasion." Therefore, it is exactly what's forbidden by FRE 404(a): evidence of D's trait of character (character for thievery) offered to prove that D acted in conformity with that trait (i.e., stole) on the present occasion.

1. **Beware stand-alone prosecution evidence:** The principle that character evidence is not admissible to prove the person acted in conformity therewith means that on the MBE, you should be very *skeptical* of any *prosecution attempt* to show, in the prosecution's *case in chief*, that the defendant has some undesirable character trait, such as a capacity for lying or dishonesty. See the further discussion of this topic *infra*, p. 18 (par. (a)).

B. **Character is essential element of case:** A person's general character, or his particular character trait, is *admissible* if it is an *essential element* of the case. As the idea is sometimes put, character (or some particular trait of character) can be proved when it is *"in issue."*

> **Example:** P says that D has libeled him by calling him a liar. D may introduce evidence of P's character for untruthfulness, since that character trait is an essential element of D's defense that his statement was true.

1. **Illustrations:** True "character in issue" situations are *rare*. Civilly, *negligent entrustment* (D gave dangerous instrumentality, like a car, to one he should have known was of careless or otherwise bad character) and *defamation* (above example) are the most common. Criminally, *entrapment* (prosecution rebuts by showing D was "predisposed" to commit the crime) is the only instance.

2. **Appears on MBE:** But "character in issue" scenarios do get tested on the MBE from time to time. For instance, the examiners may give you a defamation scenario in which the *plaintiff's reputation* for some character trait may properly be proved because it is in issue, as in the above example.

    a. **MBE trap:** But be careful: The MBE examiners *know* that defamation suits are one of the few places where character can be in issue, and they may try to fool you into reflexively thinking that because the case involves defamation, any use of character evidence will be allowable — for instance, if *P* tries to introduce evidence about *D*'s bad character in a defamation suit, that typically *won't* be a valid use.

    > **Example:** P brings a defamation suit against D, alleging that D telephoned X (who D had heard was thinking of hiring P), and falsely told X that P was a dishonest employee who couldn't be trusted to keep his fingers out of the cash drawer. At the trial, P in his case in chief calls as his first witness Wit, who testifies, "I've known D for years, and I think he's just the sort of malicious and habitual liar who wouldn't hesitate to tell the kind of lie that P is alleging here."

    > Wit's testimony is inadmissible character evidence. Even though the case involves defamation, *D*'s character is not an essential element (only *P*'s is). Therefore, Wit's testimony is being offered for the classic forbidden "propensity" inference, that because D has lied in the past, he's more likely to have lied in the situation at issue here.

3. **Types of evidence:** When character is directly in issue, *all three types of character evidence* (specific acts, W's opinion, or the subject's reputation) are admissible.

    a. **Specific acts:** Thus FRE 405(a) says that when a character trait is "an essential element of a charge, claim, or defense," it may be proved by "specific instances of ... conduct."

Example: On the facts of the above libel example, since P's character for untruthfulness is properly in issue, D may introduce specific instances in which P lied (e.g., testimony by W, "D falsified his resume by saying he graduated from Harvard").

C. Other-crimes (and "bad acts") evidence in criminal cases: A consequence of the general rule against proof of character to prove action in conformity therewith is that in a criminal case, a prosecutor may *not* introduce evidence of *other crimes* committed by D for the purpose of proving that because D is a person of criminal character, he probably committed the crime with which he is now charged. Nor may the prosecutor show, for this purpose, D's prior *"bad acts"* that didn't lead to a conviction.

1. **FRE:** This rule is spelled out in FRE 404(b), which applies to both civil and criminal cases, and which says: *"Evidence of other crimes, wrongs, or acts is not admissible to prove the character of a person in order to show action in conformity therewith[.]"*

2. **Proof of other relevant factor:** But other crimes or bad acts by D *may* be admitted if this is done *not* to show D's general criminal disposition, or specific character trait, but to establish circumstantially *some other relevant fact.* Thus FRE 404(b) says that other crimes, wrongs or acts "may, however, be *admissible* for *other purposes,* such as proof of *motive, opportunity, intent, preparation, plan, knowledge, identity,* or *absence of mistake or accident."*

   This "other purposes" clarification is probably the most important thing to remember about other-crimes-or-bad-acts evidence on the MBE, since the other-purposes clause is *very frequently tested.*

   Here are some common elements that may be circumstantially proved by other crimes or bad acts that D has committed:

   a. **Signature:** If the perpetrator's identity is in doubt, proof that D has committed prior crimes or bad acts that are *so similar in method* that they constitute his *"signature,"* and thus identify him as the perpetrator of the crime charged, may be proved. This is often described as proof of *"modus operandi"* or "m.o." (See the discussion of proof of "identity," a more general concept, below, p. 13.)

   b. **Intent:** Other crimes or bad acts may be used to prove that D had the particular *intent* required for the crime charged. Generally, this is done to rebut D's contention that he did the act charged *innocently* or *unknowingly.*

      Example: D, a mail carrier, is charged with stealing a coin from the mails. The prosecution will be allowed to show that D also unlawfully possessed credit cards taken from the mails, in order to rebut D's argument that the coin accidentally fell out of an envelope and he planned to return it.

   c. **Plan:** Other crimes or bad acts can be used to prove an overall *plan* — typically a criminal plan — by the defendant. Proof of such a plan can in turn be relevant to other disputed issues, like intent (whether the defendant intended a particular act or result), identity (whether the perpetrator was the defendant), absence of mistake, motive, etc.

      Example: D is arrested while sitting outside the First National Bank in a red Ford Fiesta rented from the local Hertz office. He is charged with attempted robbery even though he never entered the bank on that occasion. He denies having any intent to rob the bank, and says he was about to make a cash deposit. The prosecution offers evidence that in two other recent robberies, D was seen shortly before the crime sitting in a red Fiesta whose decals indicated it was rented from Hertz.

      A court would likely conclude that the evidence of these other sightings is admissible to show that D had a "plan" of robbing banks while using a rented red Fiesta, making it likely that the present occasion was part of the same plan. This evidence makes it less likely that D's explanation — "I was there to make a deposit" — is true.

d. **Motive:** Other crimes or bad acts may be used to establish the defendant's *motive* for the crime charged.

Example: D, a nurse, is charged with stealing Demerol from the hospital where she works. The prosecution may show that D is a Demerol addict, to show that she had a motive to steal the drug. [*U.S. v. Cunningham*]

e. **Identity:** Other crimes or bad acts may be used to show *"identity,"* i.e., that D was really the perpetrator, if he disputes this.

Example: D is on trial for robbing a convenience store after midnight while wearing a mask similar to the very distinctive one worn in the movie "Clockwork Orange." The prosecution shows the jury a surveillance tape in which the masked robber can be seen wearing such a mask. D testifies that he wasn't the robber, and that the man in the tape must be someone else. The prosecution asks D, "Isn't it true that you were convicted two years ago of robbing another convenience store while wearing a 'Clockwork Orange' mask?" (It's true that D was so convicted.)

The question is proper — the evidence of D's conviction is available not only to impeach him, but as substantive proof that he robbed the other store wearing such a mask. The substantive admissibility results from the fact that the other crime tends to prove D's identity as the masked robber on the present occasion, and is thus non-character other-crimes evidence offered for "[an]other purpose[], such as proof of ... identity[.]" FRE 404(b).

f. **Knowledge:** Other crimes or bad acts may be used to show that someone had particular *knowledge* of some fact or event.

Example: D is charged with possession of and intent to distribute 8 ounces of cocaine found in a secret compartment in his suitcase as he re-entered the U.S. following a business trip to Bolivia. D's defense is that the drugs must have been put there by his personal assistant, Jean, who had traveled with him on the trip. D offers testimony by Winnie, a business colleage of D, that on an occasion prior to the Bolivia trip, when Winnie and Jean were traveling out of the country with D, Winnie saw Jean pack some marijuana into the same secret compartment of D's suitcase and smuggle it into the U.S.

Winnie's testimony is admissible, even though it demonstrates a prior bad act or crime by Jean. That's because it is being offered *not* to show that "because Jean smuggled before, she [not D] is more likely to be the smuggler this time," but rather, to show that Jean *knew about the suitcase's secret compartment* and how to use it for smuggling, making it more likely that she (not D) was the smuggler of the drugs this time.

g. **"Absence of mistake or accident":** The other-bad-acts evidence will often be admissible to prove that something that the defendant said was an accident was really a consequence or act which the defendant *intended*. This comes within 404(b)'s reference to *"absence of mistake or accident."*

Example: D's wife V dies after falling off a cliff. The prosecution claims that D pushed her off. D says it was an accident, that while D was standing by, V tragically tripped right at the edge of the cliff. The prosecution offers evidence that on three prior occasions in the last four years, D hit V in the face. This evidence is admissible notwithstanding FRE 404(a), because it tends to disprove D's statement that the fall was an accident.

h. **Not an exclusive list:** The catalog of permissible "other purposes" given in 404(b) ("motive, opportunity, intent, preparation, plan, knowledge, identity, or absence of mistake or accident") is *not exclusive*. So evidence of other bad acts or crimes by a person is allowable for *any* purpose that does not amount to "proof of character," even if the purpose is *not among the ones listed in 404(b)*.

   i. **Causation:** For instance, evidence of some bad act by a person might be admissible to provide an *alternative explanation* for what *caused* a disputed event.

   Example: P, a pedestrian, is injured when a car driven by X goes off the road and hits P. P sues D, the manufacturer, in strict product liability. D offers evidence that X smoked marijuana the night of the accident. This will be admissible notwithstanding 404(a), because it is relevant for a non-character purpose, by tending to show that the accident was caused by X's stoned driving rather than by a product defect.

3. **Other aspects of other-crimes evidence:**

   a. **No conviction:** The other crimes need not have led to a conviction. In fact, in federal courts interpreting the FRE, the existence of the other crime or bad act does not even have to be shown by a preponderance of the evidence. *Huddleston v. U.S.*

   b. **Acquittal:** Even the fact that the person was *acquitted* of the other crime will not necessarily require the exclusion of the other-crimes evidence if it's otherwise admissible under the FRE (e.g., because it's for an "other purpose" than proof of character).

      i. **Prejudice:** But always remember that FRE 403 bars evidence whose probative value is substantially outweighed by the *danger of unfair prejudice*. The fact that the person was acquitted will very much reduce the probative value of the evidence. So, for instance, if the present case is a criminal prosecution of D, a prior crime of which D was charged but acquitted will almost certainly be excluded under FRE 403 even if the present judge thinks that D in fact committed that other crime. (See more about FRE 403 in this other-crimes context shortly below.)

   c. **Use by D:** It's ordinarily the prosecution that uses the proof of the defendant's prior crime or bad act to show some element of the present crime. But *the defendant*, too, may show someone's past crimes or bad acts, to suggest that *it's that other person*, not the defendant, who committed the present crime.

   d. **Rule 403 balancing:** Where other crimes or bad acts committed by the accused in a criminal trial are offered by the prosecution to show signature, identity, intent, etc., the risk of *prejudice* is especially great. Therefore, the court will often exclude such evidence based on Rule *403* (*supra*, p. 8), which you'll recall allows exclusion if *the probative value of the evidence is "substantially outweighed by the danger of unfair prejudice[.]"*

   Example: D is on trial for burglarizing a house. He denies that he was the burglar. The prosecution offers evidence that on three prior occasions, D burglarized other houses but was never charged. A court is likely to hold that the risk of prejudice from this evidence — that is, the risk that the jury will say, "He burglarized other houses, so he probably burglarized this one" — substantially outweighs the limited probative value of this evidence as showing a "signature" or "m.o." or "plan" by D.

D. **Evidence of criminal defendant's good character:**

1. **Allowed:** Evidence offered by a *criminal defendant* that he has a *"pertinent trait of character"* is *allowed* by FRE 404(a)(1).

Example: D is charged with a violent murder. He will be allowed to show that he has the general character of being law-abiding. He will also be permitted to show the narrower trait of being peaceable. But he will not be allowed to show the narrow trait of being truthful, since this is not "pertinent" to the murder charge.

2. **Method of proof:** FRE 405(a) governs the *methods* of proving a character trait when the trait is provable, as it is for an accused's proof of a favorable trait. 405(a) allows the trait to be proved by both "testimony as to *reputation*" and "testimony in the form of an *opinion*."

    a. **No specific acts:** But 405(a) does *not* allow proof by "*specific instances* of [that person's] conduct." However, "on *cross-examination*, inquiry is *allowable into relevant specific instances of conduct.*"

        i. **D's proof of character and prosecution's response:** This means that if D, the accused in a criminal case, wants to put on evidence of his own favorable character trait, D must do so by reputation or opinion testimony, not by evidence of specific instances in which he exhibited that trait. FRE 405(a). Once D puts on such reputation or opinion testimony, the prosecution may then, on cross of the witness who is giving the reputation or opinion testimony, "inquir[e] ... into relevant specific instances of conduct." *Id.* That is, the prosecution may ask the witness something like, "Would it change your opinion of D's favorable trait of [X] to know that he once did [act Y]?"

            Example: D, charged with murdering V, pleads self-defense. He puts on testimony by W that in W's opinion, D is a peace-loving man. The prosecution may not put on a rebuttal witness to testify that the witness saw D start a fight with X. But, while W is on the stand, the prosecution may ask on cross, "Would it change your opinion to know that D once started a fight with X?" (The prosecution would have to have a good-faith basis for believing that D indeed started a fight with X.)

3. **Rebuttal by prosecution:** If D puts on proof of his good character, the prosecution may *rebut* this evidence in several ways:

    a. **Own witnesses:** The prosecution may do this by putting on its *own witness* (call her Wit) to say that D's character is bad. But Wit must do this by giving reputation or opinion evidence, not specific-acts evidence (a limit discussed further below in "No extrinsic evidence of specific acts").

    b. **Cross-examination:** The prosecution may *cross-examine* D's character witness to show that D's character is not really good. The prosecutor may even do this by asking the witness on cross about *specific instances* of bad conduct by D, provided that: (i) the prosecutor has a *good-faith basis* for believing that D really committed the specific bad act; and (ii) the specific bad act is *relevant* to the *specific character trait* testified to by the witness (so if W testified that D was honest, the prosecutor could not ask about specific bad acts showing D's character for violence). FRE 405(a), last sentence. Even an arrest that did not lead to a conviction may be brought up in cross-examination, if relevant to the character trait in question.

    c. **No extrinsic evidence of specific acts:** The prosecutor's ability to show specific bad acts is *limited to cross-examination.* She *may not put on extrinsic evidence* (e.g., *other witnesses* or documents) to prove that the specific acts took place, if the character witness denied that they did. Conversely, the defendant may not put on other witnesses to show that the specific act referred to by the prosecutor on cross-examination never took place. (For more about this no-extrinsic-evidence-of-specific-acts rule, see *infra*, p. 19.)

E. Character of victim: A criminal defendant may also put on evidence of a relevant *character trait of the victim*. Thus FRE 404(a)(2) allows "evidence of a pertinent trait of character of the victim of the crime offered by an accused[.]" (But this right is very limited in sexual assault cases, discussed below.)

1. **V's violent character:** So, for instance, the defendant in a homicide or assault case who claims that the victim was the *first aggressor*, may introduce evidence that the victim had a *violent character*. This is true even if D cannot show that he was aware of the victim's violent character at the time of the assault or murder.

    a. **Reputation or opinion, not specific acts by V:** But as with evidence of D's own favorable character trait, this character evidence must be in the form of reputation or opinion evidence, not evidence of *specific past acts* of violence by the victim.

2. **Rebuttal by prosecution:** Once the defendant introduces evidence of the victim's character for violence, the prosecution may then *rebut* this evidence by showing the victim's *peaceable* character. In fact, if the defendant claims that the victim was the first aggressor, the prosecution may put in evidence of the victim's peaceable character *even though the defendant does not put in proof of the victim's general character for violence*. FRE 404(a)(2).

3. **Rape or sexual assault:** At common law, the defendant in a *rape or sexual assault* case could usually show the victim's character for *unchastity*, to show that the victim *consented* on this particular occasion. But the Federal Rules, like most states, impose a *rape shield provision* to restrict evidence of the victim's past sexual conduct.

    a. **FRE:** That federal rape shield provision is Rule 412. The most general part of this provision (412(a)) says that subject to the narrow exceptions given in 412(b), the following types of evidence are *inadmissible*: (1) "Evidence offered to prove that any alleged victim *engaged in other sexual behavior*"; and (2) "Evidence offered to prove any alleged victim's *sexual predisposition*."

        Here are some of FRE 412's more important features (some of them covered in the exceptions to the general rules quoted above):

        i. **Conduct with persons other than D:** Most significantly, FRE 412 *prevents the defendant from introducing evidence of the victim's past sexual behavior with persons other than himself, when offered on the issue of whether there was consent.*

            Example: D is charged with the date rape of V, which is alleged to have occurred at the conclusion of their second date. D defends on the ground that V consented. D offers to prove that in the year prior to the event, V slept with two other men at the conclusion of her second date with them.

            This evidence is flatly inadmissible under FRE 412, since it's evidence "offered to prove that any alleged victim engaged in other sexual behavior," and the only possible exception in 412(b) allows other sexual behavior on the issue of consent only if the other behavior was between the victim *and the accused*, not between the victim and a third person.

        ii. **Reputation or opinion evidence:** Evidence relating to the victim's *reputation* for past sexual behavior, and *opinion* testimony about that past behavior, is *generally excluded* in federal trials. That is, in those comparatively rare instances where, under other provisions of FRE 412, evidence concerning the victim's past sexual behavior is admissible, that evidence must always take the form of proof of *specific acts*.

        iii. **Specific acts evidence:** *Specific acts* evidence concerning the victim's past sexual behavior is also *inadmissible* in criminal sexual-assault trials under FRE 412, unless it falls into one of three categories:

❑ **Source of semen or injury:** The evidence concerns the victim's past sexual behavior with persons other than the accused, offered by the accused on the issue of whether the accused was *"the source of semen, injury or other physical evidence."* FRE 412(b)(1)(A).

❑ **Consent:** The evidence relates to the victim's past sexual behavior *with the accused,* and is offered by the defense on the issue of whether the victim *consented,* or is offered by the prosecution. FRE 412(b)(1)(B).

❑ **Constitutional requirement:** The evidence is *constitutionally required* to be admitted. FRE 412(b)(1)(C).

> **Example of "constitutionally required":** D is on trial for raping V on their first date. The prosecution claims that after dinner, D took V (with her consent) to her apartment, where he then had sex with her against her will. D offers testimony by V's girlfriend W, who would testify that D and V knew each other slightly before the date, and that the day before the date, V said to W, "I find D very attractive, and who knows, I might get carried away at the end of the date as I've done before." This testimony would perhaps be barred by 412(a)(2) (since it's arguably being offered to prove the V's "sexual predisposition"). But excluding it would probably violate D's constitutional due process right to show highly probative evidence on the issue of consent, so it would come in under the "constitutionally required" provision of 412(b)(1)(C). See ACN to FRE 412, Subdiv. (b).

F. **Prosecution's evidence of criminal defendant's bad character:** If a criminal defendant uses FRE 404(a)(2) to put on evidence that the victim V has a particular bad character trait, the prosecution is then automatically entitled to put on evidence that the *defendant has that same bad character trait.* See FRE 404(a)(1).

1. **Evidence of D's violent character:** Most commonly, the way this happens is that D, charged with a crime of violence against V, uses FRE 404(a)(2) to put on evidence that *V had or has a violent character* (to show that V, not D, probably started the violence). The prosecution will then be entitled to show that *D, too, had a violent disposition.*

   a. **Not applicable if D uses source other than 404(a)(2):** But this special rule applies only where D's evidence about V's violent disposition is admitted under FRE *404(a)(2),* not where D relies on *some other evidentiary theory* for the evidence of V's violent tendencies.

   Example: D is charged with murdering V by stabbing him during a barroom brawl. D defends on the grounds of self-defense, and shows that before the altercation, he knew that V had a reputation for often drawing a knife without warning. D testifies that this reputation was on his mind when he drew his own knife first. Since D is offering the evidence about V's violent reputation not under FRE 404(a)(2) (i.e., not as a way of showing that V had a generally violent disposition, making it more likely that V started the fight), but rather as a way of supporting his self-defense claim (i.e., that he reasonably feared for his life), the prosecution will not be able to show that D, too, has a previously-demonstrated propensity for violence.

G. **Limited prosecution right to use:** Let's review, in one place, the scenarios in whch the *prosecution* can put in evidence of *D's bad character trait.* It's urgent for you to remember that the prosecution can put in evidence of D's bad character trait *only if one of three conditions* applies:

   [1] D has already offered evidence that he has the *opposite (good) trait,* so the prosecution is rebutting the defendant-offered evidence;

[2] D has already offered evidence that *V has a bad character trait*, and the prosecution is now rebutting this by showing that D has the *same bad trait*; or

[3] D is a *witness* whose veracity the prosecution is now trying to *impeach* by showing that D has a *character for lying* (see *infra*, p. 32).

(This list ignores the special case of evidence showing D's propensity for sexual misconduct; see *infra*, p. 20.)

a. **Stand-alone attempts:** Because of the limited circumstances in which the prosecution can show negative defendant-character traits, on the MBE you should be very *skeptical* of the admissibility of any attempt by the prosecution *during its case in chief* to show that the defendant has a particular bad character trait — in the prosecution's case in chief, it's very unlikely that the prosecution could be fulfilling any of the three conditions listed above (since it can't be rebutting evidence already offered by D as to his own good character trait or the victim's bad character trait, and it can't be impeaching the defendant if, as is likely, the defendant hasn't yet taken the stand).

Example: D is on trial for perjury. In the prosecution's case in chief, the prosecution calls as its first witness D's former boss, Bossman, who testifies, "D has always been a pathological liar." Is the testimony admissible?

No. Despite these very skeletal facts, we already know enough to know that the evidence cannot come in. The evidence is clearly not being used to impeach D's testimony (scenario [3] above), since the fact that Bossman is the first witness in the case for either side means that D cannot yet have given any testimony to impeach. Furthermore, the fact that Bossman is the first witness means that D cannot yet have offered evidence of his own truthfulness (scenario [1] above) or evidence of any victim's untruthfulness (scenario [2] above). So we're left with the reality that the prosecution is offering evidence of D's character trait for untruthfulness for the sole purpose of showing that on the occasion in question (when D made the statement on which the perjury prosecution is based), D is more likely to have lied than he would have been without this character evidence. And that's the core "inadmissible character-trait evidence" scenario covered by FRE 404(a) (*supra*, p. 10).

H. **Must be pertinent:** In all the above situations representing exceptions to the general rule excluding evidence of character traits offered to show action in conformity with, remember that FRE 404(a) *requires that the trait be "pertinent."* So whether it's a criminal defendant's proof of his own good character, the prosecution's proof of the defendant's bad character in rebuttal, or proof by either side of the character of the victim, the requirement of pertinence always applies. This means that on the MBE, character-trait evidence offered by the defendant or in rebuttal by the prosecution will often be inadmissible because not pertinent.

Example: D is charged with beating V almost to death in a barroom brawl. D (without ever taking the stand) presents a witness, Wit, who expresses the opinion that D is a truthful person. Even though FRE 404(a)(1) allows an accused to offer favorable character evidence about himself, Wit's testimony would be excluded because it is not "pertinent" to any issue in the case. That is, to the extent that any character trait of D is an issue, it would be the trait of peaceableness, not truthfulness.

III. METHODS OF PROVING CHARACTER: REPUTATION, OPINION AND PROOF OF SPECIFIC ACTS

A. FRE: Whenever proof of a character or character-like trait is allowed under FRE 404, FRE 405(a) says that the method of the proof may be by either *reputation* or *opinion* testimony.

    1. D's good-character evidence: So D in a criminal case can show his own good character by W's testimony that D has a good reputation for, say, honesty or non-violence, or by testimony that in W's opinion, D possesses these favorable character traits. (But D *can't* show *specific instances* of his own good character.)

        a. Rebuttal: If D makes this showing (thus "opening the door"), the prosecution may *rebut* by reputation or opinion evidence of D's poor character. Also, the prosecution may use *"specific acts" evidence* during its *cross* of D's good-character witnesses.

        Example: D, accused of starting a barroom fight in which V was killed, puts on testimony by Wit that in Wit's opinion, D is a peaceable person. The prosecutor may inquire into specific-past-acts by D in the cross of Wit. For instance, the prosecutor may ask Wit, "Would it change your opinion to know that D was booked by the Muni police on charges of starting a barroom fight in November of last year?"

            i. Good-faith basis for specific-act question: Before the cross examiner may ask about a specific act during cross, she must have a *"good-faith basis"* for believing that the specific act really occurred.

            Example: In above example, the prosecutor must have a good-faith basis for believing that D was charged with starting the November barroom fight.

            ii. No extrinsic evidence of specific acts: Also, the prosecution *can't* introduce *extrinsic evidence* of the specific acts. The prosecution may merely *ask the defense's witness* about whether the witness knows about those specific acts, and how the witness's knowledge of the existence of those acts would or wouldn't affect the witness's opinion or reputation testimony. The prosecution cannot put on its own witness (or introduce documents) to rebut the first witness's reputation or opinion testimony about D's good character. In other words, the prosecution must *"take the answer of the witness."*

            Example: In the above barroom-fight Example, the prosecutor must "take the answer of the witness" (Wit) on the subject of the prior's arrest's significance. So if Wit says, "No, it wouldn't change my opinion of D's peaceable character because I don't believe that that prior arrest happened" (or "No, because if the arrest happened, it wasn't valid") the prosecutor cannot: (1) introduce the police arrest record from the prior arrest into evidence; or (2) put on Wit-2, to testify that the prior arrest occurred.

    2. Character of victim: Just as a criminal defendant may show his own relevant good character by reputation or opinion testimony, he or she may show a *pertinent trait of character of the victim* by such reputation or opinion evidence.

        Example: In murder case where D claims self-defense in the killing of V, D can put on W to testify, "In my opinion, V was always the kind of guy who liked to start fights." (But W could not testify to particular fights that V started; this would be forbidden "specific acts" evidence.)

        a. Rebuttal: Again, the prosecution in rebuttal can not only use reputation or opinion, but can also refer to specific acts on cross.

3. Proof for "other purposes": Where a party (usually the prosecution) is using D's prior crimes or bad acts for some "other purpose" (e.g., identity, knowledge, etc.), this proof *can* be by "specific acts." And it can be by extrinsic evidence, i.e., not just by cross-examination of the opposing witness.

> **Example:** D is charged with robbing the Second Nat'l Bank on Sept. 1 while wearing a blue ski mask and a yellow raincoat. D denies that he's the one who did it. The prosecution can show that on June 21, D robbed the First Nat'l Bank wearing this distinctive garb, because the apparel is so unusual as to amount to a "signature." And this proof can be in the form of direct testimony by a police detective who investigated the June 21 robbery. (In other words, the prosecution can use "extrinsic evidence" of the prior specific act by D that establishes this non-character-trait "signature" fact.)

IV. PAST SEXUAL ASSAULT OR CHILD MOLESTATION BY D

A. FRE allows: Under FRE 413, if D is accused of a sexual assault, evidence that D has *committed a sexual assault in the past* is *admissible*, and may be considered *on any relevant matter*.

> **Example:** If D's charged with raping V, the prosecution may show that 20 years ago, D raped someone else. The prosecution may also argue, "The fact that D raped before means he's extra likely to have committed the present rape."

1. Child molestations; civil suits: Similar rules (FRE 414 and 415) allow: (i) proof that D previously *molested a child* to be introduced in his present molestation trial, and (ii) proof of D's prior sexual assaults or child molestations to be introduced in *civil* proceedings where P claims D sexually assaulted or molested P.

V. HABIT AND CUSTOM

A. Generally allowable: Evidence of a person's *habit* is admissible under the FRE to show that he *followed this habit on a particular occasion*. "Habits" are thus to be distinguished from "character traits" (generally disallowed as circumstantial evidence that the character trait was followed on a particular occasion).

1. Text of FRE 406: Here's the text of FRE 406, allowing habit evidence: "Evidence of the *habit of a person or of the routine practice of an organization*, ... regardless of the presence of eyewitnesses, is relevant to *prove that the conduct of the person or organization on a particular occasion was in conformity with the habit or routine practice.*"

2. Three factors: There are three main factors courts look to in deciding whether something is a "habit" or merely a trait of character:

a. Specificity: The more *specific* the behavior, the more likely it is to be deemed a habit.

> **Example:** If V is killed when his car is hit on the railroad tracks, his estate will be allowed to show that he had almost always stopped and looked before crossing those tracks every day — this conduct will be a "habit," because it is very specific. But V's general "carefulness" will be found to be a character trait, not a habit, and will thus not be admissible to show that he probably behaved carefully at the time of the fatal crossing.

b. Regularity: The more *"regular"* the behavior, the more likely to be a habit. "Regularity" means "ratio of reaction to situations." (So something that X does 95% of the time she's in a particular situation is more likely to be a habit than something X does 55% of the time in that situation.)

c. **Unreflective behavior:** The more *"unreflective"* or *"semi-automatic"* the behavior, the more likely it is to be a habit.

Examples: Using a left-hand turn signal is probably a habit because it's semi-automatic. Going to temple for the Sabbath each Friday night is probably not a habit, because it requires conscious thought and volition.

3. **Driving practices:** On the MBE, the most common area for testing the admissibility of habit evidence is a person's *driving practices*. The two prior examples are illustrations. Especially when the driving practice in question is part of a *daily commute*, the chances are good that the three above factors — specificity, regularity and unreflective behavior — will all point toward the practice's being a habit.

Example: Passenger is killed when the car she is riding in is struck by a car driven by D. In a civil suit by Passenger's estate against D, an issue is whether Passenger was wearing her seat belt at the time of the accident. The estate offers testimony by Will, that Will commuted with Passenger to work nearly every weekday during the year prior to Passenger's death, and that Passenger almost always fastened her seatbelt.

This evidence will be *admissible* as habit evidence, tending to show that Passenger acted in conformity with this habit on the occasion in question. Fastening one's seatbelt is quite *specific* behavior; fastening it each time one gets in the car for a daily commute is quite *regular* behavior; and fastening it is relatively *unreflective*, semi-automatic, behavior. In fact, the evidence will be admissible even if the accident in question did not happen during a daily commute, since the court would almost certainly hold that the relevant habit is "fastening one's seatbelt when one rides as a passenger," not merely the more specific "fastening one's seatbelt when one rides as a passenger during a daily commute."

B. **Business practices:** Notice that FRE 406, quoted above, allows evidence of the *routine practice* of an *organization*, to show that that practice was *followed by the organization on a particular occasion.* The "organizational routine practice" aspect of FRE 406 is tested more often on the MBE than the "habit of an individual" aspect.

1. **Practices relating to copies and mailings:** On the MBE, the organizational-routine-practice provision is frequently tested in the context of proving (1) that a *copy found in the business' files* of a document sent to someone else is *authentic*, or (2) that a particular letter was *mailed* on a particular day.

Example: A business may prove that a particular letter was mailed by showing that it was the organization's routine practice to mail, that same day, all letters placed in any worker's "outgoing mail" box, and that the letter in question was placed in such a box.

VI. SIMILAR HAPPENINGS

A. **General rule:** Evidence that *similar happenings* have occurred in the past (offered to prove that the event in question really happened) is generally *allowed*. However, the proponent must show that there is *substantial similarity* between the past similar happening and the event under litigation.

1. **Accidents and injuries:** Thus evidence of past similar injuries or accidents will often be admitted to show that the same kind of mishap occurred in the present case, or to show that the defendant was negligent in not fixing the problem after the prior mishaps. But the plaintiff will have to show that the conditions were the same in the prior and present situations.

2. **Past safety:** Conversely, the defendant will usually be allowed to show due care or the absence of a defect, by showing that there have *not* been similar accidents in the past. How-

ever, D must show that: (1) *conditions were the same* in the past as when the accident occurred; and (2) had there been any injuries in the past, they would have been *reported* to D.

VII. SUBSEQUENT REMEDIAL MEASURES

A. General rule: The Federal Rules (like the common law) *do not allow* evidence that a party has taken *subsequent remedial measures*, when offered to show that the party was negligent, or was conscious of being at fault. The theory behind this rule is that if such evidence were admissible, people would be disincentivized from correcting dangers, and the world would be a less safe place.

   1. Text of FRE 407: This ban on subsequent-remedial-measures evidence is imposed by FRE 407: "When, after an injury or harm allegedly caused by an event, measures are taken that, if taken previously, would have made the injury or harm less likely to occur, evidence of the *subsequent measures* is *not admissible* to prove *negligence, culpable conduct*, a *defect* in a *product*, a *defect* in a *product's design*, or a *need for a warning* or instruction."

      Example: P trips on D's sidewalk. P may not show that just after the fall, D repaved the sidewalk, for the purpose of proving that D acknowledged the sidewalk's dangerousness.

B. Other purposes: But subsequent remedial measures may be shown to prove *elements other than culpability or negligence.* Thus the second sentence of 407 states that the rule of exclusion does not apply when evidence is offered for "*another purpose*, such as proving *ownership, control*, or *feasibility of precautionary measures, if controverted*, or *impeachment*." This list is illustrative, *not exhaustive.*

   1. Availability of alternative: For instance, such measures may be used to rebut the defendant's claim that there was *no safer way* to handle the situation.

   2. Control: Similarly, if the defendant claims that he *did not own or control* property involved in an accident, the fact that he subsequently repaired the property may be shown to rebut this assertion.

      Example: P, a pedestrian, is injured when a car driven by D runs off the road and strikes P. In the litigation, D defends on the ground that (1) the car had faulty brakes; and (2) the car was not owned by D, as proved by the fact that it was registered to X, D's brother. P may prove that after the accident, D hired a gas station to repair the brakes — this is offered not to prove D's culpability, but to prove that the person with real control (if not registered ownership) of the car was D, not X.

C. Product liability: The FRE *apply* the no-subsequent-remedial-measures rule to *product-liability* cases, just as to negligence cases. FRE 407 says that subsequent-measures evidence is not admissible to prove "negligence, culpable conduct, *a defect in a product, a defect in a product's design,* or a need for a *warning* or instruction."

      Example: P, the owner of a single-engine plane made by D, crashes in the plane when it runs out of fuel because water has gotten into the fuel tanks. P sues D on a products liability defective-design theory. P's theory is that a defective design of the fuel tanks allowed condensation to form inside the tank. In support of this theory, P offers evidence that shortly after this and two other similar accidents, D redesigned the fuel tanks to make such condensation less likely. Under FRE 407, this evidence will be inadmissible.

VIII. LIABILITY INSURANCE

A. General rule: Evidence that person carried or did not carry *liability insurance* is *never* admissible on the issue of whether he acted "negligently or otherwise wrongfully." FRE 411.

1. **Other purposes:** But evidence of the existence or non-existence of liability insurance is admissible for *purposes other than proving negligence or fault*, "such as proof of *agency, ownership, or control, or bias or prejudice* of a witness." FRE 411.

   Example: Employee sometimes uses his own car to carry out the job he does for Employer. One day, Employee gets into an accident while driving the car, injuring P. P sues Employer on a *respondeat superior* theory. In P's case in chief, P offers records from the insurance company that writes liability insurance on Employee's car, to show that the policy is billed to, and paid for by, Employer.

   The evidence is admissible. Although the evidence here is evidence that Employee "was or was not insured against liability" (the initial phrase of FRE 411), the evidence is not being offered "upon the issue whether the person acted negligently or otherwise wrongfully," which is all FRE 411 forbids. Instead, the evidence is being offered "for another purpose, such as proof of agency[.]" That is, although the fact that Employer pays for the liability insurance does not conclusively prove that on the occasion in question Employee was traveling on Employer's business, it certainly demonstrates that Employee often used the car as an agent of Employer, making it more likely that he did so on the present occasion.

   a. **Usually wrong answer:** Most MBE questions that involve admissibility of liability insurance will feature these "other purposes." Thus on the MBE, FRE 411 is more likely *not* to apply than to apply.

      Example 1: In the above example, the fact that Employee's car insurance is paid for by Employer is admissible, and is not barred by FRE 411.

      Example 2: The fact that W, a witness for D in a tort suit, works for D's liability insurance company, could be admitted to show bias on W's part, and is not barred by FRE 411.

IX. SETTLEMENTS AND PLEA BARGAINS

A. **Settlements:** The fact that a party has offered to *settle* a *claim* may *not* be admitted on the issue of the claim's validity or amount. FRE 408. Because the details of Rule 408 are often tested on the MBE, here's the entire text of the Rule:

   "Rule 408. Compromise and Offers to Compromise

   (a) Prohibited uses. Evidence of the following is *not admissible* on behalf of any party, when offered to *prove liability for, invalidity of, or amount of a claim that was disputed as to validity or amount*, or to *impeach* through a prior inconsistent statement or contradiction:

      (1) *furnishing* or *offering* or promising to furnish — or *accepting* or offering or promising to accept — a *valuable consideration* in *compromising or attempting to compromise the claim*; and

      (2) *conduct or statements* made in *compromise negotiations* regarding the claim, except when *offered in a criminal case* and the negotiations related to a *claim by a public office or agency* in the exercise of regulatory, investigative, or enforcement authority.

   (b) Permitted uses. This rule does not require exclusion if the evidence is offered for purposes not prohibited by subdivision (a). Examples of *permissible purposes* include proving a witness's *bias or prejudice*; negating a contention of *undue delay*; and proving an effort to *obstruct a criminal investigation* or prosecution."

1. **"Claim that was disputed as to validity or amount"**:   An important and non-obvious aspect of FRE 408 is that it applies only if the claim is one that is *"disputed as to validity or amount."* So if there is *no controversy* about the claim's validity or amount, an offer by the obligor to settle it for less than face value will not become inadmissible because of 408.

2. **No "claim" at all**: Similarly, if there has been no *"claim"* at all, 408 won't apply. So, for instance, an MBE fact pattern may involve a promise by one party to make good on a contractual or moral obligation (e.g., a promise make a repair for free) without the other's having asserted a "claim," in which case proof of the promise won't be barred by 408.

   Example: P, a patient, has liposuction performed on her thighs by D, a plastic surgeon. P is not completely happy with the resulting contour, and expresses that lack of complete satisfaction to D. However, P does not indicate in any way that she believes that D has failed to adhere to professional standards or to deliver a contractually-promised result; nor does she indicate that she is even considering suing D. D says, "Come back on April 1, and I'll re-do the work for free." D then re-does the procedure, but sends P a bill for the re-do. P doesn't pay, D sues for the bill, and P offers to testify to the above promise of a free re-do.

   P will be permitted to give this testimony, notwithstanding FRE 408. That's because when D made the statement, P had not asserted any "claim," let alone one "disputed as to validity or amount"; therefore, D's offer was not one "offering ... to furnish ... a valuable consideration in compromising ... [such a] claim," as 408 requires.

   a. **Incorrect "distractor"**:   This requirement of a "claim" will more often allow you to *eliminate a wrong choice* than to identify the right one — the examiners love to give you a fact pattern where the out-of-court statement is either inadmissible hearsay or admissible because the hearsay rule doesn't apply, but where one of the choices mentioning settlement offers is wrong because there's no claim (or no dispute).

3. **Collateral admissions of fact**:   Another often-tested point on the MBE is that *collateral admissions of fact* made during the course of settlement negotiations are *covered* by FRE 408 (and thus inadmissible), in the same way that the settlement offer itself is inadmissible. This is so because admissible under FRE 408(a)(2)'s exclusionary rule extends to *"conduct or statements* made in *compromise negotiations* regarding the [disputed] claim."

   Example: Pedestrian is injured by Driver. Pedestrian hires a lawyer, who threatens to sue Driver if the claim is not settled. Driver then visits Pedestrian in the hospital and says, "Don't sue. I know I was drunk when I ran over you, so I'll pay you $5,000 in damages." Driver's statement about being drunk — even if severed from the pay-damages part — is inadmissible under FRE 408. That's because the statement about being drunk was a "statement[] made in compromise negotiations regarding the claim." So even though the statement wasn't itself part of the settlement offer, it's still kept out by 408.

   a. **Speaker denies the claim's validity:**   This principle that "collateral admissions of fact" are excluded (and the more general one that settlement discussions are excluded) applies *even where the speaker makes other statements denying the validity of the claim.*

   Example: In a two-car auto-accident case, P, the driver of one car, sues D, the driver of the other. P offers to testify that after the suit was filed, D said to P, "I don't agree that I was the cause of the accident. But I guess I was speeding, so I'm willing to pay you $1,000 to cover your medical bills, in order to get rid of what I think is a nuisance case." D's reference to his speeding is excluded by FRE 408, because it was made in conjunction with a settlement offer. That's so even though in the same statement, D denied legal responsibility.

Note: In the above example, notice also that FRE 408's exclusion of the collateral statement of fact about being drunk applies even though the offer is an offer to *pay medical expenses* (independently excludible under FRE 409; see p. 25 below). That is, a statement can be simultaneously excludible as an offer to pay medical expenses under FRE 409 and an offer of settlement under 408. But the distinction matters sometimes, such as here, because collateral statements of fact are excluded by 408, whereas under 409 only the offer to pay medical expenses, not collateral statements made in conjunction with it, are made excludible (see p. 25). If *either* rule applies, the collateral statement cannot come in.

4. **Other purposes:** But settlement offers may be admissible to prove issues *other than liability*.

   Example: If W testifies on behalf of D in a civil suit, the fact that W received money from D in settlement of a related claim may be admitted to show that W is biased in favor of D and against P.

B. **Offers to plead guilty:** The fact that the defendant has *offered to plead guilty* to a crime (where no actual guilty plea ever resulted) may *not* be shown to prove that D is guilty or is conscious of his guilt. In fact, FRE 410(4) excludes not only the offer to plead guilty, but any other *statement* made in the course of plea discussions with the prosecutor, from being used against the defendant.

   1. **Withdrawn plea:** Similarly, the fact that D made a guilty plea and then later *withdrew it* may not be admitted against D in the ultimate trial.

   2. **Later civil case:** The plea offer or withdrawn plea, and the accompanying factual admissions, are also not admissible in any *later civil case*. FRE 410(4).

C. **Offer to pay medical expenses:** Offers or promises to pay "*medical, hospital* or similar *expenses* occasioned by an *injury*" are not admissible to prove *liability for the injury*. FRE 409.

   Example: After an accident in which D's car hits P (and before P has made a claim or filed a suit against D), D says to P, "I'll pay your medical expenses." D's statement is inadmissible, under FRE 409, to prove that D recognized that he was responsible for the injury. And that's true even though P has not made any claim, and there has been no discussion of settlement or release.

   1. **Does not cover collateral statements of fact:** But only offers of payment, *not collateral admissions of fact*, are excluded. This is an important distinction between offers to pay medical expenses and offers to settle (since under FRE 408, factual admissions related to settlement offers, like the offers themselves, are inadmissible).

      Example: D says to P, "I'm paying your medical expenses because if I hadn't been drunk that night, I wouldn't have hit you." D's statement, if offered by P, may be edited and then admitted to show D's drunkenness, but not to show that D paid the expenses.

      Note: Notice that a collateral factual admission, even though it's not barred by FRE 409, will still have to avoid the *hearsay rule* (perhaps via an exception or exclusion) in order to be admissible. Thus in the above example, if P is trying to prove that D was drunk, the statement will be admissible, but only because it avoids being hearsay on account of the exclusion for statements by a party opponent (see *infra*, p. 46).

CHAPTER 3

EXAMINATION AND IMPEACHMENT OF WITNESSES

I.   FLOW OF EXAMINATION

A. Four stages: The examination of a witness goes through up to four stages:

    1. Direct: First, the party who called the witness engages in the *direct* examination.

    2. Cross: After the calling side has finished the direct exam, the other side may *cross-examine* the witness.

    3. Re-direct: The calling side then has the opportunity to conduct *re-direct* examination.

    4. Re-cross: Finally, the cross-examining side gets a brief opportunity to conduct *re-cross*.

II.   DIRECT EXAMINATION

A. Leading questions: Generally, the examiner *may not ask "leading questions"* on direct.

    1. Definition: A leading question is one that *suggests to the witness the answer desired by the questioner*.

        Example: Auto negligence suit by P against D. Question by P's lawyer to P: "Was D driving faster than the speed limit at the time he hit you?" This is leading, since it suggests that the questioner desires a "yes" answer.

    2. Hostile witness: Leading questions are allowed on direct if the witness is *"hostile."* The *opposing party* will almost always be deemed hostile; so will a witness who is shown to be biased against the calling side, as well as a witness whose demeanor on the stand shows hostility to the calling side.

III.   CROSS-EXAMINATION

A. Leading questions: Leading questions are usually *permitted* during cross-examination. FRE 611(c).

    1. Exception: But if the witness is biased in favor of the cross-examiner (e.g., one party is called by the other and then "cross"-examined by his own lawyer), leading questions are not allowed.

B. Scope: Cross is ordinarily *limited* to the *matters testified to on the direct examination*. See FRE 611(b): "Cross-examination should be limited to the *subject matter of the direct* examination and matters affecting the *credibility* of the witness."

    1. Discretion: But the court has *discretion* to *allow* cross-examination that goes beyond the scope of direct. See the continuation of FRE 611(b), which, following the sentence quoted above, says, "The court may, in the exercise of discretion, permit inquiry into *additional matters as if on direct examination.*"

        a. Rarely allowed: However, on the MBE, when the fact pattern is designed to test your knowledge of the scope of cross, the fact pattern will normally be constructed so that the court would almost certainly *not exercise its discretion* to allow questions going beyond the scope of direct. Typically, the examiners will do this by having the plaintiff call a hostile witness (perhaps the defendant) and ask about a *very limited topic* on direct; then, the lawyer for the defendant tries to dramatically expand the topics covered during a non-hostile "cross." You should answer that questions are not permissible because the direct examiner has the right to *control presentation of her case.*

Example: Plaintiff brings a medical malpractice case against Defendant, a surgeon who operated on Plaintiff's infected foot. The suit claims that Defendant's poor sanitary controls during the operation caused the infection to become worse, leading to the amputation of the foot. Plaintiff calls Defendant as Plaintiff's first witness. Except for questions identifying Defendant, Plaintiff's lawyer's only question to Defendant is, "Did you perform an operation on Plaintiff's foot?" After Defendant answers "yes," Plaintiff's lawyer turns the witness over to Defendant's lawyer, who asks Defendant, "If you hadn't operated on the foot, was the existing infection so severe that the foot would likely have to have been amputated anyway?" Plaintiff's lawyer objects.

The court should *sustain* the objection. The basic rule is that questions on cross should be limited to ones that fall within the subject of direct, or that go to the witness's credibility. The question here obviously does not relate to credibility, and goes well beyond the limited scope of direct. While the judge theoretically has discretion to permit the question, the judge is extremely unlikely to exercise that discretion so as to allow the question here, since allowing it would deeply disturb Plaintiff's tactical decision to use Defendant's testimony only to establish that Defendant was the surgeon. (Defendant can and should give the "foot would have been amputated anyway" testimony as part of *Defendant's case in chief* rather than on cross during Plaintiff's case.)

C. Credibility: The witness's *credibility* may always be attacked on cross-examination.

IV. RE-DIRECT AND RE-CROSS

A. Re-direct: Re-direct is generally limited to those aspects of the witness's testimony that were *first brought out during cross*.

B. Re-cross: Similarly, re-cross is generally limited to matters newly brought up on the re-direct.

V. PRESENT RECOLLECTION REFRESHED AND OTHER TECHNIQUES

A. Present recollection refreshed: If the witness's memory on a subject is hazy, *any item* (picture, document, weapon, etc.) may be *shown to the witness to refresh his recollection*. This is the technique of *"present recollection refreshed."*

1. **Allowed in federal courts:** The present-recollection-refreshed technique is not expressly authorized anywhere in the FRE. But nothing in the FRE forbids it, and courts applying the FRE *allow it*, subject to the restrictions described below.

2. **Not evidence:** The item shown to the witness is *not evidence* at all; it is merely a *stimulus* to produce evidence in the form of testimony from the witness. So even a document that contains *completely-inadmissible testimony*, such that the document could never itself be admitted, may serve as the basis for present recollection refreshed.

    Example: D is charged with bank robbery. The prosecution offers testimony by Officer, who investigated the crime. While testifying, Officer consults notes prepared by him during the course of his investigation. D's lawyer objects on the grounds that the notes haven't been introduced into evidence, that the notes can't be introduced because they are hearsay not within any exception, and that D should therefore be barred from testifying in reliance on their contents.

    As long as the court is satisfied that D is testifying from his own now-refreshed recollection, the fact that the notes haven't been introduced into evidence (and can't be, because of hearsay problems) is irrelevant.

3. **Abuse by "reading aloud":**   The witness really has to testify from her refreshed recollection. So if the item shown to the witness is a *document* (and it does not have to be a document — it could be a tangible object) and the trial judge concludes that the witness is *really reading* the document on the stand instead of testifying from his now-refreshed recollection, she may order the testimony *stricken.*

4. **MBE tip:** On the MBE, sometimes the concept of present-recollection-refreshed will supply the answer, even though the question, including the correct choice, *never explicitly mentions the technique.* Just remember that except for the "abuse by reading aloud" problem just discussed, pretty much anything can be shown to the witness to stimulate recall, since the thing shown does not become evidence.

5. **Adversary's right to inspect document:**   When an examiner uses a document to refresh a witness's recollection, it would be unfair to prevent that examiner's adversary from seeing the document, or from using that document during the subsequent cross-examination of the witness. Therefore, FRE 612 — in the FRE's only reference to the present-recollection-refreshed technique — gives the non-calling party's lawyer some *access* to any document used to refresh the witness's recollection.

    a. **Text of FRE 612:**   Here's how FRE 612 does this: "[I]f a witness uses a writing to *refresh memory* for the purpose of testifying, either (1) *while testifying*, or (2) *before testifying*, if the court in its *discretion* determines it is necessary in the interests of justice, an adverse party is entitled to have the writing *produced* at the hearing, to *inspect* it, to *cross-examine* the witness thereon, and to *introduce in evidence* those portions which *relate to the testimony* of the witness.

    b. **Writing consulted during testimony:**   So where the witness *consults* the refreshing document *during the course* of the witness's testimony, the non-calling party *automatically* gets three rights under FRE 612:

        ❏   the right to *inspect* the document;

        ❏   the right to *cross-examine* the witness *based on the document*; and

        ❏   the right to *introduce into evidence* the *portions* of the document that *relate to the testimony of the witness.*

    c. **Writing consulted before testimony:**   But where the witness has merely consulted the document *before taking the stand* — i.e., as part of *pretrial preparation* — FRE 612 does *not* give the opposing party any automatic right to inspect the document, to cross-examine based on it, or to introduce it. Instead, as the rule puts it, the opposing party gets these rights only "if the court in its *discretion* determines it is *necessary in the interests of justice*[.]"

B. **Argumentative and misleading questions:**   A question will be stricken if it is either *argumentative* or *misleading*:

1. **Argumentative:**   An *argumentative* question is one which tries to get the witness to agree with counsel's interpretation of the evidence. It is more common on cross than on direct, and usually has an element of badgering the witness.

2. **Misleading:**   A *misleading* question is one that assumes as true a fact that is either *not in evidence* or is in dispute. It usually has a "trick" aspect.

    Example: "When did you stop beating your wife?" is misleading if there is no or disputed evidence of wife-beating, since any answer by W will be an implicit admission that he has beaten her.

VI. EXAMINATION BY COURT

A. General rule: The trial judge may call her own witnesses, and may question any witness (whether called by the judge or by a party). FRE 614(a) and (b).

VII. IMPEACHMENT — GENERALLY

A. Five types: There are five main ways of *impeaching* a witness, i.e., of destroying the witness's credibility:

(1) by attacking W's general *character* for truthfulness (e.g., by showing past crimes, past bad acts, or bad reputation, if these bear on veracity);

(2) by showing a *prior inconsistent statement* by W;

(3) by showing that W is *biased*;

(4) by showing that W has a *sensory or mental defect*; and

(5) by other evidence (e.g., a second witness's testimony) that *contradicts* W's testimony.

B. Impeaching one's own witness: The Federal Rules have *abandoned* the common-law rule prohibiting impeachment of one's own witness. FRE 607 says that "The credibility of a witness *may be attacked by any party,* including the *party calling the witness.*"

> **Example:** In a civil car-accident case in which P was injured by a car driven by D, P may call D as part of P's case in chief, and may then attack D's credibility during the "direct" examination. The same would be true if P called D's wife, W, who witnessed the accident — even though W is a non-party called by P, P can attack W's credibility.

VIII. IMPEACHMENT BY PRIOR CRIMINAL CONVICTION

A. Federal Rule: The Federal Rules allow limited use of *prior criminal convictions* to impeach the witness. Under FRE 609:

1. Crime involving dishonesty or false statement ("*crimen falsi*"): If the crime included as an element *dishonesty or false statement* (called "*crimen falsi*", Latin for "crimes of falsehood"), *it may always be used to impeach W* (subject to the special scrutiny of "older-than-10-year" convictions discussed *infra*, p. 31).

a. Misdemeanors and felonies: This rule allowing admission of crimen falsi applies *regardless of whether the crime was a misdemeanor or a felony.* This is done by FRE 609(a), which says: "For the purpose of attacking the character for truthfulness of a witness, ... (2) evidence that any witness has been convicted of a crime *shall be admitted regardless of the punishment,* if it can readily be determined that *establishing the elements of the crime* required *proof or admission of an act of dishonesty or false statement by the witness.*"

b. Not excludible under FRE 403: Where the conviction is for a *crimen falsi*, the judge *does not even have discretion to exclude* the evidence under *FRE 403*, which normally allows exclusion of evidence whose probative value is substantially outweighed by the danger of unfair prejudice. So even if the judge thinks admission of the particular conviction would be deeply unfair, the judge *must* admit it for impeachment.

> **Example:** D is charged with robbing a 7/11. D takes the stand and claims mistaken identity. The prosecutor asks D, "Isn't it true that nine years ago, when you were 18 years old, you pled guilty to the misdemeanor of embezzling $80 from your employer, and were sen-

tenced to probation?" The question is proper (and must be answered). The judge must admit it even if the judge believes that the probative value of the evidence is extremely low due to the small sum, D's youth at the time, and the lack of any real bearing on D's character for truthfulness, and even if the judge believes that the resulting prejudice to D will be great and unfair.

c.   **Illustrations of** *crimen falsi*:   Here are some crimes that constitute *crimen falsi*: *Perjury; false statement; criminal fraud; embezzlement; taking property by false pretenses; counterfeiting; forgery; filing false tax returns.*

i.   **Perjury:**   The MBE examiners are especially fond of using *perjury* convictions as the underlying crime. That's because the very definition of perjury (knowingly making a false statement under oath) means that the crime cannot be committed without "an act of dishonesty or false statement by the witness." This means that the examiners can test you on the automatic nature of the *crimen falsi* branch of 609(a), without telling you anything about the underlying crime, just the fact that there was a perjury conviction. And it also means that the examiners don't have to tell you whether the crime was a misdemeanor or felony.

Example: D is charged with possession of marijuana, found on the front seat car in which D was a passenger when stopped. The prosecution calls the owner of the car, who testifies that the marijuana was not his. D's lawyer now asks the owner, "Isn't it true that three years ago, you were convicted of misdemeanor perjury charges?" The owner denies this, whereupon D's lawyer offers into evidence proof of such a conviction.

The question and proof of conviction are admissible. That's because perjury is always a crime the conviction of which "required proof or admission of an act of dishonesty or false statement by the witness" (609(a)(2)). Therefore, the conviction is admissible even though (1) it was a misdemeanor rather than a felony (i.e., "regardless of the punishment," in the language of 609(a)(2)), and (2) regardless of the relationship between its prejudicial impact and its probative value. (Note that 609(a)(2) says that the conviction "shall be admitted," and doesn't say, as the non-*crimen-falsi* language of 609(a)(1) does, that the judge should determine whether the probative value outweighs the prejudicial effect.)

ii.   **MBE tip:**   If the MBE examiners give you a fact pattern in which the witness's criminal conviction is being offered for impeachment, and the examiners *don't tell you whether the conviction was for a misdemeanor or felony*, that's probably a *tipoff* that the crime was a "*crimen falsi*" (act of dishonesty or false statement), because only in the *crimen falsi* situation is the felony / misdemeanor distinction *irrelevant*. (As we'll see in a moment, in the non-*crimen falsi* scenario, misdemeanor convictions are *never* admissible under 609, whereas *felony* convictions may or may not be admissible based on the judge's determination of the balance between probative value and prejudicial effect.)

Example: If the above example were an MBE fact pattern, the examiners would likely not tell you whether the perjury conviction was for a felony or misdemeanor. That should be a tipoff to you to consider whether the pattern involves a *crimen falsi*, in which case the court must admit the proof of the conviction without even considering the trade-off between probative value and danger of prejudicial impact.

d.   **Other theft crimes:**   In courts interpreting FRE 609(a), *theft* crimes other than false pretenses and embezzlement have generally been held *not* to be *crimen falsi*. So *shoplifting, robbery, burglary* and *receiving stolen goods* aren't *crimen falsi* for purposes of the FRE.

e.   **Don't look to underlying facts:**   Under FRE 609(a), the court may *not* treat a crime as *crimen falsi* unless it is *defined so as to require proof of dishonesty or false statement* — it's not enough that the defendant *actually behaved in a deceitful way.*

Example: D sees V on the street, lures her into a secluded alleyway by falsely telling her he has a message for her from her husband, and then robs her. Since robbery is not defined to include dishonesty or false statement as an element of the crime, D's robbery conviction is not a *crimen falsi* under FRE 408(a) even though D committed this particular crime in a deceitful manner.

2. **Felony:** If the crime was a *felony* that is not a *crimen falsi*, i.e., not involving dishonesty or false statement, admission of it for impeachment purposes is not so cut-and-dried. And in this scenario, the test for admission varies depending on whether the witness being impeached by proof of his own conviction is a criminal defendant or a non-defendant witness:

    a. **W is a criminal defendant:** If the witness is *the defendant in a criminal case*, the conviction may be used *only if the court "determines that the probative value of admitting this evidence outweighs its prejudicial effect to the accused."* FRE 609(a)(1) So if the prejudicial effect is "the same" as the probative value, or slightly greater, the evidence can't come in.

    b. **Witnesses other than an accused:** But if the witness is *not* a criminal defendant (e.g., a prosecution witness, a witness for a criminal defendant, or any witness in a civil case), the witness *gets no special protection against impeachment* as a criminal defendant witness does. Instead, the *general balancing test of FRE 403* applies, allowing the prior conviction to be excluded only if the person opposing its introduction shows that the conviction's probative value is *"substantially outweighed by the danger of unfair prejudice."*

    c. **Comparison:** So *criminal defendants get more protection* against being impeached by their own convictions than all other witnesses do. Thus if the judge thinks the prejudicial effect and the probative value from the conviction are about the same, the judge must let in the conviction against the non-criminal-defendant witness, but not let it in against the criminal-defendant witness.

3. **Other misdemeanors:** If the crime was a *misdemeanor not involving dishonesty or false statement*, the fact of conviction may *not* be used for impeachment at all under FRE 609. (The misdemeanor might still be admissible for impeachment when brought out on cross of the witness under FRE 608(b) as a prior bad act, as discussed *infra*, p. 33.)

4. **Old convictions:** If *more than 10 years* have elapsed from *both* the conviction and the prison term for that conviction, the conviction may not be used for impeachment unless the court determines that there are "specific facts and circumstances" that make the *probative value* of the conviction *substantially outweigh* its prejudicial effect. FRE 609(b). So the presumption is against the admissibility of such "old" convictions. This makes it *much harder* to get more-than-10-year-old convictions into evidence.

5. **Ineligible convictions:** Certain types of convictions are excluded by special rules:

    a. **Pardon:** If W was *pardoned*, based on a finding of *innocence*, the conviction may never be used. (If the pardon was because W was rehabilitated, it may be used for impeachment only if W has been convicted of a subsequent felony.) FRE 609(c).

    b. **Juveniles:** A *"juvenile adjudication"* of D may not be used to impeach him. FRE 609(d).

6. **Must be actual conviction:** FRE 609 applies only where there has been an *actual conviction*. Where the witness has committed a crime that has not resulted in a conviction, the underlying criminal act does not qualify for the special treatment of FRE 609, and is merely a "bad act" to be evaluated pursuant to FRE 608 (*infra*, pp. 32-33). The MBE examiners will sometimes try to trick you by using an unconvicted bad act, and then giving you a choice saying something like "admissible because it involved dishonesty or false statement" — dishonesty

or false statement matters only under FRE 609 as applied to an actual conviction, not under FRE 608 as applied to an unconvicted bad act.

> **Example:** Wit appears as a character witness for D in a civil case. P's lawyer asks Wit on cross, "Isn't it true you embezzled $80 from your last employer, Boss?" Wit denies this. (Assume that Wit really did this, but was never charged.) P's lawyer now offers testimony by Boss that Wit did this embezzlement. The fact that this conduct was a crime of dishonesty or false statement doesn't bring the question or the underlying act within FRE 609, since Wit was never convicted. Instead, the question and Boss' testimony are to be evaluated under the "bad acts" provision of FRE 608 (under which the question to Wit was proper under 608(b), but the testimony of Boss was inadmissible as extrinsic character evidence under that same section).

IX. IMPEACHMENT BY PRIOR BAD ACTS

A. Federal Rule: The Federal Rules basically follow the common-law approach to impeachment by the witness's *"prior bad acts."* See FRE 608(b). 608(b) is so often-tested on the MBE that it's worth reading and more or less memorizing:

> *"Specific instances* of the *conduct of a witness,* for the purpose of attacking or supporting the witness's *character for truthfulness, other than conviction of crime* as provided in Rule 609, *may not be proved by extrinsic evidence.* They may, however, in the *discretion* of the court, if *probative of truthfulness or untruthfulness,* be *inquired into on cross-examination* of the witness (1) concerning the witness's *character for truthfulness or untruthfulness,* or (2) concerning the character for truthfulness or untruthfulness of *another witness* as to which character the witness being cross-examined has testified."

1. May bring out on cross: The cross-examiner may, subject to the discretion of the court, bring out the fact that the witness has committed the prior bad acts *even though these have not led to a criminal conviction.*

> **Example:** W testifies for the defense in a murder trial. On cross, the prosecution asks him, "Isn't it true that you lied on your job application by falsely stating that you had never used drugs?" This is allowable under 608(b) — it is "prior bad act" evidence tending to show that the witness is not worthy of belief. And it's admissible even though W was not convicted of the falsehood.

a. Applies to any witness: This principle that the cross examiner may bring out unconvicted acts of the witness during cross applies to *any* witness, whether the witness is giving substantive testimony or merely impeaching another witness.

> **Example:** Car accident, in which P asserts that D drove negligently. D takes the stand and testifies that he drove carefully on the occasion in question. P offers rebuttal testimony by Wit, D's neighbor, that D has a reputation in the neighborhood for being a liar. D's lawyer asks Wit on cross, "Isn't it true that when you were looking for a job last year, you falsified your resume?" (Assume that the lawyer has a good-faith basis for asking this.) The questioning is proper, in the discretion of the court. The fact that the examiner is asking about specific acts of misconduct doesn't matter, nor does the fact that Wit was called merely to give reputation or opinion testimony bearing on the truthfulness of another witness (D), rather than giving "occurrence" testimony.

2. Probative of truthfulness: However, only prior bad acts that are *probative of the truthfulness* of the witness may be asked about.

> **Example 1:** W's prior act of lying on a job application or embezzling from an employer could be asked about, because each of these is probative of W's truthfulness. But the fact that W

killed his wife and was never tried could not be asked about, because this act does not make it more likely than it would otherwise be that W is now lying.

> **Example 2:** In a civil car-accident case, P claims that D was speeding at the time of the accident. D, as a witness on direct in his own case, denies speeding. P's lawyer proposes to ask D on cross, "Isn't it true that you've gotten two speeding tickets in the last 3 years?" D's lawyer objects.
>
> The question is not proper. The fact that D sped on two occasions doesn't bear on his general character for truthfulness. And it doesn't shed any real light on whether he's telling the truth on this particular occasion, since he could well have been driving within the speed limit this time even though he's sped in the past. (It's really inadmissible character-trait evidence, implying, "He sped before, therefore he's probably lying when he says he didn't speed this time"; such evidence is inadmissible under FRE 404(a) and (b); see *supra*, p. 10.)

3. **No extrinsic evidence:** Most importantly, the prior bad acts *must* be introduced solely through the *cross-examination, not* through *extrinsic evidence.* This rule is imposed by the first sentence of FRE 608(b): "*Specific instances* of the conduct of the conduct of a witness, for the purpose of attacking or supporting the witness's character for truthfulness, *other than conviction of crime* as provided in Rule 609, *may not be proved by extrinsic evidence.*" (As used in the just-quoted sentence, "extrinsic evidence" means "evidence other than from the mouth of the witness whose credibility is being attacked or supported.") As the concept is often expressed (though not stated this way in the FRE), the examiner must *"take the answer of the witness."*

    This rule against extrinsic evidence of bad acts, but allowing cross-examination into bad acts, is very frequently tested on the MBE, so be on the lookout for situations in which it applies.

    > **Example:** Car accident case. P calls Wit-1, who testifies that he saw D speeding just before the accident. On cross by D's lawyer, Wit-1 is asked, "Didn't you lie on your job application?" Assuming that the lawyer has a good-faith basis for believing Wit-1 really did this (see *infra*, immediately below), this question is *proper.*
    >
    > But D's lawyer must "take the answer of the witness." Therefore, if Wit-1 denies having lied on the application, D's lawyer cannot: (1) show Wit-1 the false job application and ask him to explain why a statement on it isn't false; (2) present testimony by Wit-2 that Wit-1 lied on the application (though Wit-2 could give opinion or reputation testimony about Wit-1's bad character for truth, such as "I think Wit-1 is generally a liar" or "Most people around town think Wit-1 is a liar." The only thing to which 608(b)'s ban on extrinsic evidence applies is evidence of "specific acts.")

4. **Good-faith basis:** Before the prosecutor may ask a witness about a prior specific bad act, he must have a *good-faith basis* for believing that the witness really committed the act.

5. **Discretion of court:** All questions about prior bad acts are in the *discretion of the court.* The extent to which the questioner has a good-faith basis for believing W really committed the act will, of course, be one factor the court normally considers.

X. IMPEACHMENT BY OPINION AND REPUTATION REGARDING CHARACTER

A. **Federal Rules:** The Federal Rules allow the credibility of a witness to be attacked by evidence that is in the form of *opinion or reputation evidence,* even if that evidence comes in the form of *evidence by a second witness about the first witness's credibility.* FRE 608(a) says:

"The credibility of a witness may be attacked or supported by evidence in the form of *opinion* or *reputation*, but subject to these limitations: (1) the evidence may refer only to character for *truth-fulness or untruthfulness*, and (2) evidence of *truthful* character is admissible only after the character of the witness for truthfulness *has been attacked* by opinion or reputation evidence or otherwise."

1. **Reputation:** So W1's credibility may be impeached by testimony from W2 that W1 has a *bad reputation for truthfulness*.

2. **Opinion:** Similarly, W2 may state his own *opinion* that W1 is untruthful.

3. **No specific instances:** But W2 may not describe *specific instances* of conduct by W1 that led to W1's bad reputation for truthfulness, or to W2's opinion that W1 has a character for untruthfulness. This is forbidden "extrinsic evidence" of a witness's character; see *supra*, p. 33.

4. **Truthfulness only:** W2 must testify *only* about W1's character trait for *truthfulness*, not W1's general bad character, or his character for something not having to do with veracity (e.g., violence or peaceableness).

5. **Opening issue:** As soon as a criminal defendant takes the stand, she opens herself up to this kind of evidence, even if she does not affirmatively state that she is a truthful person.

XI. IMPEACHMENT BY PRIOR INCONSISTENT STATEMENT

A. **General rule:** W's credibility may generally be impeached by showing that on some point covered by W's testimony, W has made a *prior inconsistent statement.* And, subject to the non-impeaching party's rights described below, p. 35, the impeaching party can prove the prior inconsistent statement by *extrinsic evidence*, and need not just "take the answer of the witness" as the impeacher must do for impeachment by prior-bad-acts evidence (*supra*, p. 33).

> **Example:** D is on trial for burglary of a farmhouse. The prosecution calls Wit, who testifies, "I saw a man I recognized as D coming out of the farmhouse at about the time of what turned out to be the burglary." On cross, D's lawyer asks Wit, "Didn't you tell the police that you didn't recognize the person you saw?" Wit says, "No, I never told the police that." D's lawyer may show Wit — and read to the jury — a properly-authenticated tape recording made by a police investigator of an interview with Wit, in which Wit says, "I didn't recognize the person coming out of the farmhouse." The recording is not substantively admissible to prove that Wit didn't see or recognize D at the farmhouse (that would be hearsay not within any exception), but the recording *is* admissible to impeach Wit by showing he made a prior inconsistent statement.

B. **Special rules from FRE 613:** FRE 613 makes it easier than it was at common law for the examiner to impeach by means of the witness's prior inconsistent statement:

1. **Not required to be shown to W:** Most importantly, the prior statement *does not have to be shown to the witness* — or its contents disclosed to him — *prior to or during the questioning.* 613(a). On the other hand, 613(a) says that "on request, the same shall be *shown or disclosed to opposing counsel*."

> **Example:** W is called by P in a car accident case, and testifies that "I saw the accident, and D was travelling 70 mph." D's lawyer knows that W previously signed an affidavit that D was travelling "no more than 60," and handed the affidavit to D's investigator. D's lawyer can ask W on cross, "Have you ever signed an affidavit that D was 'traveling no more than 60'?" If W says, "No I didn't," D can excuse the witness and introduce the affidavit later (see Par. (2) below). D's counsel does not have to disclose to the witness at the time of the question that

counsel has such an affidavit, or show W a copy. (But if P's counsel asks for it, D's counsel must show the affidavit to him.)

2. **"Extrinsic evidence," and the "explain or deny" and "interrogate" rules:** FRE 613 contains special rules limiting the questioner's ability to prove that W1 made a prior inconsistent statement by *"extrinsic"* evidence, i.e., by evidence other than W1's admitting that he made the statement (e.g., testimony by W2 about hearing W1 make the statement, or admission of a copy of W1's prior written statement). FRE 613(b) says that such extrinsic proof can only be made where *two requirements* are satisfied:

❑ The witness who made the prior inconsistent statement must be "afforded an opportunity to *explain or deny*" it; and

❑ The opposite party (the proponent of the testimony of the witness being impeached by the prior inconsistent statement) must be given "an opportunity to *interrogate* the witness [who made the inconsistent statement] thereon."

(But both of these requirements may be dispensed with if "the interests of justice otherwise require.")

These two requirements mean that, as a practical matter, if W1 is to be impeached by a prior inconsistent statement, the impeacher will have to be sure that, after the extrinsic evidence is presented, W1 remains *physically available* to "explain or deny" it and to be interrogated about the statement by W1's proponent.

> **Example:** W testifies in an auto accident case, "D was travelling over 70 mph." W is excused by P, and leaves the country. D presents testimony by Officer that when Officer interviewed W two days after the accident, W said "D wasn't going more than 60 mph." Since W is no longer available to explain or deny making this statement, or to be interrogated about the alleged statement by P's counsel, FRE 613(b) prevents Officer's testimony.

a. **Doesn't apply to hearsay declarants:** The "opportunity to explain or deny" rule does not apply when the prior inconsistent statement is offered against a *hearsay declarant*, rather than against a "live" witness. In other words, when FRE 613(b) says that "extrinsic evidence of a prior inconsistent statement by a witness is not admissible unless the witness is afforded an opportunity to explain or deny the same," the rule is referring only to a witness *at the trial*, not one who made an out-of-court statement being proved at trial. The MBE examiners will sometimes try to trick you into thinking that the "opportunity to explain or deny" rule applies to hearsay declarations.

> **Example:** Accident case, in which Pete claims that Dave was speeding at the time of the accident. Pete offers, as her first witness, Wanda, who testifies, "Right after the accident, I heard Fred say, 'Look at that idiot Dave — he was speeding and he just crashed.'" Dave's lawyer asks Wanda on cross, "Isn't it true that the day after Fred allegedly saw the accident, Fred told you, 'Dave wasn't really speeding, I just made that up'?" Pete objects on the grounds that Fred is not present, and therefore doesn't have an "opportunity to explain or deny" the statement.
>
> The objection will be overruled. Fred is a hearsay declarant, not a live witness. Therefore, Dave was entitled to attempt to impeach Fred's credibility by asking questions of Wanda designed to expose Fred's inconsistent statement. FRE 613(b)'s "opportunity to explain or deny" rule does not apply when the prior inconsistent statement is offered against a hearsay declarant like Fred, only when the statement is offered to impeach a "live" witness.

3. **Can be used by calling witness:** By the way, as you would expect, the right to use the prior inconsistent statement to impeach the witness also applies while the witness is *still on the stand.* And less-obviously, the right to use it applies *even when it's used by the party who called that witness* (i.e., it's being used on direct), as long as this is a situation in which the calling party is truly attempting to impeach the witness (e.g., the witness has given testimony that is either unhelpful to the calling party and/or has taken the calling party by surprise).

> **Example:** Auto accident case, in which P claims that D was speeding when the accident occurred. P's lawyer calls Wit, who P expects to testify that he saw D speeding at the time in question. But Wit says, "No, I saw D driving just before the accident and he wasn't speeding." While Wit is still on the stand, P's lawyer offers a properly-authenticated tape recording in which Wit can be heard telling an investigator working for P that Wit saw D speeding.

> This tape recording is admissible as a prior inconsistent statement used to impeach Wit. The fact that Wit was called by the impeaching party (P) doesn't matter, and the fact that Wit is still on the stand doesn't matter. (By the way, the tape recording is not substantively admissible to prove D was speeding — it's hearsay not within any exception, so it's admissible *only* to impeach Wit's testimony.)

XII. IMPEACHMENT FOR BIAS

A. **Generally allowed:** The FRE, like all jurisdictions, allow proof that the witness is *biased.* W may be shown to be biased in favor of a party (e.g., W and P are friends or relatives), or biased against a party (e.g., W and D were once involved in litigation).

1. **Motive for false testimony:** One form of bias that may always be brought out is W's *interest in the outcome.*

> **Example:** If W is an expert, the fact that he is being paid a fee for his testimony is allowed, as tending to show that he has an interest in having the case decided in favor of the party retaining him.

B. **Extrinsic evidence:** Bias may be shown by use of *extrinsic evidence.* See *infra*, p. 38.

XIII. IMPEACHMENT BY SENSORY OR MENTAL DEFECT

A. **Generally allowed:** W may be impeached by showing that his capacity to *observe, remember,* or *narrate* events correctly has been impaired.

> **Example:** W may be shown to have such poor eyesight that he couldn't have seen what he claims to have seen.

B. **Alcohol and drugs:**

1. **Use during event:** W may be impeached by showing that he was *drunk* or *high on drugs* at the time of the events he claims to have witnessed.

XIV. IMPEACHMENT BY CONTRADICTION; THE "COLLATERAL ISSUE" RULE

A. **Showing of contradiction allowed:** W1 may be impeached by presenting W2, who *contradicts* W1 on some point.

Example: W1 says that the perpetrator of a robbery had red hair. The defense can put on W2 to testify that the robber had brown hair — this not only is evidence of a material fact, but also impeaches W1.

1. **Must be direct contradiction:** But on the MBE, be sure that what's claimed to be evidence that contradicts the witness really *does* contradict him. "Contradiction" requires a *pretty direct inconsistency* between what the witness says and what the impeacher is asserting is the truth. And sometimes the examiners will present you with a piece of evidence that casts a little doubt on the witness's veracity but doesn't directly contradict — in this situation, the "impeachment by contradiction" rationale can't be used.

   > **Example:** Car accident case. P claims that D caused the accident by speeding. D takes the stand on direct and denies having sped. P's lawyer asks on cross, "Isn't it true that you've gotten two speeding tickets in the past three years?" (Assume it's true that D got these tickets.)
   >
   > The question does not fall within the right to impeach by contradiction, because D's having sped in the past is not inconsistent with his having driven under the speed limit on the occasion in question. (P's lawyer is really asking for character-trait evidence, offered to show action in conformity with that character trait; such evidence is inadmissible under FRE 404(a); see *supra*, p. 10.)

B. **Collateral issue rule:** Also, the right to put on a second witness to impeach the first by contradicting him is limited by the common-law *"collateral issue"* rule. By this rule, certain types of testimony by W2 are deemed to be of such collateral interest to the case that they will not be allowed if their sole purpose is to contradict W1.

   1. **Federal Rule:** The Federal Rules do not contain an explicit "collateral issue" rule. However, the trial judge can and often will apply the policies behind the rule by using FRE 403's balancing test (evidence excludible where its probative value is substantially outweighed by confusion, prejudice, or waste of time) to bar such extrinsic evidence on a collateral issue.

   2. **Disallowed:** Thus, most judges interpreting the FRE say that W2 *may not testify* as to:

      [1] prior *bad acts* by W1 that *did not lead to a conviction and that bear on W1's character for truthfulness* (we already saw this principle *supra*, p. 33);

      [2] prior *inconsistent statements* made by W1 that *do not relate to a material fact* in the case; or

      [3] things said by W1 in his testimony that according to W2 are *not true*, unless these facts are *material* to the case (i.e., are *not "collateral"*).

      > **Example of [3]:** Wit-1, called by P in a car accident case, testifies that he saw D speeding just before the accident. Wit-1 also mentions that the accident happened on the corner of Main & Park, "in front of the sign advertising '20 Billion McDonald's Sold.' " In rebuttal, D offers testimony by Wit-2, that on the day in question, the McDonald's sign said "15 Billion Sold." Since the precise contents of the sign are not material to the case, a judge under the FRE would likely hold that this extrinsic evidence is inadmissible on account of the general rule against extrinsic evidence to contradict another witness on collateral matters.

   3. **Allowed:** On the other hand, testimony by W2 will *not* be deemed to be collateral, and will thus be *allowed*, as to the following subjects:

      [1] prior *criminal convictions* by W1 (if the convictions meet the requirements of FRE 609; see *supra*, p. 29);

      [2] W1's *character for untruthfulness* (if proved by *opinion or reputation testimony*, as opposed to testimony about specific acts of untruthfulness by W1);

[3] W1's *bias*; or

[4] W1's *sensory or mental defect* that prevents W1 from observing, remembering or narrating events correctly.

a. Bias: Item [3] on the above list, *bias*, is especially important, both in real life and on the MBE. As the saying goes, *"Bias is never collateral."* So if W1 gives testimony, W2 may be put on the stand in rebuttal, to impeach W1 by showing that he is biased and thus may not be telling the truth.

Example: Car accident case. P calls Wit-1, who testifies that D was speeding. In rebuttal, D calls Wit-2, who testifies that Wit-1 owes money to P, and that the money is past due. Wit-2's testimony is evidence that Wit-1 is or may be biased in favor of P; therefore, the testimony is not collateral, and is admissible.

XV. REHABILITATING IMPEACHED WITNESS

A. No bolstering: A lawyer may not offer evidence *supporting his witness's credibility*, unless that credibility has first been *attacked* by the other side. This is known as the rule against *"bolstering one's witness."*

Example: On direct, W tells a story favorable to P. P's lawyer will not be permitted to bring out on direct the fact that prior to the trial, W told the same story to the police — W's credibility has not yet been attacked, so it may not be bolstered by a showing that W made a prior consistent statement.

B. Rehabilitation: On the other hand, W's credibility *may* be supported to *rehabilitate* it, i.e., to repair the damage done by the *other side's attack* on that credibility.

1. Meet attack: The rehabilitating evidence must *"meet the attack."* That is, it must support W's credibility *in the same respect* as that in which the credibility has been attacked by the other side.

Example: P attacks W as being biased because he is D's son. D may rehabilitate W's credibility by showing evidence of non-bias. But D may not rehabilitate W by showing W's good reputation for truthfulness, or W's prior out-of-court statements that are consistent with his trial testimony — these attempts by D at rehabilitation do not respond directly to the charge of bias.

2. Good character: If W's credibility is attacked by evidence tending to show that he is generally untruthful, the proponent may show that W has a good character for truthfulness. Thus evidence of W's *good character for truthfulness* may be used to rebut evidence that: (1) W has a *bad reputation* for truthfulness; (2) that W2 has a *bad opinion* of W's truthfulness; (3) that W has been *convicted* of a crime bearing on his truthfulness; or (4) that W has committed a *prior bad act* bearing on his truthfulness.

3. Prior consistent statement: The fact that W has made a *prior consistent statement* (i.e., an out-of-court statement that matches his trial testimony) may be used only to rebut an express or implied charge that W's trial testimony is a *recent fabrication* or the product of *improper influence or motive*. This is the common-law rule, and is also carried out by FRE 801(d)(1)(B). Thus 801(d)(1)(B) says that the witness's prior consistent statement is admissible (and is non-hearsay) if offered to *"rebut an express or implied charge against the [witness] of recent fabrication or improper influence or motive."*

a. Rebutting proof of improper motive: On the MBE, the most common way you will see the admissibility of prior consistent statements by a witness (W) is where W gives particular testimony on direct, the cross examiner shows that W had a motive to lie in that direct testimony, and the direct examiner now tries to show that even if W had such a motive, W made a *prior* *statement consistent with W's trial testimony*, and this prior statement was made *before W even had the supposed motive to lie*. In this scenario, the direct examiner is indeed "rebut[ting] an express or implied charge ... of recent fabrication or improper ... motive," so the prior consistent statement will be *admissible*.

Example: P sues D, alleging that D fraudulently sold P counterfeit securities. As part of P's direct case, P puts Wanda on the stand, who testifies that D told her, "I sold the phony securities to P, and I knew they were phony when I did it." On cross, D's lawyer induces Wanda to admit that, just prior to trial, Wanda told her friend Fred, "P promised to buy me a new diamond necklace if I helped him win his trial." Now, P's lawyer calls another friend of Wanda's, Gwen, who testifies that the day after the stock sales (and before Wanda supposedly made the buy-me-a-necklace statement to Fred), Wanda told Gwen, "D admitted to me that he sold phony stock to P."

Gwen's testimony is admissible in order to rehabilitate Wanda's credibility. Gwen's testimony, since it alleges a statement made by Wanda that is consistent with Wanda's trial testimony on direct, and that was made the very day after the stock scam (and thus presumably before P would even have known about the scam, let alone have had a chance to contemplate a trial and promise Wanda a necklace for aiding him in that trial), is offered for the purpose of rebutting D's lawyer's explicit charge that Wanda lied in her direct testimony because of P's improper influence over her (the bribe). Therefore, Gwen's testimony as to what Wanda said is admissible under 801(d)(1)(B).

i. **Substantively admissible:** Also, under the FRE the witness's prior consistent out-of-court statement is *substantively admissible* for what it contains, not just admissible to rehabilitate the witness's credibility at trial. That is so because 801(d)(1)(B), the provision that makes the prior statement admissible, makes that statement *non-hearsay*. Since the statement is non-hearsay, the proposition asserted in it is admissible for its truth.

    Example: Consider the above example, in which the issue is whether Gwen's testimony that Wanda told her, "D admitted to me that he sold phony stock to P" is admissible. We've already seen that Gwen's testimony is admissible for the purpose of rehabilitating Wanda's credibility. But Gwen's testimony — repeating Wanda's out-of-court statement that D admitted selling phony stock to P — is also *substantively admissible* to prove that D really made the admission to Wanda asserted in Wanda's out-of-court statement. So if you were asked on the MBE about the admissibility of Gwen's testimony, the correct answer would be something like "admissible both to rehabilitate Wanda's credibility and as substantive evidence of the truth of the matter asserted in Wanda's statement to Gwen."

b. **Attack on W's general character:** On the MBE, make sure that the witness's prior consistent statement really *is* being offered to rebut a charge of recent fabrication or improper influence. The mere fact that the cross-examiner has somehow attacked the witness's credibility does *not* mean that there has been a charge of recent fabrication or improper influence, and therefore does not necessarily entitle the proponent of the witness to introduce the witness's prior consistent statement. For instance, if W is attacked by showing his *prior criminal convictions*, *prior bad acts*, or his general *bad reputation* for veracity, his credibility may *not* be rehabilitated by a showing that he made prior consistent statements, because these attacks normally don't constitute charges of recent fabrication or improper influence.

Example: P sues D in an automobile accident case. W testifies for P, "After the accident, D told me, 'The accident happened because I ran a red light.' " On cross, D's lawyer gets

W to admit that 2 years ago, W pleaded guilty to perjury. P's lawyer now offers testimony by W2 that right after the accident, W told her that D had admitted to W that D ran a red light.

W2's testimony is not admissible. It's evidence of a prior consistent statement by a testifying witness, but it's not being offered to rebut an express or implied charge of recent fabrication or improper influence. D's lawyer, by offering a perjury conviction, may be attacking W's *general character for truthfulness*, but is not charging that W recently fabricated her story about D's confession, or that P improperly influenced W to give favorable testimony. Therefore, the fact that W made an out-of-court statement consistent with her present trial testimony is not a rebuttal of anything that D's lawyer did or tried to do on cross. W2's testimony is, consequently, completely inadmissible hearsay — it cannot be used either to rehabilitate W's credibility or to prove substantively that D made the admission to W that W's out-of-court statement to W2 asserted D did.

   c. **Before motive arose:** The proponent who wants to use a prior consistent statement must show that the prior statement was made *before* the alleged motive to fabricate or improper influence arose. This rule applies both at common-law and under FRE 801(d)(1)(B). [*Tome v. U.S.*]

Example: Same facts as the Example on p. 39, in which Wanda says on direct that D admitted to her that he had knowingly sold phony stock to P. As in the original example, assume that D's lawyer, on cross, brought out the fact that W had told Fred that P promised to buy her a necklace if she helped P at trial. Now, however, assume that P's lawyer tries to rehabilitate Wanda by putting on testimony by Gwen that *the night before the trial*, Wanda told Gwen, "D admitted to me that he sold P phony stock." Gwen's testimony will *not* be admissible. Why? Well, Wanda's out-of-court statement was not made until very recently (i.e., long after P is alleged to have tried to improperly influence Wanda), so we know that the out-of-court statement by Wanda was not made before Wanda's alleged motivation to lie arose, which is what 801(d)(1)(B) requires in order for the prior consistent statement to be admissible as rehabilitation.

CHAPTER 4

HEARSAY

I. DEFINITION

   A. **General rule:** A statement constituting *"hearsay"* is *inadmissible* unless some exception to the general rule making hearsay inadmissible applies.

   B. **Definition:** According to the FRE, hearsay is "a *statement, other than one made by the declarant while testifying at the trial or hearing, offered in evidence to prove the truth of the matter asserted.*" FRE 801(c).

      1. **Meaning of "statement":** FRE 801(a) defines a "statement" for these purposes as "(1) an *oral or written assertion* or (2) *nonverbal conduct* of a person, if it is *intended* by the person as an assertion." (For more about nonverbal conduct, see *infra*, p. 44.)

Example of hearsay: At D's murder trial for poisoning V, Wit testifies on behalf of the prosecution, "One week before V's death, V told me, 'D tried to poison me last night.' " If the prosecution is offering this testimony to prove that D really did try to poison V one week before V's death, Wit's testimony is hearsay. V is the declarant (the person who made the out-of-court statement); the declarant is not making the statement while testifying at the trial; and the proponent of the testimony (the prosecution) is trying to prove the truth of the matter asserted in the out-of-court statement (that D really did try to poison V one week before V's death).

2. **Writing:** Hearsay may be *written* as well as oral.

> **Example:** A letter written by V to her mother, "D tried to kill me last night," would be hearsay if offered to prove that D really did this, just as would V's oral statement to her mother to the same effect.

3. **Hearsay may be by the present witness:** A statement may be hearsay, and thus inadmissible, even if it was made (out-of-court) *by a person who is presently repeating it in court.* The MBE examiners like to trick you with this one — it seems as though, if the declarant is in court to repeat, and be cross-examined about, the out-of-court statement, that statement can't be hearsay. But it *can* — if it's outside of the present trial, not made in some other trial or in a hearing, and offered to prove the truth of what's asserted in it, it's inadmissible hearsay unless it falls within an exclusion or exception.

> **Example:** Car accident, in which P claims that D, driving a purple Camry, was speeding just before the accident. Wit is called by P to testify, "The day after the accident, I told my friend Fiona, 'You know, I saw an accident, and it was caused by a purple Camry that was speeding.'" This is hearsay — Wit is repeating Wit's own statement made out of court, offered to prove that the Camry was indeed speeding. The fact that the declarant is the present witness doesn't change anything about this analysis. (Of course, Wit can testify now, "I saw the Camry speeding"; but what Wit said to Fiona in the past is hearsay, so unless there's some applicable exception — which nothing in these facts suggests — it can't come in.)

> a. **Statement about what declarant previously said:** Similarly, if the out-of-court statement is of the form "I [the declarant] *told* X fact Y," then if the statement is now being offered to prove that the declarant told X fact Y, the statement is hearsay even if it's not being offered to prove fact Y. In other words, *A*'s out-of-court statement that *A* told *B* something is hearsay even if offered to prove *only the fact of the telling.*

> **Example:** P sues D, a grocery store, for failing to clean a spill before P tripped at 10 a.m. one morning. It is uncontested that P was with Fred when the fall occurred. P offers testimony by Wit that "The day after the accident, Fred told me, 'I told the store manager about the spill 10 minutes before P tripped.'" Even if Wit's testimony is being offered only to show notice (i.e., to show that Fred made the statement to the manager), not to show that there really was a spill, it's still hearsay — the matter being asserted in Fred's statement to Wit is that Fred made a statement to the manager, and proof that Fred said something to the manager (regardless of the truth of the something) is the reason for which Fred's statement to Wit is being repeated in court.

C. **Four dangers:** The use of hearsay testimony presents four main dangers:

[1] *ambiguity*;

Example: Murder case accusing D of stabbing V to death on the evening of Feb. 1 about 7 p.m. At trial, Witness says, "Declarant told me he saw D leave V's house with bloody-looking hands on Feb. 1 about 7:15 p.m." Declarant's statement may have been ambiguous; for instance, Declarant may have merely said, "D had something red and sticky on his hands," and not characterized the substance as looking like blood. Because Declarant is not there to be cross-examined, D's lawyer can't directly explore exactly what Declarant meant or said, so the potential ambiguity makes Declarant's statement as repeated at trial less likely to be accurate than if Declarant were testifying directly.

[2] *insincerity*;

Example: Same murder case as above Example. Declarant may have been lying, to falsely impli-cate D. Again, since Declarant isn't there to be cross-examined, D's lawyer has no chance to directly expose his insincerity.

[3]   *incorrect memory*;

Example: Same murder case. Declarant may have misremembered or inadvertently confabulated what he saw (especially if, between the event witnessed and the making of the statement to Wit-ness, Declarant learned that D had been charged with stabbing V at the time in question). And Declarant isn't there to be cross-examined to expose this risk of incorrect memory.

[4]   *inaccurate perception.*

Example: Same murder case. Declarant may have misperceived one or more things about the event, such as what time it was, or what the color of the substance on D's hands was. Once again, Declarant isn't there to be cross-examined to expose this risk of incorrect perception.

Note that all of these four risks relate to the fact that the person making the out-of-court statement (the declarant) is *not available for cross-examination.*

1.   **MBE tip:** So on the MBE, if you're in doubt about whether the statement is hearsay, consider whether the statement poses any of the above four risks. The presence or absence of any/all of these risks won't be dispositive, but it can help you raise the odds that you'll classify the statement correctly as hearsay/non-hearsay in a close case.

D.   **Illustrations of hearsay on MBE:** Most of the time when an MBE question poses a hearsay issue, the item will turn out not to be hearsay, or to fall within a hearsay exception. But a substantial minority of the time, the item will be "hearsay not within any exception," and thus inadmissible. Here are a couple of illustrations of the kind of out-of-court statements that may pop on the MBE and be inadmissible hearsay.

Example 1: D, who is 6' 4", is charged with murdering V by throwing him off the roof of an office building. At D's trial, the prosecution offers the testimony of Officer, a police officer who arrived at the scene moments after V's death. The prosecutor asks Officer whether he interviewed any of the people in the crowd. Officer replies that he interviewed an eyewitness, Eye. Eye is since deceased. Officer said that he accurately recorded the contents of Eye's state-ment in his notebook as she was making it and that he has brought the notebook to court with him. The prosecutor proposes to have Officer read the contents of the statement to the jury. The statement says, "I saw a man about 6' 4" throw V off the roof." D's attorney objects.

Officer will not be permitted to read Eye's statement to the jury, because it is hearsay not within any exception. It's obviously an out-of-court declaration. It is being offered to prove the truth of the matter asserted, that the one who threw V off the roof was 6' 4" tall. And it's not within any exception. (For why it's not admissible as past recollection recorded, see p. 57; for why it's not admissible as a business record, see pp. 59-60. In brief, the problem is that this is two-level hearsay, and nothing makes the "inner" statement by Eye admissible, even if the "outer" statement — the written record — is admissible.)

Example 2: D is being prosecuted for assault of V. Freda is called by the prosecution to testify that two days after the accident, V complained to Freda (who is V's friend) that D was the source of V's black eye.

Freda's testimony is hearsay not within any exception, and thus inadmissible. She's repeating V's out-of-court statement ("It was D who gave me this black eye"), and the out-of-court statement is being offered to show that D really was the assailant, so the statement is being offered to prove the truth of the matter asserted. And no exception applies.

II. SPECIAL ISSUES

A. "Out-of-court" statement: An out-of-court statement is any statement except one made "by a witness during the trial while testifying before the trier of fact." Therefore, the following will be out-of-court statements (and thus might be hearsay):

❑ Any oral or written statement by *someone other than the at-trial witness*; and

❑ A prior statement by the *at-trial witness*, where the prior statement was not made in the present trial before the trier of fact. Therefore, W's prior statement made in a *deposition* or at an *earlier trial*, or even W's statement made in the judge's chambers during the present trial, are all "out of court" and so may be hearsay.

B. "Truth of matter asserted": Here are some uses to which a statement may be put that do *not* constitute offering the statement for the "truth of the matter asserted":

1. **Verbal acts:** A statement that is a "*verbal act*," i.e., an *operative fact* that gives rise to *legal consequences*, is not hearsay.

   Example: D says to W (a vice officer), "If you pay me $25 I will have sex with you." If D is prosecuted for solicitation, her statement will not be hearsay because it is not offered to show its truth (that D would really have had sex with W had he paid her $25); rather, the crime of solicitation is defined so as to make an offer to have sex for money be an act with legal consequences, and the prosecution is proving that D made such an offer.

   a. **Verbal parts of act:** Similarly, a "*verbal part of the act,*" i.e., words that accompany an ambiguous physical act, is not typically offered for truth and thus is not hearsay.

      Example: O gives X money, saying, "This will repay you for the money you lent me last year." If offered by X in defense of a bribery charge, this will be non-hearsay because the words that accompanied the payment give the payment its particular legal effect — loan repayment.

2. **Effect on hearer/reader:** A statement offered to show its *effect* on the *listener* or *reader* will generally not be hearsay. Thus if a statement is offered to show that the listener or reader was *put on notice*, had certain *knowledge*, had a certain *emotion*, or behaved *reasonably* or unreasonably, this will not be hearsay.

   Example: Malpractice suit by P against D, a hospital, for having negligently hired as a doctor X, whom P alleges to be incompetent. P offers written statements by two other hospitals refusing to allow X on their staffs because he was incompetent. If P shows that D saw the letters before admitting X to the staff, the letters will not be hearsay — the letters are not being offered to prove the truth of the matters asserted (that X was really incompetent), merely to show that a reasonable person in D's position would have doubted X's competence.

3. **Declarant's state of mind:** Statements introduced to show the *state of mind* of the *declarant* are not offered for the "truth of the matter asserted" and thus are not hearsay.

   a. **Knowledge:** Thus a statement offered to show the declarant's *knowledge* is not hearsay.

      Example: D says to X, "I need to get my brakes checked because they haven't been working well." In a negligence suit by P against D, that statement is not hearsay, because it is not offered to show that the brakes really were defective, merely that D had knowledge that the brakes might be defective.

b. Other mental state: Statements offered to show the declarant's *sanity* or *emotion* (e.g., fear) are similarly not offered for truth and thus are not hearsay. (Also, there is an exception for "statements evidencing states of mind.")

4. Reputation: Statements about a person's *reputation* may not be hearsay.

> **Example:** Libel action; W testifies at trial, "O told me that P has a reputation for thievery." If offered to show that O's statement caused this false reputation of P, this will not be hearsay — it is not offered to prove that P is really a thief, merely to prove that P has been given a false reputation for thievery.

5. Impeachment: If W makes a statement at trial, use of a prior inconsistent statement made out of court by W will not be hearsay when used to *impeach* W's present testimony — what is being shown is not that the prior out-of-court statement was truthful, but that the conflict between the two statements raises questions about W's credibility.

C. "Statement" and conduct: The hearsay rule applies only to "*statements*." An oral or written assertion is obviously a statement. But certain types of *conduct* may also be statements:

1. Assertive conduct: *Assertive conduct* is treated as if it were a "statement," so that it can be hearsay.

> **Example:** O pulls D's mug shot out of a collection of photos; since by this act O intends to assert, "That's the perpetrator," this act will be hearsay if offered on the issue of whether D was the perpetrator.

2. Silence: A person's *silence* will be treated as a "statement," and thus possibly hearsay, only if it is *intended* by the person as an assertion.

a. Absence of complaints: The fact that one or more people have *not made complaints* about a situation will *not* usually be treated as the equivalent of a statement by them that there is nothing to complain about. Therefore, *absence of prior complaints* can usually be admitted *without* hearsay problems.

3. Non-assertive conduct: Conduct that is *not intended as an assertion* will *never* be hearsay, under the Federal Rules.

a. Non-assertive verbal conduct: Even a verbal statement will not be hearsay if it is not intended as an assertion.

> **Example:** D is charged with running a bookmaking operation out of his premises. W testifies that he answered D's phone, and the caller on the other end said, "Seabiscuit to place in the third." The caller's statement will not be hearsay, because even though it was verbal, the caller did not intend to assert, "I am talking to a betting parlor," or anything else.

b. Non-verbal conduct: Similarly, *non-verbal conduct* that is not intended as an assertion will not give rise to hearsay.

> **Example:** O, while walking down the street, suddenly puts up his umbrella. If this act is introduced to show that it was raining, it will not be hearsay — O was not intending to assert to anyone, "It's raining."

D. Multiple hearsay: If one out-of-court declaration *quotes or paraphrases another* out-of-court declaration, there is a problem of *"multiple hearsay."* The evidence is inadmissible if *any* of the declarations is hearsay not falling within an exception.

1. FRE provision: This principle is reflected in FRE 805, entitled "Hearsay Within Hearsay": "*Hearsay included within hearsay* is *not excluded* under the hearsay rule if *each part of the com-*

bined statement conforms with an exception to the hearsay rule provided in these rules." So by negative implication, if *any level* is hearsay not within any exception, the *entire combined statement is inadmissible.*

> **Example:** W, an insurance investigator, investigates a car accident involving D and then writes a report saying, "D told me that at the time of the crash, he was travelling at 65 mph." If this report is offered by P to show that D was indeed travelling at 65 mph, there are two levels of hearsay: D's original oral statement and W's out-of-court written paraphrase of it. But each would probably fall within an exception — D's original statement as an admission, and W's report under the business records rule. If so, the report could come into evidence, under FRE 805. But if *either* level did not fall within any hearsay objection, then *both* levels (i.e., the entire statement) would be excluded.

a. **Written report of what someone said orally:** On the MBE, a common scenario for a multiple-hearsay problem is that *A* says something orally out of court, and *B* makes some type of written record of the oral statement; the written record is then offered in court.

 i. **Police report:** For instance, on the MBE the prosecution will often offer a *police report* in which the officer records the fact that some out-of-court declarant (call him X) has made some statement (call it an assertion of "Fact Y") implicating D. Typically, the police report will be *inadmissible* if offered to prove Fact Y. That's because even though the outer level (the police report) might be admissible as a business record, the inner level (the statement by the witness to the officer) usually does not fall within any hearsay exception.

 [1] **MBE tactic:** So as a general tactic on the MBE, if one side offers a police report containing an occurrence-witness's statement, offered for the truth of that statement, you should strongly presume that the report is inadmissible as long as the occurrence witness is not the party against whom the report is being offered.

 > **Example:** Officer, a police officer, investigates a car accident soon after it happened. Officer writes up a report on the scene, and includes the following sentence: "I interviewed Wit, who saw the accident, and who told me that the driver in the blue Ford jumped a red light and hit the driver of the red Chevy." The lawyer for P (the driver of the red Chevy) calls Officer to the stand, asks Officer to describe making the report, and then offers the report into evidence to prove that the blue Ford (driven by D) jumped a red light.
 >
 > The report is inadmissible multiple-level hearsay. The outer level — the police report — is probably admissible as a business record (see p. 59). But the inner level — Wit's statement that he saw the red Chevy jump the light — is hearsay not within any exception. P is offering Wit's statement to show that the red Chevy really did jump the light. Therefore, the statement is an out-of-court statement offered to prove the truth of the matter asserted therein. So unless it falls within an exception, the document containing it is inadmissible. It does not in fact fall within any exception. For instance, Wit's statement does not fall within the business records exception, because even though Officer may have been making the report pursuant to a duty, Wit as a civilian had no business duty to make or participate in the making of the record. (See *infra*, p. 61.)

b. **Oral report of what someone else said orally:** Another common MBE scenario is that *A* tells the trial witness, out of court, what *B* told *A* some time previously. The trial witness then wants to testify, "*A* told me that *B* told him [thus and such]." As with the above "written report of what someone else said orally" scenario, it will often be the case that A's statement (the outer level) meets some hearsay exception, but B's statement (the inner level) doesn't.

   c. **Split of outcomes on the MBE:**   There seems to be roughly a 50/50 split on the MBE between multiple-hearsay questions in which both levels satisfy some exception or exclusion, and those in which at least one level is hearsay not within any exception, knocking out the entire statement. So you'll just have to fight your way through an analysis of both levels — there's no single rule of thumb to help you once you've identified a multiple-level problem on the MBE.

   Example of admissible multiple-hearsay statement: P sues Doc, a doctor, for malpractice during a heart operation on P. To prove that Doc inadvertently caused a small cut in P's aorta, P offers a properly-authenticated hospital record made during the operation, in which Resident wrote, "Doc says he just nicked the aorta and is trying to patch it up."

   The outer level — the written record — falls within the business-records exception (called "records of regularly conducted activity") given in FRE 803(6); see *infra*, p. 59. Doc's statement falls within FRE 803(1)'s present-sense-impression exception (see *infra*, p. 56). Since both levels fall within hearsay exceptions, the entire record can come in.

   Example of inadmissible multiple-hearsay statement: Wanda sues Dave for killing Wanda's husband Herb. Herb was found shot to death, and Dave denies being responsible. Widow offers to testify, "The week before Herb's death, he said to me, 'Last week Dave told me, "I hate your guts, so you'd better be looking over your shoulder," but I didn't take him seriously.'"

   This is multiple-level hearsay, and is inadmissible. The "inner" level is Dave's statement to Herb. Although it's common-law hearsay (it's being offered to show that Dave hated Herb), it's an admission by a party opponent (see *infra*, immediately below), which is a hearsay exclusion under the FRE. But the "outer" level is Herb's statement to Wanda, and that's hearsay not within any exception — it's being offered to show that Dave actually made the statement to Herb, since if Dave didn't make the statement to Herb, Herb's statement to Wanda would not be relevant in the case. So the entire statement will have to be excluded.

CHAPTER 5

HEARSAY EXCEPTIONS AND EXCLUSIONS

I. ADMISSIONS

   A. **General rule:**   *"Admissions"* are *"excluded"* from the definition of hearsay under the FRE. That is, *a party's words or acts may be offered as evidence against him,* even though these would be inadmissible hearsay if said or done by someone other than a party. See FRE 801(d)(2), which lists five different varieties of admissions — all receiving an exclusion from the definition of hearsay — in subsections 801(d)(2)(A) through (E). We review each of the five varieties below.

      1. **Opinion:**   An admission is non-hearsay even though it contains an *opinion* or a *conclusion of law,* and even though it is not based on the maker's *first-hand knowledge.* Thus it can be admitted more easily even than the same statement when made at trial.

   B. **Personal admissions:**   One type of admission is a *party's own statement,* offered against him (a *"personal admission"*). See FRE 801(d)(2)(A), treating "a party's own statement, in either an individual or representative capacity," as being non-hearsay.

Example: Accident case, in which P claims that D was travelling faster than the 30 mph speed limit at the time of the collision. In P's case in chief, P calls Officer, who proposes to testify that when Officer investigated the crash several hours after it occurred, D told him, "I was doing 40 mph just before the accident."

Officer's repetition of D's statement would normally be hearsay (since D's statement was made out of court, and is offered to prove the truth of what the statement asserts, i.e., that D was travelling 40 mph). But since the statement was made by a party to the litigation, and is offered against that party, it's admissible as a "hearsay exclusion" (i.e., as non-hearsay) under 801(d)(2)(A).

1. **Can be exculpatory:** Admissions by a party-opponent are admissible in criminal cases even if the statement appeared to be *exculpatory* (negating the speaker's criminality) at the time it was made. This is one thing that distinguishes them from *declarations against interest* (*infra*, p. 71).

   Example: D is charged with murdering his wife by stabbing her. At the beginning of their investigation, police believe that the stabbing took place at 7:00 p.m. D tells them, "I left the house at 6:45 p.m." It later turns out that the murder probably took place at 6:30. The prosecution may introduce D's statement against him (assuming that there are no *Miranda* problems), since it is an admission. This is so even though the statement is not a "declaration against interest," since at the time he made it, D believed the statement was exculpatory.

2. **Question may not say "admission":** On the MBE, you may be required to spot that something is an admission, and thus admissible notwithstanding the hearsay rule, *without the examiners' ever using the word "admission"* (or even "hearsay") anywhere in the fact pattern or in the correct choice. That's because the examiners can construct a correct choice that merely combines the fact that the party's statement is substantively admissible and the fact that it is, say, also available for impeachment.

   Example: The correct choice on an MBE question may merely be something conclusory like, "Admissible both substantively [or admissible to prove that X really happened] and to impeach Wit." You may have to notice that the reason the statement is substantively admissible is because it was made by a party and is being used against that party. In other words, it may well be the case that neither the fact pattern nor any choice uses the word "admission" to remind you that the question turns on the hearsay exclusion for admissions.

3. **May be part of multi-level problem:** On the MBE, an admission will often be buried within a multi-level hearsay problem, usually as the inner-most level (see *supra*, p. 44). So if the statement being made out of court by the declarant, and then repeated at some remove in-court, is being offered *against the declarant*, the hearsay problem disappears, at least to the declarant's statement itself, by virtue of the hearsay-exclusion for admissions.

   Example: Dave and Derrick were charged with robbing the First National Bank together. Derrick has since died, and the prosecution is proceeding against Dave only. At trial, Wanda testifies for the prosecution, "A week after the robbery, Derrick told me, 'Dave said he regretted robbing the First National with me, because he thought we'd probably get caught.' "

   This is multi-level hearsay, but it is admissible against Dave. The "inner" level is Dave's statement to Derrick about his regret; that's non-hearsay because it's an admission (statement by a party, Dave, offered against that party). The outer level is a declaration against interest (see *infra*, p. 71) because it exposed Derrick to criminal liability. So the entire statement can come in.

4. **Must be against, not for, party or privy:** On the MBE, if you think the statement is an admission, make sure you check that the statement is offered *against* (not for) the declarant or a person in privity with the declarant. The examiners will sometimes try to trick you by giving you a scenario in which a party offers a statement by that party, or by someone in privity with that party — it's not an admission, because it's not offered against that party.

    Example: Widow sues Insurer for payment on a life insurance policy on Hubby, Widow's husband who was found dead of a gunshot wound. The policy has an exclusion for suicides, and Insurer claims that Hubby committed suicide. (Widow claims it was murder by persons unknown.) Widow offers to testify, "The day before he was found shot to death, Hubby said to me, 'I've never been happier in my life.'" This is not admissible as an admission, because it's not being offered *against* the declarant (Hubby) or against a person in privity with him; instead, it's being offered *by* someone (Widow) who is aligned with the declarant.

5. **Can be inadmissible for other reason:** Remember that the "admissions" exclusion just solves any hearsay problem — it doesn't prevent the statement from being inadmissible due to some other evidence rule.

    Example: In an accident case, P offers to testify at trial, "One day after the accident, D offered to pay my medical bills." D's statement isn't hearsay, because it falls within the exclusion for admissions offered against a party opponent. But it's still inadmissible because of the rule excluding offers to pay medical expenses (*supra*, p. 25).

6. **Pleadings:** Statements a party makes in his *pleadings* are treated as personal admissions for most purposes, and are thus admissible.

C. **Adoptive:** Under the Federal Rules, a party may be deemed to have *adopted* another person's statement, in which case the statement will be admissible as an admission by the former party. See FRE 801(d)(2)(B), making non-hearsay a statement offered against a party if that party "*manifested an adoption or belief* in [the statement's] truth."

1. **"Real and knowing" test:** If a party is claimed to have adopted another's statement and the adoption is merely *implied*, the test is: whether, taking into account all circumstances, the party's conduct or silence justifies the conclusion that he *knowingly agreed* with the other person's statement.

2. **Silence:** Often, the party's *silence* in the face of the other person's statement will, under the circumstances, indicate that the party agrees with the statement. If so, he will be held to have made an adoptive admission, which will thus be admissible.

    a. **"Partners in crime":** When MBE questions test the adoptive-admission doctrine, most of the time the fact pattern will involve whether the defendant's silence in the presence of a statement demonstrates real-and-knowing agreement with the statement. For instance, if the speaker and the defendant are *"partners in crime"* in some sense, the adoptive-admission exception is likely to be satisfied.

        Example: While D flashes a large wad of bills, X, his girlfriend, says to W, "D got that money as his piece of the National Bank job we did together last week." D's silence in the face of this statement will probably be found by the court to show D's knowing agreement with X's statement, since otherwise, D would have denied the statement. Therefore, the statement will be admissible against D as an adoptive admission.

b. Analyze surrounding circumstances: But the adoptive-admission exception always requires you to *analyze the precise surrounding circumstances* — unless the circumstances are such that the defendant would probably have objected had she not agreed with the statement, the statement won't be deemed to have been adopted.

    i. Statements made while declarant is in police custody: This principle means that the defendant's failure to respond to accusations made by the police (or others) while defendant is in police *custody* will ordinarily not be admissible against him as an adoptive admission, because the defendant may merely have been trying to avoid incriminating himself to the police.

    Example: D1 and D2 are arrested for conspiring to burglarize the First National Bank. They are put in the same room at police HQ, and are interrogated. (They are given *Miranda* warnings but indicate that they're willing to listen to the police's questions, though they don't promise to answer them.) D1 says, "D2 planned it, and I was just going along." D2 says nothing (now or at any time during the interrogation). D1's statement implicating D2 will not be admissible against D2 as an adoptive admission, because the circumstances show that D2's silence did not mean that he necessarily agreed with the truth of what D1 was saying; he may just not have wanted to risk implicating himself by taking any position on the truth of what D1 was saying.

c. Writing: A party's silence in the face of a *writing* can be an adoptive admission, if the party can reasonably be expected to have objected were the writing untrue.

Example: D receives a bill from a creditor, reciting certain sums owed for specified work. If D does not respond, his silence in the face of the bill will be treated as an adoptive admission by him of the truth of the bill's contents.

    i. Surrounding circumstances: But with adoption of a writing, as with an adoption of an oral statement, you have to *analyze the surrounding circumstances*. So if either of the following is true, the adoptive exception won't apply: (1) there's no evidence that D *actually read* the writing; or (2) it's not more-probable-than-not that had D disagreed, he would have somehow indicated his lack of assent to the statement contained in the writing.

    Example: P and D have been partners in a business firm. An issue is whether D approved of the firm's plan to sell a particular widget to X. P testifies that he wrote down in a ledger that he kept on behalf of the firm, "Told D about the proposed widget sale to X and he approved." P also shows that D had access to this ledger and sometimes read it. These facts are not enough to make the statement in the ledger that D approved the sale be an adoptive admission by D, because there is no evidence that would justify the conclusion that D read that particular ledger entry.

D. Representative and vicarious admissions: Even if a party did not make (or even learn of) another person's admission, that admission may be admissible against the party because he *authorized it* in some way. This is a "representative" admission. The FRE recognize *two different sorts* of representative admissions, one covering explicitly-authorized admissions and the other covering admissions that are "vicarious" (implicitly authorized) because the statement relates to a transaction within an agent's authority.

1. Explicitly authorized: The provision making *explicitly-authorized* admissions non-hearsay is FRE 801(d)(2)(C), excluding from hearsay "a statement [offered against a party] by a person *authorized by the party to make a statement concerning the subject matter.*" So this provision covers the situation in which a party explicitly authorizes another person to speak for her, and that person's statement is being offered against the authorizing party.

Example: BusCo., a bus company, authorizes any employee who is involved in an accident while driving for BusCo. to make a statement to the police about the accident. Driver has an accident while driving a bus for BusCo. Any statement made by Driver to the police about the accident will be admissible against BusCo. in any litigation, because FRE 801(d)(2)(C) makes the statement a non-hearsay representative admission.

    a. Statements to principal: Even if the principal authorizes the agent only to make the report *to the principal,* the federal approach is to treat this as an adoptive admission. Thus, an employee's accident investigation report, given only to the employee's boss, would nonetheless be admissible against the boss.

  2. Vicarious: Even if an agent is not explicitly authorized to make statements, statements he makes arising from a *transaction within his authority* will, under the FRE, be deemed to be authorized admissions by the principal. These are called *"vicarious"* admissions. They are covered by FRE 801(d)(2)(D), which admits as non-hearsay a statement offered against a party if made "by the party's *agent or servant concerning a matter within the scope of the agency or employment, made during the existence of the relationship."*

    Example: Trucker, who drives a truck for Transport Co., makes a statement to the police about an on-the-job accident in which Trucker has recently been involved. Even if Transport Co. never authorized Trucker to make accident reports, under FRE 801(d)(2)(D) Trucker's statement will be admissible against Transport because the statement relates to a matter — an accident while driving on the job — that was within Trucker's employment.

      i. How to prove: The proponent of the admission may *use the statement itself as one item of evidence* to show that the agent was acting within the scope of his agency or employment relationship when the declaration was made. But the statement *cannot be the sole item of evidence* demonstrating this point. See FRE 801(d)(2), last sentence (saying that "The contents of the statement shall be considered but are *not alone sufficient* to establish ... the agency or employment relationship and scope thereof under subdivision (D)[.]")

      Example: Same facts as above example. Suppose that in Trucker's accident statement to the police, he says, "I was making a delivery for Transport Co. at the time of the accident." When the trial judge determines whether Trucker was acting on behalf of Transport at the time of the accident, the judge can consider, as one piece of evidence, the fact that in the statement at issue, Trucker confirmed that he was acting on Transport's business. But there must be some additional evidence, beyond the statement, that Trucker really was on company business at the time of the accident.

E. Co-conspirators:

  1. General rule: FRE 801(d)(2)(E) gives a hearsay exclusion for use against a party of "a statement by a *coconspirator* of [that] party [made] *during the course and in furtherance of the conspiracy."*

    a. Two requirements: So the coconspirator's statement has to be made: (1) *during the course* of the conspiracy; and (2) in *furtherance* of the conspiracy.

    Example: *A* says to *X,* "Don't you want to join *B* and me in robbing the First National Bank next Thursday?" *X* may repeat this statement against *B* in a prosecution for the robbery of that bank that took place on that date, since the statement was made by a member of the same conspiracy, was made while the conspiracy was taking place, and was made for the purpose of furthering the conspiracy's aims by recruitment of members.

  2. "During course of": The requirement that the statement take place *"during the course of"* the conspiracy means that:

a. **After end:** Statements made *after the conspiracy has ended* are admissible only against the declarant, not against the other members. Thus, if the conspiracy is broken up by the *arrest* of A and B (the only members of the conspiracy), anything B says to the police will likely not be admissible against A, since the arrest has terminated the conspiracy.

b. **Conspirator leaves:** If A leaves the conspiracy, but B and C continue the conspiracy without him, statements made by B and C after A leaves may not be admitted against A. (But the converse is not true: statements made by A to the authorities after he has left the conspiracy might be admissible against B and C, since their conspiratorial activities are still continuing at the time of A's statement.)

c. **Statements before:** Statements made by early conspirators *before* a later entry joins are admissible against the latter — when a conspirator enters an ongoing conspiracy, he is held to have adopted the earlier statements of fellow co-conspirators, so these are admissible against him.

3. **In furtherance:** The "in furtherance" requirement means that a statement should be admitted against a co-conspirator only if it was made for the purpose of somehow *advancing the conspiracy's objectives.*

> **Example:** Six months after D and Declarant allegedly rob the First National Bank together, Declarant says to his girlfriend Jill, solely to impress her, "You know, that First Nat Bank job was done by D and me." Jill's testimony about this conversation, if offered against D, will not be rendered non-hearsay by the coconspirator provision, because Declarant's statement was not made, even arguably, for the purpose of advancing the conspiracy's objectives.

4. **No need to charge conspiracy:** Statements by one co-conspirator against another may be admitted under the exception *even if no conspiracy crime is ever formally charged.*

5. **Procedure:** It is the judge who decides whether a conspiracy has been shown, so that the exception applies. He reaches this decision as follows:

a. **Preponderance:** He need only find that a conspiracy exists by a *preponderance of the evidence*, not "beyond a reasonable doubt."

b. **Statements:** In determining whether a conspiracy exists by a preponderance, he may *consider the alleged statement itself.*

i. **May not be sole proof of conspiracy:** But the contents of the statement *may not be the sole proof* that the conspiracy existed (or that the defendant and the declarant were members). FRE 801(d)(2), final sent. In other words, there must be *some independent evidence* that the conspiracy existed.

II. AVAILABILITY IMMATERIAL — GENERALLY

A. **List of exceptions:** Five major categories of hearsay exceptions apply even where the declarant is *available* to give courtroom testimony:

1. *Spontaneous, excited,* or *contemporaneous utterances* (including statements about *physical or mental condition*);

2. *Past recollection recorded;*

3. *Business records;*

4. *Public records and reports;* and

5.   *Learned writings.*

III. SPONTANEOUS, EXCITED, OR CONTEMPORANEOUS UTTERANCES (INCLUDING STATEMENTS ABOUT PHYSICAL OR MENTAL CONDITION)

A.   **Several exceptions:** We group together here four somewhat-related exceptions available under the FRE for statements about the declarant's present state of mind or physical or mental condition:

❏   Statements made for purposes of *medical diagnosis or treatment*;

❏   Statements of *then-existing mental, emotional, or physical condition*;

❏   *Present sense impressions*;

❏   *Excited utterances.*

B.   **Statements made for purposes of medical diagnosis or treatment:**   There is a hearsay exception for statements by a person made in order to receive medical diagnosis or treatment. See FRE 803(4), covering statements made "for *purposes of medical diagnosis or treatment* and *describing medical history, or past or present symptoms, pain, or sensations,* or the *inception or general character* of the *cause or external source* thereof insofar as *reasonably pertinent to diagnosis or treatment.*"

1.   **Past symptoms:**   The statement may be about *past* pain or past symptoms.

2.   **Cause:**   The statement may include references to the *cause* of the bodily condition.

     a.   **Does not cover fault:** However, statements about whose *fault* the condition is will generally *not* be covered, on the theory that they are not "reasonably pertinent to diagnosis or treatment." The MBE examiners like to test you on this one, because it's easy for them to distract you into wrongly thinking that if the disclosure is made to a doctor, and made as part of a seeking of medical treatment, everything in the statement is admissible under the 803(4) exception.

          Example 1: Declarant's statement to a treating physician that he was hit by a car will qualify, but his statement that the car was driven through a red light would not.

          Example 2: Peter sues Devon for assaulting him. P offers a record from the hospital E.R. where he was treated after the episode. The record contains a notation by the treating E.R. physician: "Patient says he was attacked by Devon." This is multiple-level hearsay. The outer level (the physical hospital record) qualifies for the business-records exception (see *infra*, p. 59). But the inner level (what Peter told the doctor about Devon) does not qualify for the treatment-or-diagnosis exception, because the identity of the attacker is not "reasonably pertinent to diagnosis or treatment." (This is in fact hearsay not within any exception.)

3.   **Statement by friend or relative:** A statement made *by a third person* (e.g., a friend or relative of the patient) is also covered, if made to help the patient get treatment.

4.   **Non-M.D.:**   Statements made for purposes of getting medical treatment that are made to non-M.D.'s, such as a *nurse*, ambulance driver, hospital admitting clerk, or other third person involved in the health-care process, are covered by the 803(4) exception.

5.   **Non-treating physician:**   If the statement is made to a doctor who is not furnishing *treatment*, but who is consulted so that he can testify about the patient's condition at trial, the statement is still covered by 803(4), since it relates to "diagnosis."

C. Declaration of present mental, emotional, or physical condition: There is a hearsay exception for statements by a person concerning his *present mental, emotional or physical condition*. See FRE 803(3), giving an exception for:

> "a statement of the declarant's *then existing state of mind, emotion, sensation, or physical condition* (such as *intent, plan, motive, design, mental feeling, pain, and bodily health*), but *not* including a statement of *memory or belief to prove the fact remembered or believed* unless it relates to the execution, revocation, identification, or terms of declarant's will."

1. **State of mind directly in issue:** The exception is often used where a declarant's state of mind is directly in issue. Often, the declarant's state of mind on a particular day will be directly at issue, and the declarant's state of mind about the same issue before that day will be relevant — the state-of-mind exception can be used here, as long as the declarant is making that statement about the declarant's then-present state of mind.

   Example: D is charged with the shooting death of V, D's girlfriend. D claims self-defense, testifying that V pulled a gun on D, saying, "I've known for a long time you've been cheating on me, and now you're gonna pay," and that D had to shoot his own gun first to prevent V from firing. The prosecution offers testimony by Wit, V's best friend, that the day before the shooting, V told Wit, "I love D completely, even though I know he's the unfaithful sort." This statement will be admissible under the present-state-of-mind exception, since: (1) it shows V's state of feelings for D at the moment she made the statement, which in turn (2) bears on whether she would have tried to kill D out of jealousy the next day.

   a. **Presently existing:** The statement must relate to the declarant's *presently existing* state of mind, not to the state of mind at a prior time.

      Example: "I hate my husband," is acceptable to show the declarant now hates her husband. But, "Yesterday I was really furious at my husband," is not admissible, because it relates to a prior mental or emotional state, rather than the declarant's present one.

   b. **Surrounding circumstances:** If statement of present mental state includes a reference to surrounding circumstances, the entire statement will normally be admitted, but with a limiting instruction.

      Example: "I hate my husband because he's an adulterer." The whole statement will be admitted under the exception, if offered to prove that the declarant hated her husband at the time of the statement; the jury will be instructed that it may not use the statement as proof that the husband was an adulterer.

2. **Proof of subsequent event:** The 803(3) exception also applies where a declaration of present mental state — especially present *intent* — is offered not because the mental state itself is in issue, but because that mental state is circumstantial evidence that a *subsequent event* actually took place.

   a. **Most common on MBE:** This use of a statement of *intent*, to show that the declarant probably later *carried out the intended act,* is the *most common use* of the statement-of-existing-state-of-mind exception on the MBE.

      Example: O says, "I plan to go to Crooked Creek." This statement of present intent is admissible under the present-state-of-mind exception to show that O probably subsequently went to Crooked Creek. [*Mutual Life Ins. v. Hillmon*]

   b. **Cooperation of other:** If the statement of present intent concerns an act which requires the *cooperation* of a third person, most courts will allow the statement to be used as circumstantial evidence that the declarant did the contemplated act with the third person's cooperation. However, in this situation, courts usually require that there be *independent evidence* either that declarant really did the intended act, or that the third person actually participated.

Example: V says, "I'm going to buy drugs from D in the parking lot." This statement of present intent will be admissible to show that V probably did meet D in the parking lot, but only if there is some independent evidence — other than the statement — either that D really went to the parking lot or that V did. [*U.S. v. Pheaster*]

3. **Statements of memory or belief:** The "state of mind" exception does *not* apply to statements of *memory* or belief about *past actions or events*, when offered to prove that the past action or event took place. Thus FRE 803(3) excludes "a statement of memory or belief to prove the fact remembered or believed..."

Example 1: O says, "I believe that my husband has poisoned me." Even though this is a statement of present belief, it is not admissible under the "state of mind" exception to prove that the husband really did poison O, since it is offered to prove the fact believed. [*Shepard v. U.S.*]

Example 2: Accident case, in which Paula sues Driver for causing the death of Paula's mother Miriam in a car accident. Driver calls Sis — who is Paula's sister and Miriam's mother — who testifies that one week after the accident (which was one day before Miriam died of her injuries), she said to Sis in great pain, "I feel so badly about the accident, because I know it was entirely my own fault." This is hearsay that's not covered by the present-state-of-mind exception, because it's essentially backward-looking — it's mainly a "statement of memory or belief" offered to "prove the fact remembered or believed" (that Miriam caused the accident). By the way, the statement is also not a dying declaration (because there's no evidence that Miriam believed her death was imminent; see *infra*, p. 70). But it *is* a declaration against interest (see *infra*, p. 71).

   a. **Execution of will:** A declarant's statement relating to his *will* is covered by the "state of mind" exception, even though the statement may be one of memory or belief offered to prove the fact remembered or believed. See FRE 803(3), making the hearsay exception applicable to a statement of memory or belief that "relates to the execution, revocation, identification, or terms of declarant's will."

   Example: O says, "I changed my will yesterday to disinherit my no-good husband." If offered in a will contest to show that O intended to disinherit her husband, this statement will be admissible even though it is a statement of memory offered to prove the truth of the fact remembered.

D. **Excited utterance:** FRE 803(2) gives a hearsay exception for certain statements made under the influence of a *startling event*; this is called the *"excited utterance"* exception. The exception covers "A statement relating to a *startling event or condition* made *while the declarant was under the stress of excitement caused by* the event or condition."

1. **Requirements:** So there are two requirements for the excited-utterance exception: (1) the statement must relate to a *startling event* or condition; and (2) the statement must have been made while the declarant was still *under the stress* of excitement caused by the event or condition.

   Example: D is charged with seriously beating V, who survived the beating, in a barroom brawl. V does not testify. The prosecution calls Wit, who testifies that moments after the last blow to V, while V was lying on the floor of the bar, Wit heard V say in an agitated voice, "In case I die, know that V started the fight. Don't let him claim it was me who started it."

   V's statement is admissible under the excited-utterance exception: (1) the statement relates to a startling event (the fight); and (2) the short passage of time, and what the facts tell us is

V's "agitated voice," show that V was still under the stress of the event. (By the way, this is not a dying declaration even though V thought he would die — if the case is a criminal prosecution, the dying declaration exception applies only if it's a homicide case. See *infra*, p. 71.)

2. **Must cause "stress of excitement":** The startling event must *cause* the declarant to be under a *"stress of excitement."* So on the MBE, scrutinize the facts to make sure that the declarant really was "excited," and that the excitement was caused by the event in question.

   Example: Ralph, a realtor, is charged with violating a state statute that forbids persons involved in the real estate sales industry from discriminating against members of any race in making recommendations about where to buy a house. The discrimination is alleged to have taken place the prior year in the Oak Tree neighborhood. In its case in chief, the prosecution introduces Wit, who testifies, "I was in a café last year and I heard my friend Frank say in a matter-of-fact voice, 'Oh, look, there's Ralph putting up a flyer saying "Let's make sure no more black people move into the Oak Tree neighborhood." ' "

   Wit's testimony cannot be admitted under the excited-utterance exception. Frank is the declarant, and the statement is being offered for its truth, to show that Ralph put up a poster with a racially-discriminatory message. Since the facts say that Ralph was speaking in a "matter of fact voice," he was not under the "stress of excitement" from the putting up of the poster, so the excited-utterance exception doesn't apply.

3. **Relate to the startling event:** The declaration must *"relat[e] to [the] startling event."* Be sure to check this element out mentally before you conclude that a declaration on the MBE qualifies. The MBE examiners will often try to trick you by giving you a statement that is clearly made while the declarant is still under the stress of some startling event, but the statement does not relate in any way to the event.

   Example: Charlie, who is standing in the street in front of his house, is struck by a car. Moments later, as Charlie lies injured at the side of the road, his wife, Wanda, runs out. Charlie, believing he is going to die, says to her, "I never told you this, but Dennis and I were the ones who did that robbery of the First National Bank in Smallville last year." Charlie then dies. Dennis is prosecuted for this robbery, and the prosecution calls Wanda to testify to the above statement by Charlie.

   The statement is hearsay (offered to prove that Dennis really did rob the bank), and is not admissible under the excited-utterance exception. That's because, while Charlie was under the stress of excitement caused by an event (the accident), his statement did not "relate to" the event. (As as to the dying declaration exception, it doesn't qualify there either, because it doesn't concern the cause or circumstances of declarant's impending death; see *infra*, p. 71.)

4. **Time factor:** In determining whether the declarant was still under the influence of the startling event, the *time* that has passed between the event and the statement is of paramount importance. Usually, statements made during the exciting event or within half an hour afterward are admitted, statements made more than an hour later are not, and statements between a half hour and an hour are decided based on the surrounding circumstances.

   a. **"Immediately":** On the MBE, be on the lookout for an indication that the declarant described a stressful event *"immediately"* after it occurred — this should be a clue to you that perhaps the excited utterance exception applies.

5. **Reflection:** Since the rationale behind the exception is that statements made by a declarant who does not have the *opportunity to reflect* should be admitted as unusually reliable, facts showing that the declarant really did reflect will cause the exception not to apply. Thus if the

statement is very self-serving, or is in response to a detailed question, the court is likely to find that the declarant reflected (rather than speaking spontaneously), so that the exception should not apply.

6. **Need for inference:** Sometimes on the MBE, you will have to make some slight *inferences* to satisfy yourself about the existence of one or more elements needed for an exciting utterance. For instance, the fact pattern may not say expressly that the declarant was under stress from excitement, but may tell you that the declarant "screamed" — you will then be expected to infer from the scream that the declarant was "under the stress of excitement" caused by the startling event to which the scream refers.

E. **Present sense impression:**   The Federal Rules recognize an exception for *"present sense impressions,"* even where the declarant is not excited. FRE 803(1) gives an exception for a statement *"describing or explaining an event or condition* made *while the declarant was perceiving the event or condition, or immediately thereafter."*

Example: O sees a car speed by in the opposite direction, and says, "If the driver keeps up that rate of speed, he'll surely crash." This statement is admissible to show that the car was traveling fast. [*Houston Oxygen Co. v. Davis*]

1. **Immediacy:**   In contrast to the excited-utterance exception, the present-sense-impression exception applies only if *virtually no time passes* between the event being perceived and the declarant's statement about it.

2. **Must describe or explain:**   The present sense impression must *describe or explain* the event that the declarant has perceived (in contrast to the rule for excited utterances, where the utterance need not explain the event or condition that is causing the declarant to be excited, as long as it somehow "relates to" that event or condition).

3. **Declarant must perceive:** The present-sense-impression applies only when the declarant is describing an event that *he himself is perceiving* (or has just finished perceiving). If the declarant is "speaking hearsay" — describing something that he knows from someone else's statement or by some *means other than the declarant's first-hand perception*, the exception *won't* apply.

> **Example:** Car accident case, in which P claims D was speeding. P offers testimony by Wit as follows: Just prior to the accident, Wit was listening to the local police-dispatcher frequency, and heard the dispatcher say, "Police cars are chasing a blue Mustang at a high rate of speech down Main near the corner of South." Wit heard a crash and looked out her window to see police cars driving down Main coming up to a crashed Mustang (undisputedly belonging to D) just beyond the intersection with South. The issue is whether Wit's testimony can be admitted, in reliance on the present-sense-impression exception, for the purpose of demonstrating that the blue Mustang was speeding down Main.
>
> The answer is, "no." First, the dispatcher's statement is hearsay (offered to show that the Mustang really was speeding at the relevant moment). And the present-sense-impression exception doesn't apply because the dispatcher was not speaking of his own first-hand knowledge — he wasn't directly observing the Mustang (or the pursuing officers); he must have learned of the pursuit from them, and was merely "rebroadcasting" what he had learned. So even though the dispatcher was describing or explaining an event that was still occurring, the exception doesn't apply.

4. **Declarant need not be excited:**   The declarant *need not be excited* for the present-sense-impression exception to apply.

IV. PAST RECOLLECTION RECORDED

A. Exception under the FRE: A *written* record of an event, made shortly after the event has occurred, may be admissible under the hearsay exception for *"past recollection recorded,"* given by FRE 803(5). That rule gives an exception for:

> "a *memorandum or record* concerning a matter about which a witness *once had knowledge but now has insufficient recollection* to enable him to testify fully and accurately, *shown to have been made or adopted by the witness when the matter was fresh in his memory* and to *reflect that knowledge correctly*. If admitted, the memorandum or record *may be read into evidence* but *may not itself be received as an exhibit unless offered by an adverse party*."

1. Four requirements: So under 803(5), for the past-recollection-recorded exception to apply, four requirements must be met:

a. First-hand knowledge: The memorandum must relate to matters of which the sponsoring witness (or witnesses) once had *first-hand knowledge*.

Example: W writes down an inventory. If he says at trial that some of the information in the inventory was known only to his assistant who supplied the information, not to W, the memorandum will not be admissible under the past recollection recorded requirement unless the assistant is also available to testify.

b. Made when fresh in memory: The record must have been *made or adopted by the sponsoring witness* when the matter was *fresh in the witness's memory*.

i. Permissible delay: Under cases interpreting FRE 803(5), even a record made several days after the events in question might be held to satisfy this requirement if there was evidence that the person doing the recording would still have had a clear memory of it.

c. Impaired recollection: The sponsoring witness's memory of the event recorded must now be *impaired* — if he can clearly remember the events, he must testify from memory rather than have the document admitted. But he must merely have *some* impairment of his memory, not total lack of recall.

d. Accurate when written: Someone — typically the sponsoring witness at the trial — must testify that the record was *accurate* when it was made. (But the sponsoring witness does not have to be the person who made the record; thus if X made the record, it may be sponsored by W, X's assistant, who can testify that after the record was made, W checked it and determined it to be accurate.)

i. Multi-party problem: If *A* knows the facts and *B* records them, both *A* and *B* will probably have to testify at the trial for the record to be admissible: *A* will testify that the facts he told *B* were ones that he, *A*, knew to be accurate; then *B* will testify that he accurately recorded what *A* told him.

Example: Wit-1 works as a packer in the shipping department of Corp. When a shipment is completed, Wit-1 orally tells Wit-2, who is a clerk in the billing department, that the shipment has gone out. Wit-2 then makes a notation on a shipment ledger to that effect. Corp. now wishes to prove that a particular shipment was sent to Cust. No person who works for Corp now has a recollection of this particular shipment.

Using past recollection recorded, Corp can introduce the ledger as substantive evidence to prove the shipment was sent. But to do so, Corp will likely need testimony of both Wit-1 and Wit-2. The two will together have to establish that: (1) Neither has sufficient recollection now to testify about whether the shipment was made; (2) Wit-1 spoke from personal knowledge when he told Wit-2 to make the notation; (3) Wit-2 made the entry based on what Wit-1 told her to do; and (4) Wit-1, while his memory of the transaction was fresh, looked at the ledger entry or had Wit-2 read it back to him (or did something else so that Wit-1 could "adopt" the entry, since the entry must be "made or adopted" by a person with first-hand knowledge of the fact recorded).

2. **MBE Tip ("think hard before picking this answer"):** *Think long and hard* before selecting "past recollection recorded" as the answer. The doctrine has very strict requirements, and the MBE examiners are more likely to give you a fact pattern in which at least one requirement is *not satisfied* than one in which all requirements are satisfied. (For instance, out of all the released questions, we could find only one in which past-recollection-recorded was the correct answer.)

3. **Distinguish from present recollection refreshed:** Be sure to distinguish past recollection recorded from *present recollection refreshed* (p. 27). In past recollection recorded, the record becomes evidence. In present recollection refreshed, the witness gives the evidence, and the record just helps refresh her memory. The following table gives further differences between the two doctrines.

Past Recollection Recorded	Present Recollection Refreshed
W (sponsoring witness) *must not now remember* (at least not perfectly)	W *must remember*, so as to be able to testify
Record must be *shown to have been accurate* when made	Record *need not be shown to have been accurate* when made
W is *not now testifying* about underlying events (the record is the evidence)	W *is now testifying* about underlying events (the record is not the evidence)
Record must have been *made when maker's memory was fresh*	Record *need not have been made when maker's memory was fresh*
Record must have been *made or adopted by W*	Record *need not be either made or adopted by W*
Record *becomes evidence* (though can't be taken into jury room)	Record *never becomes evidence*

B. **Status as exhibit:** Under the Federal Rules, the record *cannot be taken into the jury room as an exhibit*, unlike other forms of real or demonstrative evidence — the theory is that the record is in lieu of testimony, so it should not be given greater weight than testimony by being taken to the jury room. But the record, as read to the jury, is *evidence.*

1. **Distinction:** This is one of the most important differences between past recollection recorded and *present recollection refreshed*: In the former, the record becomes evidence. In the latter, the document used to jog the witness's memory does not become evidence, but is merely an aid to stimulate memory and thus facilitate testimony.

2. **Trap on MBE:** In those relatively rare instances on the MBE when a fact pattern *qualifies* for the past recollection recorded exception, the examiners will often try to trip you up by specifying that the underlying document is *offered as an exhibit*. This usage is *not permissible* — as noted above, the last sentence of FRE 803(5) says that "If admitted [i.e., if the requirements for past recollection recorded are all satisfied], the memorandum or record may be read into evidence *but may not itself be received as an exhibit unless offered by an adverse party.*" So even where the requirements are met, if it is the proponent of the evidence that offers the physical memorandum or record as an exhibit, the document will not be admissible.

Example: P sues D for running a factory that spews pollutants into the air, harming P's ability to enjoy his next-door property. While P is on the stand, his lawyer shows P a diary that P maintained, showing P's day-by-day reactions to the pollution over a particular two-week period. P agrees that the diary entries were likely accurate when made. P's memory of his reaction is not fully refreshed by looking at the diary. If the physical diary is now offered into evidence as an exhibit by plaintiff's lawyer, it will be inadmissible.

To analyze what's going on here, let's first examine whether P's lawyer could *read aloud* various passages from the diary. The answer is *yes*. That's because all four of the requirements for past recollection recorded are satisfied: (1) the diary relates to matters of which the sponsoring witness, P, *once had first-hand knowledge* (his reactions to that day's pollution); (2) each day's diary entries were made by the sponsoring witness, P, when the matter was *fresh in his memory*; (3) the sponsoring witness now has at least a *partially-impaired memory* of events covered in diary (since we're told that showing P the diary did not fully refresh his recollection); and (4) the diary has been shown (by P's testimony) to have *correctly reflected P's knowledge when written* (i.e., P's reactions to that day's pollution).

On the other hand, because of the last sentence of 803(5), P is still not entitled to have the *diary itself* entered as an exhibit. However, once P has jumped through all the hoops (i.e., has shown that at least some parts of the diary meet the past recollection recorded exception), the *other side* (the "adverse party," meaning adverse to the party who has tried to use the past recollection recorded doctrine, i.e., D) *is* entitled to offer the diary as an exhibit. So, for instance, after P or P's lawyer has properly read some passages into evidence by using the exception, *D is* entitled to offer the *entire diary* to show that other parts of the diary — ones not read to the jury by P's lawyer — do not support P's case.

V. RECORDS OF REGULARLY CONDUCTED ACTIVITY (a/k/a "BUSINESS RECORDS")

A. Federal Rule: FRE 803(6) contains the FRE's version of the *"business-records"* exception. Because of the exception's considerable importance on the MBE, we reproduce it here:

> *"Records of regularly conducted activity.* A memorandum, report, record, or data compilation, in any form, of acts, events, conditions, opinions, or diagnoses, made at or near the time *by*, or from *information transmitted by*, a *person with knowledge*, if *kept in the course of a regularly conducted business activity*, and if it was the *regular practice* of that business activity to *make the memorandum*, report, record, or data compilation, all as shown by the *testimony of the custodian or other qualified witness*, or by certification that complies with Rule 902(11), Rule 902(12), or a statute permitting certification, unless the *source* of information or the *method* or *circumstances* of preparation indicate *lack of trustworthiness*. The term 'business' as used in this paragraph includes business, institution, association, profession, occupation, and *calling of every kind*, whether or not conducted for *profit*."

B. Various requirements: So taking apart FRE 803(6), a record is admissible as a record of regularly conducted activity if it meets the following requirements:

1. Business activity: The record must have been kept in the course of a *"regularly conducted business activity."*

    a. Non-profits: This formulation covers *non-profits* and other types of entities or individuals, as long as they are the records of a "business activity."

b. Personal records: Individual business proprietors are also covered, as long as they're acting in the course of the business. But a person's record made for purely *personal* purposes (e.g., personal diaries, shopping lists, etc.) are *not* covered.

2. Regular practice: It must have been the *"regular practice"* of that business activity to make the record. So sporadic, occasional notes about a business activity will not suffice — the records must be kept in the *regular routine* of the business.

    a. Ad hoc or special-occasion documents don't qualify: So a document *created for a special one-time purpose won't* qualify.

    Example: Doc examines Patient, who is complaining of a bad back following an automobile accident she alleges was caused by Derrick. Doc then writes a letter to Employer, Patient's boss, saying "Patient cannot safely lift weights over 10 pounds due to her recent back injury." The letter will not be admissible if offered by Patient pursuant to the business-records exception of FRE 803(6), because it was not the "regular practice" of Doc to write such a letter — he wrote this letter for the particular occasion of setting restrictions at Patient's place of employment. (On the other hand, Doc's notation in Patient's chart at Doc's office, "Patient complains of back pain," *would* be admissible, if Doc kept similar notes for all visits by patients.)

    b. Litigation purposes: Records that are made *in anticipation of particular litigation* probably *won't* meet this requirement of being kept in the "regular practice" of the business.

    Example: D is a construction company. At a building D is constructing in New York City, a crane collapses, injuring two pedestrians. D's manager requests that all of D's employees thenceforth create a daily record of "any communication or event relating to the crane collapse." These records will not meet the business-records exception, because they're being made in conjunction with a particular one-time event, and are thus not kept in the "regular practice" of the business. (Also, the fact that they're being kept for purposes of litigation probably means that "the source of information or the method or circumstances of preparation indicate lack of trustworthiness," a second ground of disqualification under 803(6) as discussed below.)

3. Knowledge: The record must have been made by, or from information supplied by, a person with *personal knowledge* of the matter recorded and who is *working in a business.*

    a. Writer need not have first-hand knowledge: Notice that the person making the record *need not have first-hand knowledge* of the facts recorded. All that FRE 803(6) requires is that the record be made "by, or *from information transmitted by,* a person with knowledge[.]" So if *A* reports a fact to *B* of which *A* has first-hand knowledge, and *B* immediately records that fact, this suffices.

    b. Source must be acting in the routine of business: If the person creating the record does not have first-hand knowledge, then the record must be made from information "transmitted by" a person with knowledge. Since the record must be "kept in the course of" regularly-conducted business activity, this means that the *source of the information* must be acting as *part of a business operation* when she transmitted the information, unless some other hearsay exception applies to the source's statement. See *infra*, p. 61, for more about this requirement.

4. Timeliness: The entry must have been made *"at or near the time"* of the matter recorded.

    Example: The shipping department of Store records every shipment sent out to a customer. Store's ledger showing a shipment made to D will be admissible under FRE 803(6) if Store establishes that: (1) it regularly kept a written record of every shipment that went out; (2) the person who wrote the ledger entries did so either from his personal knowledge that a given shipment had gone out, or by being told that this had happened by a person with such direct knowledge and a business duty to disclose that knowledge; and (3) the ledger entries were made shortly after each shipment actually went out.

C. Person supplying info: The person who *originally supplies the information* that goes into the record must satisfy two requirements: (1) he must have first-hand knowledge of the fact he reports; and (2) he must do his reporting *pursuant to a business duty*. The latter requirement means that if the source of the information is not an employee of the business that keeps the record, or at least of some business operation, the exception does not apply. (But as we discuss more below, if the statement by the person supplying the information falls within some other hearsay exception apart from business records, then the requirement that the person making the report be acting pursuant to a business duty does not apply.)

   1. **Witnesses to accidents:** Thus statements by consumers who are *witnesses to an accident*, even if made to a police officer or other person with a business duty to compile a report, will typically *not* be admissible. [*Johnson v. Lutz*]

   2. **Consumer complaints or reports:** Similarly, *complaints* by *consumers*, if offered for the truth of the complaint asserted by the consumer, will not qualify, unless the consumer's statement falls within some other exception. The MBE examiners like to test this point.

      > **Example:** P, the owner of the trademark "Ray's Pizza" for purposes of the New York City pizza-parlor industry, operates a Ray's Pizza Restaurant at No. 20 Park Avenue. P has reason to believe that other businesses with similar names are sometimes causing consumer confusion, in possible violation of P's trademark. P therefore asks its employees to keep a record of any phone call in which the customer thinks he is speaking to a Ray's Pizza at an address other than No. 20 Park Ave. The employees record such consumer statements (e.g., "This is the Ray's on Fifth Ave., right?") in a notebook. In a trial by P against D, which operates a "Ray's Pizza" on Fifth Ave., P offers the notebook as a business record, to show that many consumers are confused about which Ray's Pizza they're calling.
      >
      > The notebook does not meet the business records exception for several reasons. One reason is that, to the extent the notebook is being offered to prove that individual customers are in fact confused, the source of each statement is not a person acting pursuant to the requirements of a business (whether P's business or some other business); instead, each statement is being made by a consumer, so the statements do not meet the requirement of being made by one with a business purpose (and no other hearsay exception applies to each consumer's statement). (Also, the record is of suspect trustworthiness, since it's being made in anticipation of various litigations, and finally, it probably isn't being made sufficiently routinely to be in the "regular practice of" P's business activity.)

   3. **Other exception covering source of info:** But if the third-party information (from a source who is not an employee of the business that keeps the record) falls within *some other hearsay exception*, then by a *two-step process* the *entire report* may nonetheless be admissible.

      > **Example 1:** P accuses her employer D, a business, of sexual harassment, because P's boss X made advances to her. D hires Security Co., a private-investigation firm, to investigate P's claim; D tells all its employees to cooperate with the investigation. Security Co. interviews W, who works for D; W tells Security Co., "Yes, I saw X make advances to P at the office." Security Co. prepares a report which repeats W's statement. At trial, P now seeks to introduce the report as evidence that W saw X make advances to P.
      >
      > The business-records exception won't by itself be enough to get the whole report into evidence, because W (the source of the information) didn't work for Security Co. (the

business keeping the record, i.e., the report). But since W was an employee of D at the time he made the statement to Security Co., and did so as part of his job (which included cooperating with the investigation), W's statement will be admissible against D as an agent's admission, admissible against the principal. So the "outer layer" (the report) is admissible as a business record, and the "inner layer" (W's statement to Security Co.) is admissible as an admission by an agent.

Example 2: Hospital directs its emergency room personnel to keep a chart on every patient who is treated. P, who is injured in a car accident allegedly caused by D's negligence, immediately after the accident comes to Hospital's E.R. for treatment. There, P tells Doc, the doctor who treats him, "I have back pain from the car accident I was just in." Doc records this statement on the hospital chart. In P's suit against D, P offers the record to show that P suffered from back pain right after the accident.

Even though the particular statement at issue (P's statement that he has back pain from the car accident) comes from a person (P) who is acting as a consumer rather than as a person with a business duty to make the statement, the record will be admissible. That's because P's statement itself falls within a non-business-records hearsay exception (803(4)'s exception for statements made for purposes of medical diagnosis or treatment), and Doc's entry of the statement into the hospital record met the requirements of being made pursuant to the business-records exception (e.g., the hospital records were routinely kept, and Doc was acting in the course of Hospital's regular business activity when he recorded P's statement). So the fact that P was not acting in the course of Hospital's or any other business when he made the statement does not prevent the business-records exception from applying.

D. Untrustworthy: If the surrounding circumstances make the record seem *untrustworthy*, the court must find that it does not satisfy the business records exception. See the last phrase of the main sentence of FRE 803(6), making the exception applicable "unless *the source of information or the method or circumstances of preparation indicate lack of trustworthiness*."

1. **Self-serving record:** For instance, if the facts indicate that the business that made the record had a strong motive to create a *self-serving* record, the court is likely to exclude it.

   Example: After every train crash, Railroad conducts an internal investigation, and makes a report. One such report completely absolves the engineer, based on what the court determines was an incomplete investigation that overlooks some aspects indicating negligence by the engineer. Railroad then offers the report at trial. The court is likely to conclude that the "method or circumstances of preparation" indicate that the report lacks trustworthiness. If so, the court must exclude the record from the coverage of the business-records exception.

E. Don't use where record is kept by D and offered by P: If the record is *kept by the defendant and offered by the plaintiff,* the business-records exception will almost certainly *not* be the best choice on the MBE. That's because in this scenario, the record ought to always be admissible as an *admission.* So the business-records exception is likely to be the best choice only where the record is being offered by either the business that *made* the record, or by a *third party*, rather than by the litigation adversary of the business that made the record.

F. Proving the record: The business record is not "self admitting." Instead, a *sponsoring witness* must normally be called, who can testify that the requirements of the business-records statute were satisfied. Typically, this will be someone who knows enough about the record-keeping routine of the business to testify that the records were appropriately kept in the particular instance (even if this witness did not make or observe the particular entry in question).

1. **Certification as alternative:** However, FRE 803(6) (together with FRE 902(11)) gives an alternative method for a business record to be admitted, a method that does not need a "live" sponsoring

witness. Instead, the proponent can supply a written *"certification,"* by a person who would be qualified to be a live sponsoring witness. As long as the certification document describes how the record meets the requirements for a business record, the hearsay rule does not bar the document, and no live sponsoring testimony is needed.

2. **Need records, not just testimony about what they say:** The business record *itself* must be admitted, *not merely oral testimony about what the business record says.* That's because the Best Evidence Rule of FRE 1002 (discussed in detail *infra*, p. 90) says: "To prove the contents of a writing ... the original writing ... is required, except as otherwise provided in these rules[.]"

> **Example:** P, a business, sues D for non-payment of 3 invoices. D claims the items were never delivered. P's bookkeeper testifies, "I kept regular contemporaneous records of every delivery during the time in question. I have personally reviewed the records, and find a delivery receipt for each shipment covered by these 3 invoices." Even if the delivery records would otherwise qualify for the business records exception, the bookkeeper's testimony standing alone must be excluded — the underlying delivery receipts (i.e., the business records themselves) must be produced, because what is being proven is the "contents" of these delivery records, and the Best Evidence Rule (*infra*, p. 90) says that to prove the contents of a writing, the writing itself is required.

G. Special situations: Here are two recurring situations where the business records exception is often applied:

1. **Hospital records:**   *Hospital records* are often introduced to prove the truth of statements contained in them. Even statements contained in the record that are not declarations of symptoms (e.g., "Patient said he was hit by a truck") may be admitted if part of the record. But totally extraneous matter (e.g., "Patient says that the car that hit him ran a red light") will not be admitted.

   a. **Patient under no duty:**   If the information comes from the patient, the situation will not normally satisfy the requirement that the person supplying the information must have been acting pursuant to the requirements of a business. However, the hospital record can usually be admitted for the limited purpose of showing that the patient made a particular statement; then, *some other exception* may apply to allow the patient's statement to be offered for the truth of the matter asserted. For instance, if the patient is the plaintiff, the defendant will be able to introduce the statement against him because it is an admission; similarly, if the patient was reporting his current symptoms or other bodily condition, the "statement of present physical condition" or "statement for purposes of medical diagnosis or treatment" exception will likely apply.

2. **Computer print-outs:**   *Computer print-outs* will often be admissible to prove the truth of matters stated in the print-out. However, the proponent must show that: (1) the print-out comes from data that was entered into the system relatively promptly; and (2) the procedures by which the data was entered, the program written, the report prepared, etc., are all reasonably reliable.

H. Absence of entry: If a particular type of regularly kept business record would qualify under 803(6), a party may instead prove that a particular entry in the records is *absent*, if such an entry would normally have been made had a particular event occurred.

1. **FRE 803(7)**   This ability to prove *"absence of a record"* is granted by FRE 803(7), which gives a hearsay exception for:

> "Evidence that a matter is *not included in the memoranda, reports, records, or data compilations*, in any form, kept in accordance with the provisions of [803(6), the regularly-kept

records exception], to prove the *nonoccurrence or nonexistence of the matter,* if the matter was of a kind of which a memorandum, report, record, or data compilation was *regularly made and preserved*, unless the sources of information or other circumstances *indicate lack of trustworthiness*."

2. **Testimony about search of records:** Most commonly, the way this exception is employed is by *testimony by someone who works for the business* that kept the records, who says that she *searched the relevant records* and *could not find any mention* of the matter in question. M&K, §8.48.

    Example: Merchant keeps regular records of every payment by a customer. The issue is whether Customer has paid a particular bill. Merchant may offer testimony by its office manager that the manager searched Merchant's records of all dealings with Customer, and that there is no indication in those records of any payment by Customer of the bill in question.

VI. PUBLIC RECORDS AND REPORTS

A. **Public records and reports:** The Federal Rules, like the common law, give a hearsay exception for a *written report or record* of a *public official* if: (1) the official has *first-hand knowledge* of the facts reported; and (2) the official had a *duty* to make the record or report.

1. **Federal Rule:** Actually, the FRE recognize three conceptually-distinct exceptions, all involving public records and reports. These are all spelled out in FRE 803(8):

    a. **Agency's own activities:** Subsection (A) allows admission of a government agency's records of its *own activities*, if offered to show that those activities occurred.

        Example: P sues the FBI for invading his privacy. He can introduce the agency's own surveillance records to prove that the agency tapped his phone.

    b. **Matters observed under duty:** Subsection (B) makes the written records of *observations* made by public officials admissible if: (1) the observation was made *in the line of duty*; and (2) the official had a *duty to report* those observations.

        Example: An IRS agent does a field audit of Smith's tax return at Smith's house. If Smith claims a deduction for "home office," and the agent finds no evidence of one, his written report to his superior can be introduced by the government in a later civil suit on the issue of whether Smith had a home office. But the agent's observation that Smith possessed cocaine would not be admissible, since the agent had no duty to report non-tax related matters.

    c. **Investigative reports:** Subsection (C) allows the admission of *"factual findings"* resulting from *investigations*, except when used against a criminal defendant.

        Example: Following an accident, the police send an accident investigator, who writes a report that concludes that the crash was caused when the vehicle traveling east-west went through a stop light. This report would be admissible in a civil suit arising out of the crash.

B. **Criminal cases:** Use of FRE 803(8) in *criminal cases* raises special issues:

1. **No use of (B) and (C):** Subsections (B) and (C) expressly *limit* the use of these subsections *against the defendant in a criminal case.* (B)'s "matters observed through duty imposed by law" provision does *not* apply "in criminal cases [to] *matters observed by police officers* and other law enforcement personnel." (C)'s "factual findings resulting from an investigation made pursuant to authority granted by law" provision *excludes use by the government* in criminal proceedings.

    Examples: A police officer's written report stating that he has seen D commit a robbery, or a detective's report concluding that a previously unsolved crime has probably been committed by D, could not be admitted against D in his trial. (Probably each of these reports, however, could be used *by* D against the government in the criminal trial, under subsection (C)'s provision allowing "factual findings resulting from an investigation made pursuant to authority granted by law.")

    a. "Other law enforcement personnel": Notice that Subsection (B), by its terms, does not apply in criminal cases to matters observed by police officers and *"other law enforcement personnel."* Observations by *laboratory technicians* working in government laboratories (e.g., the results of substance analysis performed by a police department chemist) will likely be excluded under this "other law enforcement personnel" provision.

C. Other issues: Other issues arise in both a civil and criminal context:

  1. Evaluations: Subsection (C) refers to the "factual findings" in investigative reports. But so long as an investigative report includes factual findings, other *"evaluative"* parts of the report — *opinions*, *evaluations* and *conclusions* — may *also* be admitted. [*Beech Aircraft Corp. v. Rainey*]

    Example: The government, after investigating the crash of a Navy plane, produces a report containing numerous factual findings. The report then says that "the most probable cause of the accident was pilot error." This statement may be admitted, even though it is an "opinion" or "conclusion." See *Beech Aircraft, supra.*

  2. Multiple hearsay: A government report must be carefully scrutinized for *multiple hearsay* problems.

    a. Report by one government agent to another: If government employee *A* tells facts to employee *B*, who writes them up into a government report, *A*'s statements will be admissible if *A* had a duty to give the report to *B*.

    Example: Officer Jones witnesses a car accident, and later says to Officer Smith, "I saw the green Plymouth run a red light and cause the accident." Smith includes this statement in a report on the accident. The entire report, including Jones' quoted statement, will be admissible under 803(8)(B), because Jones had a duty to furnish the information to Smith, and Smith's report was otherwise covered as a "report of matters observed."

    b. Statement by one without duty to talk: But if information is supplied by one who does *not* work for the government and does not have a duty to give the report, the resulting written report may not include the quoted statement, unless the quoted statement independently falls within some exception.

    Example: After an accident, Bystander tells Officer Jones, "I saw the blue car jump the light and cause the accident." Jones' report on the accident will be generally admissible as an investigative report under subsection (C), but Bystander's statement will have to be removed, because he did not observe the accident pursuant to any duty, or have any duty to make a report.

  3. Trustworthiness: If the "sources of information or other circumstances indicate lack of *trustworthiness*," the judge can keep the report out of evidence. This is probably the case with respect to reports falling under any of the three subsections.

    Example: Evidence that the public official who prepared a report had been bribed, or was motivated to minimize the government's culpability in the episode being reported on, would cause the report to be excluded for lack of trustworthiness.

D. Absence of public record: Sometimes a party may wish to prove that there is *no* entry in the public records about a certain event, or that a particular document or filing does not exist in the public records. Just as there is an exception allowing proof of the absence of a particular business record (see *supra*, p. 63), so there is an exception to prove *absence of a public record.* That's FRE 803(10), which gives a hearsay exception as follows:

> "To prove the *absence* of a record, report, statement or data compilation ... or the *nonoccurrence or nonexistence of a matter* of which a record, report, statement, or data compilation ... was regularly made and preserved by any public office or agency, *evidence* in the form of a *certification* in accordance with rule 902 [covering, among other things, certified copies of public records], or *testimony*, that *diligent search failed to disclose* the record, report, statement, or data compilation, or entry."

    a. **Certificate or testimony:** So by this language, the absence of a particular public record can be proved in either of two ways: (1) by a *certificate* by the keeper of the records in question, that diligent search has failed to find the record; or (2) by testimony of the record keeper to that effect.

        Example: In a prosecution of D for failure to file tax returns, the IRS could prove failure to file either by a certificate from a person who works in the relevant IRS records center that a search of the Service's records failed to disclose the relevant return, or by live testimony of that custodian that the return could not be found when such a search was conducted.

VII. LEARNED WRITINGS AND COMMERCIAL PUBLICATIONS

A. **Learned writings:** A *learned writing* (e.g., a *scientific treatise* or *article*) may be admitted *for the truth of the matter asserted,* under FRE 803(18).

    1. **Text of FRE 803(18):** Because 803(18) is tested with some frequency on the MBE, here's its full text:

> "To the extent *called to the attention* of an *expert witness* upon *cross-examination* or *relied upon by the expert witness in direct examination*, statements contained in *published treatises, periodicals, or pamphlets* on a subject of history, medicine, or *other science or art*, established as a *reliable authority* by the *testimony or admission of the witness* or by *other expert testimony* or by *judicial notice*. If admitted, the statements may be *read into evidence* but may *not be received as exhibits*."

        Example: P sues Doc, a heart surgeon, for malpractice in the performance of a heart bypass operation. P calls Serge, another heart surgeon, as an expert witness. During Serge's direct testimony, Serge identifies a book, "Coronary Bypass Surgery," as a reliable authority in the field. Serge now seeks to read to the jury passages from this book on which Serge relied in concluding that Doc performed the operation negligently.

        As long as the judge believes that the passages are relevant to some issue (e.g., whether Doc was negligent), Serge may read those passages, and they will be admissible substantively, i.e., to prove the assertions they make about proper heart surgery techniques.

    2. **Details:** Here are some details of how learned writings (e.g., scientific or technical treatises or articles) can be substantively admitted under this provision:

        a. **Use on direct:** The publication may come in as part of a party's *direct* case, if a favorable expert testifies that the treatise is authoritative.

        b. **Cross-examination:** Alternatively, the publication can be used as part of the *cross-examination* of the other side's expert.

            i. **Expert refused to concede authoritativeness:** The publication can be used on cross even if the expert *refuses to admit that the publication is authoritative.* (But in that event, the cross-examiner must establish the authoritativeness of the publication by some other means, such as another witness.)

c. **Expert must be on the stand:** Whether the publication is introduced as part of the direct or cross-examination, the publication may only be introduced if there is an *expert on the stand* who can help the jury interpret its meaning.

    i. **Use in cross-examination:** This "interpretation" may (and often will) be by a *hostile* expert under cross-examination.

    Example: P brings a medical malpractice action against D, arising out of coronary bypass surgery. D calls an expert witness, W, to testify that what D did was not negligent. On cross, P's counsel calls W's attention to a treatise called "Coronary Bypass Surgery." If W concedes that the treatise is authoritative, P's lawyer may cross-examine W by reading to him portions of the treatise. The "interpretation" of the treatise may consist of W's saying why the treatise does not help P's case. For instance, W may point out that the treatise is out of date, that it doesn't say what P says it says, or that it is too general and fails to deal with the particularities of P's situation under litigation. Nonetheless, any statement from the treatise read by P's counsel during the cross counts as substantive evidence of the truth of the matter asserted in the portion being read. (See "Use for truth," immediately below.)

d. **Use for truth:** Remember, under the FRE any statements read in from a treatise that has been "qualified" in this manner can come in *for their truth*, not merely for impeachment purposes. (That's what's happening in the above example involving medical malpractice.)

e. **Not admitted as exhibit:** Even if all of the requirements are met, the treatise *may not* be admitted as an *exhibit*. The jury has to be content with *hearing* the appropriate portions read to it (and "interpreted" for it by the expert who is on the stand at the time). This safeguard prevents the jury from misunderstanding and misusing a work written for professionals. (Observe that this no-exhibits policy is similar to that for past recollection recorded, *supra*, p. 58.)

    i. **MBE tip:** The MBE examiners like to test this point — they give you a situation in which portions of a learned treatise are (properly) read to the jury, and then ask you whether the jury can "examine the book" or "take the book with them into the jury room." The answer is "no" — the only use the jury can make of the treatise is to hear it be read to them and then be "interpreted" by an expert witness (whether she agrees or disagrees that it's authoritative).

f. **Other types of materials:** The classic use of FRE 803(18) is for a scientific or medical book. But the rule is written more broadly. It includes *periodicals or pamphlets*, and it includes materials not only on the sciences and medicine, but also on "*history* ... or other ... *art*[.]" This language is broad enough to include "*standards and manuals* published by government agencies and *industry and professional organizations*." McC., p. 534.

Example: P is injured by a power saw, and sues on a product liability claim based upon defective design. He should be able to use FRE 803(18) to put into evidence Underwriters Laboratory Standards, and to show that the saw in question did not satisfy those standards. (Remember that he would have to have an expert on the stand while doing so. He might, for instance, call the chief engineer of D, and ask him whether Underwriters Laboratory Standards are recognized in the power saw industry as being a measure of the safeness of a saw.)

B. Commercial publications: The Federal Rules recognize a similar exception for *commercial publications* that are commonly relied upon by business people. See FRE 803(17), allowing admission of "market quotations, tabulations, lists, directories, or other *published compilations*, generally *used and relied upon by the public or by persons in particular occupations.*"

VIII.   UNAVAILABILITY REQUIRED — GENERALLY

A. Four exceptions: Under the FRE, there are four significant hearsay exceptions that require that the declarant be *unavailable* to testify at trial:

1.   *Testimony* given in a *prior proceeding*;

2.   Statements made while the declarant believed his death was impending (so-called *"dying declarations"*);

3.   Statements which were *against the declarant's interest* when made; and

4.   Statements offered against a party that has engaged in (or acquiesced in) *wrongdoing* that was intended to, and did, *procure the unavailability* of the declarant as a witness.

   See FRE 804(b)

B. Meaning of "unavailable":

1.   **FRE 804(a):** FRE 804(a) defines five situations in which the declarant will be deemed to be unavailable:

   a.   He is *privileged* against testifying about the subject matter of his out-of-court statement;

   b.   He *refuses* to testify despite a court order;

   c.   He testifies that he *cannot remember* the statement's subject matter;

   d.   He cannot be present to testify because of *death*, or physical or mental *illness*; or

   e.   He is absent, and the proponent of his statement has been unable to procure his attendance (or his deposition) by *process* or other reasonable means (e.g., persuasion).

2.   **Proponent's fault:** But none of the above reasons will make the declarant "unavailable" if his unavailability is due to "procurement or *wrongdoing*" by the *proponent*.

IX.   FORMER TESTIMONY

A. General rule: The FRE give a hearsay exception for *former testimony* — that is, testimony given in an *earlier proceeding* — if the witness is unavailable for trial. This is done by FRE 804(b)(1), which gives an exception for:

> "[t]estimony given as a witness at *another hearing* of the *same or a different* proceeding, or in a *deposition* taken in compliance with law in the course of the same or another proceeding, if the party against whom the testimony is now offered, or, in a civil action or proceeding, a *predecessor in interest*, had an *opportunity* and *similar motive* to develop the testimony by *direct, cross, or redirect examination.*"

1.   **Requirements for 804(b)(1):** So 804(b)(1) imposes these requirements:

   a.   **Hearing or deposition:** The testimony was given either at a *hearing* (including a *trial*) in the same or earlier action, or in a *deposition* in the same or different proceeding;

b. Party present: The party against whom the testimony is now offered was *present* at the earlier testimony (or, in a civil case, that party's *"predecessor in interest"* was present); and

c. Opportunity to cross-examine: The party against whom the testimony is offered had the *opportunity* and *similar motive* to develop the testimony. Usually, this opportunity will have been the chance to *cross-examine*, but it may have been a chance to expand the testimony by *direct* or redirect examination.

Example (opportunity to cross-examine): P sues D for negligence. At a deposition in which D is present, P asks questions to X, a witness to the accident. Because D has had the chance to cross-examine X during the deposition, X's deposition answers may be introduced against D in the eventual suit, if X is unavailable to testify at trial (even if D did not use his right to cross-examine X at the deposition).

Example (no opportunity to cross-examine): W gives testimony unfavorable to D before a grand jury while D is not present. At D's eventual criminal trial, this testimony cannot be introduced against D even if W is now unavailable, because D had no opportunity to cross-examine.

2. **MBE Tip:** On the MBE, most of the time when there's a plausible former-testimony scenario, the former-testimony *won't apply.*

a. Most likely reason: The most likely reason why former-testimony won't apply is that neither the party against whom the former testimony is now offered nor any predecessor in interest was *present* with the *opportunity to cross-examine* the maker of the former testimony.

Example: Dave is charged with murdering Victor. Dave defends on the grounds that the murder was really committed by Molly, a woman who has since died. Dave offers a properly-authenticated photocopy of a transcript of a deposition in a civil suit brought against Molly by Victor's family for Victor's death, in which Molly said, "Yes, I killed Victor because I hated him." The civil suit was brought because Molly was known to have quarreled with and disliked Victor. The prosecution objects.

The judge may not admit Molly's deposition testimony under the former-testimony exception. That's because the exception applies only if "the party against whom the testimony is now offered ... had an opportunity and similar motive to develop the testimony by direct, cross, or redirect examination." FRE 804(b)(1). Since the "party against whom the testimony is now offered" is the government, the statement could qualify only if the government had the opportunity and similar motive to "develop" (i.e., undermine) the woman's testimony in the earlier civil suit. Since the prosecution was not part of that suit, this requirement was not satisfied. (But Molly's deposition statement *is* admissible as a declaration against interest; see *infra*, p. 71.)

i. Criminal trial or grand jury followed by civil case: If the present case is a *civil trial* not involving the government, and one party is offering former testimony of someone other than the present opponent, taken from a *criminal trial* or a *grand jury proceeding*, you can be confident that the exception *can't possibly apply.* That's because the private party against whom the prior testimony is now being offered cannot possibly have had the opportunity or motive to cross-examine the testifier at the prior criminal trial or grand jury proceeding. (In a criminal trial, no private party other than the defendant himself would ever have the opportunity or motive to cross-examine a witness; and in a grand jury proceeding, no private party, even a suspect on whom the proceeding is focusing, would ever have the opportunity to cross-examine a witness.)

b. Criminal defendant was earlier party: On the other hand, if a person, D, who is *now a criminal defendant* was a *party to an earlier civil or criminal trial,* and the prosecution is now offering testimony that was given against D in the earlier proceeding, then the chances are good that the former-testimony exception will apply if the former witness is now unavailable.

Example: D is now charged with involuntary manslaughter, arising out of a collision between a car driven by D and one driven by V, who died in the accident. In a prior civil case against D brought by V's estate, Wit, who saw the accident, gave a deposition in which he said, "D was speeding." Wit has since died. The prosecution can use the former-testimony exception to get Wit's deposition testimony admitted against D in the manslaughter prosecution — D as a defendant to the earlier civil suit must have had the opportunity and motive to cross-examine Wit during the deposition (and it does not matter that he didn't actually use that opportunity).

B. Meaning of "hearing" and "proceeding": "Hearing" and "proceeding" include any official inquiry in which *sworn testimony* is taken. So a *prior trial,* a *preliminary hearing* in a criminal case, a *grand jury* hearing, and a *deposition,* all qualify.

1. Not covered: But *affidavits,* and *statements* (written or oral) made to *law enforcement officials during investigations, aren't* covered because they're not truly hearings or proceedings.

C. Identity of parties: The *proponent* of the former testimony need *not* have been a party to the taking of the former testimony. Only the *opponent* must have been present.

1. Similar party in interest: Furthermore, even if the opponent was not present, under the Federal Rule the testimony can be used so long as the present opponent's "predecessor in interest" was present, if the case is a civil case. This probably means merely that a person with a very similar motive must have been present. (But in criminal cases, there is no "predecessor in interest" provision. Thus a statement may not be offered against a criminal defendant who was not present, even if another person — e.g., a co-defendant — was present at the prior proceeding and had a highly similar motive to cross-examine.)

X. DYING DECLARATIONS

A. General rule: There is an exception for *"dying declarations."* The Federal Rules broaden the common-law exception; FRE 804(b)(2) reads as follows:

"The following are not excluded by the hearsay rule if the declarant is unavailable as a witness: ... (2) *Statement under belief of impending death.* In a prosecution for *homicide* or in a *civil action* or proceeding, a statement made by a declarant while *believing that the declarant's death was imminent,* concerning the *cause or circumstances* of what he believed to be his impending death."

B. Requirements in detail: So under the FRE's version of the dying-declaration exception, the following principles apply:

1. Awareness of imminent death: The declarant must, at the time he made his statement, have been *aware of his impending death.* It is *not* enough that he knows he is seriously ill or wounded, or that he will probably die at some point soon. As FRE 804(b)(2) puts it, the declarant must *"believe ...* that his death [is] *imminent."*

a. Declarant wrongly believes he'll live: So even if the declarant *ends up dying* from the event to which the declaration relates, the dying declaration exception won't apply if at the time of the statement the declarant thought he would probably live, or even thought that his death would not be imminent.

2. **Actual death:** The declarant *need not in fact be dead* by the time the evidence is offered. The declarant must of course be unavailable, since this is one of the "unavailability required" exceptions — but if the declarant recovers from his life-threatening condition, and then, say, pleads the Fifth Amendment or moves beyond the court's subpoena power, the exception can apply.

   a. **Don't overlook "unavailability" requirement:** Where the declarant recovers, don't forget to check whether she's *unavailable*, as required for dying declarations. The MBE examiners like to trick you with a fact pattern in which the witness makes a declaration under imminent expectation of death, recovers, and then is available at trial (perhaps having already testified at trial). In this scenario, of course the exception doesn't apply.

3. **No non-homicide prosecutions:** Dying declarations are usable in both *civil suits* and *homicide* prosecutions, but *not in non-homicide criminal cases.*

   a. **Usable in civil cases:** The MBE examiners will sometimes try to trick you into thinking that dying declarations can't be used if the case is a civil case. Don't be fooled: if it's a civil case, the dying declaration exception *can* be used.

4. **Indirect reference:** On the MBE, if the choice specifically *names* the "dying declaration" exception, and asserts that the exception applies, the choice is *less* likely to be correct than if the reference is more *indirect*, like "Admissible, because [declarant] believed he would probably die of his injuries."

5. **Relating to circumstances of killing:** Under the Federal Rules, as at common law, the declaration must relate to the *causes or circumstances of the killing*.

   Example: Declarant, while dying, says to his wife, "I overpaid Contractor by $10,000; make sure you get it back." The exception does not apply, since it does not relate directly to the causes or circumstances of declarant's death. But, "X has been stalking me for two days," where X is later tried for killing Declarant, would satisfy this test.

6. **For accused:** The statement may be admitted *on behalf of* the accused (though usually, it is admitted *against* him).

XI. DECLARATIONS AGAINST INTEREST

A. **Generally:** There is a hearsay exception for declarations which, at the time they are made, are *so against the declarant's interest that it is unlikely that they would have been made if they were not true.*

1. **Text of Federal Rule:** The Federal Rules apply more or less the common-law version of the declaration-against-interest rule. FRE 804(b)(3), entitled "Statement against Interest," gives a hearsay exception, but only if the declarant is unavailable, for:

   "A statement which was *at the time of its making* so far *contrary* to the declarant's *pecuniary or proprietary interest*, or so far tended to subject the declarant to *civil or criminal liability*, or to render invalid a claim by the declarant against another, that a *reasonable person* in the declarant's position *would not have made the statement unless believing it to be true*. A statement tending to expose the declarant to *criminal liability* and offered to *exculpate the accused* is not admissible unless *corroborating circumstances clearly indicate the trustworthiness* of the statement."

So for a declaration to qualify under the FRE statement-against-interest exception, the declaration must satisfy these elements:

(1) **Against interest:** The declaration must have (i) been against the declarant's *pecuniary or proprietary* interest, (ii) tended to subject him to *"civil or criminal liability"*; or (iii) tended to *"render invalid a claim* by [him] against another."

(2) **Belief in truth:** The declaration must be such that, due to the against-interest element summarized in the prior paragraph, the declarant would not have made the statement *unless he believed it to be true.*

(3) **Unavailability:** The declarant must now be *unavailable.*

(4) **Corroboration:** If the against-interest element comes from the statement's tendency to expose the declarant to *criminal liability,* and it's offered to *"exculpate"* (take the blame off) a criminal defendant (an "accused"), there must be *"corroborating circumstances* [that] clearly indicate the *trustworthiness* of the statement."

> **Example 1:** P sues D for damages from the death of P's husband Hubby in an auto collision between Hubby and D. At trial, D calls Wit, who testifies that one day before Hubby's death from his injuries incurred in the accident, Hubby told Wit, "I feel terrible — the accident was all my fault." This is admissible as a declaration against interest: (1) Hubby is now dead and thus unavailable; (2) Hubby was exposing himself to civil (tort) liability by making the statement; and (3) therefore, Hubby would be unlikely to make the statement if he didn't believe it was true.

> **Example 2:** Dave is charged with murdering Victor. Dave defends on the grounds that the murder was really committed by Molly, a woman who has since died. Dave offers a properly-authenticated photocopy of a transcript of a deposition in a civil suit brought against Molly by Victor's family for Victor's death, in which Molly said, "Yes, I killed Victor because I hated him." The family brought the suit because Molly was known to have quarreled with and disliked Victor.

> Molly's deposition testimony is admissible under the statement-against-interest exception, since: (1) at the time Molly made the statement, she was exposing herself both to criminal liability and civil (tort) liability; (2) the consequences of such a statement are so adverse to the maker (criminal and civil liability) that a person in Molly's position would be unlikely to make it unless she believed it was true (and there's no hint of any other motivation on her part); (3) Molly is now dead and thus "unavailable" to testify at Dave's trial; and (4) the requisite "corroborating circumstances" indicating trustworthiness are present, because Molly is known to have quarreled with and disliked Victor.

B. Meaning of "against interest":

1. **When made:** The declaration must have been made against the declarant's interest *at the time it was made.* The fact that later developments have turned what was an innocent-seeming statement into one that now harms some interest of the declarant is *not* enough to satisfy this requirement.

2. **Pecuniary interest:** Statements against the declarant's *pecuniary* or *proprietary* (i.e., financial) interest qualify.

> **Examples:** Thus the declarant's statement limiting his own *property* rights (e.g., "I only have a one-half interest in this house") will qualify. Similarly, if the declarant is or was a *creditor,* his statement that the debt has been paid will qualify.

   a. **Tort liability:** Also, a statement subjecting the declarant to possible *tort liability* will qualify.

> **Example:** Declarant is a driver who has had a car accident. His statement to a police officer later, "I had a couple of drinks before I got in the car" qualifies, because it exposes him to tort

liability; that's true even if Declarant didn't believe that he had enough alcohol to pose any risk to him of criminal liability.

> **i. No tort liability:** But you've got to analyze the facts closely to make sure that declarant really *is* — or at least believed himself to be — possibly exposing himself to tort liability. For instance, if declarant is *exposing only a third person to tort liability,* that won't be enough even if the declarant and the third person are good friends or otherwise closely linked.
>
> **Example:** P sues D, the driver and owner of a car that crashes into P's car. D was carrying Pass, D's close friend, as passenger at the time of the accident. Pass tells Officer, a police officer investigating the accident, "D and I had a few drinks about 30 minutes before the accident." Pass' statement, if offered by P against D, is not admissible as a declaration against interest, because it did not expose the maker (Pass) to tort or other liability. That's because Pass was not driving, so his having had some alcohol before the trip didn't matter legally. And the fact that Pass' statement was against *D*'s interest doesn't matter either — only a statement against the declarant's *own* pecuniary or other interest counts.

3. Penal interest: The FRE treat statements against *penal* interest — i.e., statements exposing the maker to prosecution — as *qualifying.* However, a statement against penal interest that is offered to *exculpate the accused* is not admissible unless "*corroborating circumstances* clearly indicate the trustworthiness of the statement."

> **Example:** D is charged with burglary. W offers to testify that while in jail, he heard X, another inmate, confess to having done this burglary alone. Because both W and X are felons whose word is somewhat doubtful, this testimony will be allowed only if there is independent evidence that X may well have done the burglary — e.g., he was out of prison at the time, and is known to have performed other, similar burglaries.

4. Collateral statements: If a statement includes a disserving part but also a self-serving part, the court will try to *excise the self-serving part.* If the statement has both a disserving and a neutral part, the court will probably let in the whole statement.

> **Example:** "It was Joe and me that pulled off that bank job," will be admissible against Joe, even though the part of the statement referring to Joe was not directly against the declarant's interest.

> **a. Neutral or self-serving statements not allowed as collateral:** But a *neutral* or *self-serving* declaration *won't* be allowed in merely because it's part of the same broader statement that includes against-interest declarations — *each individual declaration* must be scrutinized to see if it's against interest.
>
> **Example:** W, in custody for a particular crime, says, "I participated in a small way." W then goes on to describe D's participation in detail, and says that D was the ringleader. The description of D's participation won't be allowed in as against-interest, because that description isn't specifically against W's interest. [*Williamson v. U.S.*]

5. Unavailability: Don't forget that the declarations-against-interest exception requires that the declarant be *unavailable to testify.* The MBE examiners like to trick you by giving you a fact pattern that might qualify, except that the declarant has testified at trial, proving she is not "unavailable."

C. Constitutional issues:

1. **Use by prosecution:** When the prosecution tries to introduce a third party's declaration to inculpate the accused, the Sixth Amendment *Confrontation Clause* rights of the accused may help him keep the statement out. For instance, a statement exposing the declarant to criminal liability, given while the declarant is under *police interrogation* in connection with a criminal investigation, will always be excluded from being used against the accused, if the declarant doesn't take the stand (and undergo cross on behalf of the accused) at the accused's trial. [*Crawford v. Washington*]

    Example: X is arrested on suspicion of burglary. While under police interrogation, he confesses to the burglary, and says he did it with D. At D's burglary trial (X hasn't been tried yet), the prosecution puts X on the stand. X pleads the Fifth. The prosecution now offers X's confession, to show that D did the crime with X. Even though the confession was against X's interest, the Confrontation Clause prohibits its being used against D, because X is unavailable for cross on behalf of D.

XII. FORFEITURE BY WRONGDOING

A. **The problem generally:** A party, especially a criminal defendant, will often have an incentive to attempt to keep a witness from testifying against him at trial. A defendant might do this by *intimidating* the witness, *bribing* him, or even *murdering* him. However, in many instances the witness will previously have made an out-of-court declaration (e.g., a statement to the police, "D did it.").

B. **FRE 804(b)(6)'s solution:** To remove the incentive for witness-tampering, FRE 804(b)(6) gives a hearsay exception for "[a] statement offered against a party that has *engaged or acquiesced* in *wrongdoing* that was *intended* to, and did, *procure the unavailability of the declarant* as a witness."

    Example: W is arrested at an airport when large quantities of cocaine are discovered on his person. While under arrest, he tells DEA agents, "I was doing this smuggling for D [a drug kingpin], who promised to pay me $1,000 when the drugs got through." D is then arrested and charged with conspiracy to import narcotics. D learns of W's statements, and wants to make sure that W does not testify at D's (or W's own) trial. D therefore tells W that if W testifies at D's trial he will be killed. W is frightened, and refuses to testify.

    Under 804(b)(6), the government will be able to introduce at D's trial W's original out-of-court statement to the agents that D was W's boss. This is true even though the statement does not fall under any other hearsay exception. D has, through his threats, committed "wrongdoing that was intended to, and did, procure the unavailability of [W] as a witness."

    1. **Common scenarios:** The out-of-court statements to which 804(b)(6) is often applied include:

        ❏ Statements made by W while under *police interrogation* (as in the above example);

        ❏ Statements made by W in a *grand jury proceeding* or preliminary hearing;

        ❏ Statements made by W in *W's own criminal trial*, or in a criminal trial of some third person.

    2. **No reliability requirement:** Rule 804(b)(6) does not contain any requirement that the out-of-court declaration be *reliable* in order to be admitted. This makes the exception much easier to use than, say, the residual exception of FRE 807 (which requires "circumstantial guarantees of trustworthiness").

        Example: A suspect, W, is being interrogated by the police for a particular robbery. W admits to some involvement, but says that the robbery was masterminded by someone else, D. W's statements implicating D are probably not especially trustworthy, given W's strong incentive to get rid of the blame by putting it on someone else. Therefore, W's statements are unlikely to make it into evidence against D under the residual exception.

But now suppose that the prosecution can show that D threatened W so that W refused to testify at D's trial even under a grant of immunity. Here, W's prior statement under police interrogation is exempt from the hearsay rule, no matter how untrustworthy the statement appears to be.

XIII. PRIOR STATEMENTS OF AVAILABLE WITNESS

A. Prior inconsistent statements: FRE 801(d)(1) makes certain prior *inconsistent* statements of a trial witness substantively admissible (i.e., not hearsay). If a declarant testifies at trial and is *subject to cross-examination* concerning his prior statement, that statement is admissible if it is "*inconsistent* with the declarant's [trial] testimony, and was given *under oath* subject to the penalty of perjury at a *trial, hearing,* or other *proceeding*, or in a *deposition*."

1. **Proceeding:** In other words, only statements given *under oath* as part of a *formal proceeding* — generally a *trial, preliminary hearing, or deposition* — may be *substantively introduced* if the witness's trial testimony differs. A prior inconsistent statement that was *not* given under oath, or not given at a formal proceeding, is *not* substantively admissible.

   Example (substantively admissible): In an accident case, Wit testifies at trial on behalf of P, "D went through the red light." D may introduce a statement made by Wit at a deposition (whether the deposition was given in the present P-vs-D case or some other case) in which Wit says, "The light was green when D went through it." Since this deposition testimony is inconsistent with Wit's trial testimony, it will be substantively admissible — admissible to prove the light was green when D went through — because FRE 801(d)(1) makes it non-hearsay. The same would be true if Wit made the "light was green" statement at an earlier trial (e.g., a criminal trial of D).

   Example: (not substantively admissible): Same basic facts as above example. Now, however, after Wit testifies that "D went through the red light" and leaves the stand, D offers testimony by Walt that two weeks after the accident, Wit told him, "The light was green when D went through it." Although this is a prior inconsistent statement, it does not qualify as non-hearsay under 801(d)(1), because: (1) it was not made in a trial, hearing, other proceeding or deposition; and (2) it was not made under oath. Therefore, it's not substantively admissible to prove the light was green, and can be used *only* to impeach Wit.

   a. **MBE tip:** Be careful to distinguish between the two scenarios covered in the two above Examples. Only prior inconsistent statements made *under oath at a trial, proceeding or deposition* are substantively admissible as non-hearsay; other types of prior inconsistent statements (e.g., oral statements to someone in an informal setting) are merely usable for *impeachment*, not as substantive proof of the matters asserted in the statement. The MBE examiners like to test you on this point, by giving you a prior inconsistent statement not made under oath at a proceeding, and hoping you'll say that the prior statement is substantively admissible.

      i. **Admissible for impeachment only:** So when you see a question on the MBE in which the cross-examiner wants to use the witness's prior inconsistent statement, and that statement was *not made under oath*, the answer will typically be that the statement is usable for *impeachment only*, not to prove the truth of the matter asserted in that statement.

Example: P sues D in a suit arising out of an auto accident at an intersection. P calls Wit-1, who witnessed the accident. P's lawyer expects that Wit-1 will say that the light was in favor of P. Instead, Wit-1 testifies, "I saw the accident, and the light was in favor of D." P's lawyer now calls Wit-2, Wit-1's next door neighbor, who proposes to testify that the day after the accident, Wit-1 told Wit-2, "The light was in favor of P."

Wit-2's testimony is admissible *only to impeach Wit-1, not to prove substantively* that the light was in favor of P. That's because: (1) Wit-1's statement was of course made out of court, and if offered substantively would be offered to prove the truth of the matter asserted in it (so it's hearsay unless some exclusion or exception applies); (2) the only plausible exception or exclusion is the exclusion given by 801(d)(1)(A) for a statement that is "inconsistent with the declarant's testimony and was given under oath subject to the penalty of perjury at a trial, hearing, or other proceeding, or in a deposition"; and (3) the statement here, made the day after the accident to a next-door neighbor, obviously was not made under oath or at a trial, hearing or other proceeding, so the exclusion does not apply. (But if Wit-1 had made the statement during, say, testimony at a criminal trial of P for running the light, it *would* be substantively admissible now by virtue of the exclusion. And that would be true even if the party now opposing Wit-2's testimony [i.e., D] did not have the opportunity to cross examine the declarant, Wit-1, at the time of the prior testimony.)

2. **Cross-examination not required:** FRE 801(d)(1)'s exclusion for prior inconsistent statements made under oath at a trial or other proceeding allows the prior statement into evidence even when there was *no cross-examination*, or even any *opportunity* for cross-examination, in the prior proceeding or deposition.

    Example: W testifies in favor of D at a criminal trial. The prosecution may substantively introduce W's prior inconsistent grand jury testimony, even though D and his lawyer were not present and had no opportunity to cross-examine W at that grand jury session — the theory is that D has the opportunity to cross-examine W *now*.

B. **Prior consistent statements:** If the prior statement is *consistent* with the witness's trial testimony, it is substantively admissible, but only if it is "offered to *rebut an express or implied charge* against [the witness] of *recent fabrication or improper influence or motive*." FRE 801(d)(1)(B).

    Example: W, a witness to a robbery, testifies at trial that the robber was not D. The prosecutor asserts in cross-examination that D has recently intimidated W and gotten him to change his story. D's lawyer may substantively introduce a statement made long ago by W at a grand jury, in which W told the same story, because the prior statement rebuts the prosecution's charge that W recently made up the story.

C. **Prior identifications:** A statement of "*identification* of a person made after perceiving him" is substantively admissible, if the declarant testifies at the trial and is available for cross-examination. FRE 801(d)(1)(C).

1. **No oath or proceeding:** Unlike a prior inconsistent statement, a statement of identification is substantively admissible under this provision even though it was *not made under oath* or at a formal *proceeding*.

    Example: V, a robbery victim, is walking down the street the day after the robbery when she spots D. She says to H, who is with her, "That's the robber." H will be permitted to repeat this statement at D's trial, even though W's statement was not made under oath or at a proceeding. And the statement is substantive evidence that V identified D as the robber.

XIV. RESIDUAL ("CATCH ALL") EXCEPTION

A. Federal Rule generally: Modern courts now tend to admit hearsay evidence that does not fall within any well-defined exclusion, if it is highly reliable and badly needed in the particular case. The Federal Rules codify this *residual* or *"catch all"* exception in FRE 807. FRE 807 imposes five requirements:

1. Circumstantial guarantees of trustworthiness: The statement must have *"circumstantial guarantees of trustworthiness"* that are equivalent to those inherent in the other, more specific, federal hearsay exceptions.

2. Material fact: The statement must be offered as evidence of a *material fact.*

3. More probative: The statement must be *"more probative"* on the point for which it is offered than any other evidence which is available through reasonable efforts.

> **Example:** If the declarant can give equally probative live testimony, or if there is some other witness who can give the same evidence as that contained in the out-of-court declaration, the catch all exception does not apply.

4. Interests of justice: Use of the evidence must be consistent with "the general purposes of [the Federal] Rules and the interests of justice."

5. Notice: The proponent of the evidence must give *notice* of his intention to offer the statement "sufficiently in advance of the trial or hearing to provide . . . a fair opportunity to prepare to meet it." The notice must include the particulars of the statement, including the declarant's name and address.

> **Example 1:** W has given detailed, credible, and important *grand jury testimony*, and is not available to testify at a civil trial. The residual exception will probably apply. (The "former testimony" exception of 804(b)(1) does not apply to this testimony, because the opponent did not have the opportunity to cross-examine.)

> **Example 2:** X took contemporaneous *hand-written notes* of an event he witnessed, but is not available to testify at a civil trial. If the notes seem to be reliable, and there is no equally probative or better testimony available, the notes will be admitted under the residual exception. (The document cannot constitute Past Recollection Recorded, under FRE 803(5), because the author is by hypothesis not available as a witness to authenticate it.)

B. Grand jury testimony: Prior to 2004, the most common use of the residual exception was to allow *grand jury testimony* to be used against a *criminal defendant* when the testifier isn't available to testify at trial. But the 2004 decision in *Crawford v. Washington* means that because of the *Confrontation Clause* of the Sixth Amendment, grand jury testimony can't be used against a criminal defendant (other than the testifier, that is) unless the testifier takes the stand and is available for cross-examination.

> **Example:** W witnesses a fatal shooting of V. W tells a grand jury looking into the shooting, "I saw the shooter, and it was D." At D's later criminal trial, W can't be found (he's moved out of state, with no forwarding address). Since W is not available to be cross-examined by D's lawyer at trial, and since D didn't have the opportunity to cross-examine W at the time of the grand jury, W's grand-jury testimony can't be used against D on account of D's Sixth Amendment right to be confronted with witnesses against him. And that's true even if the trial court is convinced that the grand-jury testimony has circumstantial guarantees of trustworthiness, and that it meets all the other requirements for the residual exception.

CHAPTER 6
CONFRONTATION AND COMPULSORY PROCESS

I. INTRODUCTION

A. Confrontation Clause: The Confrontation Clause of the Sixth Amendment guarantees a criminal defendant the right "to be confronted with the witnesses against him." This Clause gives a criminal defendant the right to keep out of evidence certain out-of-court declarations, where the declarant is not available to be cross-examined in court.

B. Compulsory process: The Sixth Amendment's Compulsory Process Clause gives the criminal defendant the right "to have compulsory process for obtaining Witnesses in his favor." This Clause may allow the defendant to *gain admission* of otherwise-inadmissible evidence. For instance, this Clause may give the defendant the right to introduce an out-of-court declaration (e.g., a confession to the crime by someone else) that would otherwise be excluded under traditional hearsay principles.

II. CONFRONTATION CLAUSE

A. First thing to decide: When you analyze hearsay evidence used against a criminal defendant to see whether it violates the Confrontation Clause rights of the accused, you must first decide whether the out-of-court statement at issue is *"testimonial."* That's because the testimonial/nontestimonial distinction makes a huge difference in how or whether the Confrontation Clause applies. [*Crawford v. Washington*; *Davis v. Washington*]

   1. Summary of rule: In brief, here's why the testimonial/non-testimonial distinction is key:

   ❏ an out-of-court *testimonial* statement by W *can't be admitted* in a criminal case against D unless W is *made available for cross-examination* at D's trial (or was subject to cross by D at the time W made the statement), but

   ❏ an out-of-court *non-testimonial* statement by W *can* be admitted against D *without any Confrontation Clause problem* even if W is never made available for cross by D.

   2. What is "testimonial":   Here's an overview of when a statement will be considered *"testimonial"*:

   a. Rough definition: The rough meaning of "testimonial" is "bearing testimony." The idea is that the declarant has some idea that the statement will be or may be *used in a serious legal proceeding*, such as a *criminal investigation*. So a *casual offhand remark* to a friend or acquaintance who happens to be standing near the declarant would typically *not* be testimonial.

   In the case of a *police interrogation,* a testimonial statement is one where "the primary purpose of the interrogation is to *establish or prove past events potentially relevant to later criminal prosecution."* [*Davis v. Washington*]

   b. Listing of "testimonial" statements: At a minimum, the following types of statements *will* be considered testimonial under *Crawford* and *Davis v. Washington*:

   ❏ *prior testimony* at a *preliminary hearing*;

   ❏ *prior testimony* before a *grand jury*;

   ❏ testimony at a *former trial* (whether of the present defendant or of someone else);

❏ an *affidavit* issued as part of a law-enforcement proceeding;

❏ perhaps most significantly, *statements made during the course of police interrogations,* including interviews by police at *crime scenes,* as long as the focus of the interrogation was on investigating a completed crime, not on managing a present emergency.

> **Example:** The police get a report that a domestic disturbance is occurring at V's house. They show up, and determine that sometime previously, V may have been attacked by her husband D, but that there is no present danger. An officer asks V, "What happened?" and V answers, "My husband John attacked me." V's statement is "testimonial" (made as part of an investigation into a completed crime rather than in response to a present emergency); therefore, as we'll see below it can't be introduced against D unless V is available for cross-examination. [Cf. the "Hammon" fact pattern portion of *Davis v. Washington*]

c. **Non-testimonial statements:** The following types of statements are probably *not* "testimonial," because the circumstances surrounding them don't suggest that the statement will be used in a later proceeding:

❏ statements by a *co-conspirator* during the course of the conspiracy, and in furtherance of it;

❏ *excited utterances,* spoken to a friend or relative who happens to be nearby, or spoken to a *911 operator* under emergency conditions;

> **Example:** V phones a 911 line, and tells the operator, "My boyfriend is attacking me." The operator, in order to do a records search to find out whether the boyfriend is likely to be dangerous to police officers, asks, "What's your boyfriend's name?" V answers, "His name is John Smith." Because this statement, although made in response to official interrogation, was made under emergency circumstances (rather than as part of an investigation into a completed crime), it is non-testimonial (and therefore may be admitted against Smith in a criminal trial without Confrontation Clause review). [Cf. the "Davis" fact pattern of *Davis v. Washington.*]

❏ *present sense impressions, spoken to a friend or relative who happens to be nearby;*

❏ *state-of-mind statements, spoken to a friend or relative who happens to be nearby;*

❏ *dying declarations, spoken to a friend or relative, and not intended to be used in an investigation or prosecution.*

B. **Rule for testimonial statements:** If the statement *is "testimonial," Crawford v. Washington* imposes a bright-line rule: the statement *may not be admitted against the accused unless the declarant is made available for cross-examination by the accused,* either at the *time of the statement,* or at the *time of the accused's trial.*

1. **Two important scenarios:** There are two especially important scenarios in which the bright-line rule of *Crawford* is likely to apply: (1) statements made *during police interrogations;* and (2) *grand jury testimony.*

   a. **Police interrogations:** The situation in which the *Crawford* rule probably applies most often is where W is *interrogated by the police,* perhaps while under suspicion of some sort of criminality, and W implicates D. If W doesn't testify at D's trial, W's statement can't be used against D (unless somehow D had a prior opportunity to cross-examine W about the statement).

Example: X is questioned by the police about the fatal shooting of V. X says, "I didn't shoot V, but I did lend my gun to D knowing that D wanted to shoot V, and I then watched as D did the shooting." At D's murder trial, X pleads the Fifth Amendment. The prosecution then offers (as a declaration against interest) testimony by Ollie, the police detective who interviewed X, about what X said concerning the shooting. Because X's statement during interrogation is "testimonial," it can't come in against D unless X is made available for cross by D. Since X has pleaded the Fifth, he's deemed not available for cross. Therefore, the Confrontation Clause blocks X's statement from being used against D.

    b. Grand jury testimony: Another important instance in which the rule of *Crawford* will lead to the declaration's being kept out is where the declaration is made in *grand jury testimony*, and the declarant refuses to testify at D's later trial.

Example: Same basic fact pattern as above Example in which X says he lent his gun to D. Now, however, assume that X makes his statement — "I didn't shoot V, but I did lend my gun to D knowing that D wanted to shoot V, and I then watched as D did the shooting" — not to the police, but to a grand jury. This, too, is obviously a "testimonial" statement. And, of course, D's lawyer doesn't have the opportunity to cross-examine X about it in front of the grand jury (since lawyers for the suspect never get the right to cross-examine grand jury witnesses). Then, suppose the prosecution wants to use this against D at his trial, under the hearsay exception for declarations against the speaker's (X's) interest. If X pleads the Fifth at D's trial instead of repeating the remark, his grand jury testimony inculpating D can't be used against D.

C. Rules for nontestimonial statements: Next, let's look at the rules governing use of *"non-testimonial"* statements. The *Confrontation Clause plays no role where a non-testimonial statement is concerned.* That's true even if circumstances surrounding the statement's making suggest that it is unreliable. [*Crawford v. Washington; Davis v. Washington*]

Example: Suppose that X and W are old friends, who have committed various crimes together and who trust each other. One day, while the two are having a casual conversation, X says to W, "You know that murder of V last year — well, D and I were the doers." (X is not intending to supply "evidence" against D – he's just gossiping.) Later, in a prosecution of D for the murder, the prosecution would like to offer W's testimony about what X told him. X refuses to repeat the remark at D's trial, pleading the Fifth Amendment.

The remark is *non-testimonial* (since X was not speaking as part of a formal proceeding or a police investigation, and had no reason to believe that the remark would become part of a criminal proceeding). Therefore, under *Crawford* and *Davis*, this non-testimonial declaration *doesn't get Confrontation Clause analysis at all*, and there is no constitutional barrier to its use against D in the form of W's live testimony about what X said to him.

D. Confession implicating someone else, used during joint trial: Special problems arise when *A* and *B* are tried together, and *A*'s confession implicating himself and *B* is sought to be used by the prosecution. If the same jury hears *A*'s confession implicating *B* (and *A* doesn't take the stand), then *B*'s Confrontation Clause rights are violated even if the prosecution only purports to be offering the confession against *A*. That's true even if the judge warns the jury not to consider *A*'s confession as evidence against *B*. [*Bruton v. U.S.*]

    1. The "two jury" technique: One way around this problem is to use *two juries* when co-conspirators are being tried. The trial court empanels a separate jury for each defendant. Then, D1 is allowed to withdraw his jury during presentation of evidence that D2 confessed and implicated D1. This saves the necessity of conducting two entirely separate trials.

CHAPTER 7

PRIVILEGES

I. PRIVILEGES GENERALLY

A. Federal: There were a number of specific proposed federal rules of privilege. But these were never enacted. Instead, FRE 501 is the only Federal Rule dealing with privileges. It provides that

❑ In general, privileges "shall be governed by the principles of the *common law* as they may be interpreted by the [federal] courts in the light of reason and experience." That is, normally federal judges will decide what privileges to recognize based on *prior federal case law* and the court's *own judgment.*

❑ But "in *civil actions* and proceedings, with respect to an element of any claim or defense as to which *State law supplies the rule of decision* [essentially *diversity* cases] the competency of a witness [i.e., availability of a privilege] shall be determined in accordance with *State law*."

1. Summary: So in summary, federal courts handle privileges as follows under the FRE:

a. Criminal and federal question cases: If the case is a civil case involving a *"federal question,"* or is a *criminal case,* the court will apply the *federal common law* of privileges;

b. Civil diversity cases: But if the case (or the particular claim or defense at issue) is a civil case based on state law — in essence, if it's a *diversity case* — the court will apply the privilege law of the *state whose substantive law applies.*

Example 1: In a federal civil case alleging that D violated P's civil rights under a federal statute forbidding sex discrimination, the issue of whether P's medical records are privileged will be determined by reference to the federal common law governing privileges. Since federal courts interpreting federal common law have generally not recognized a doctor-patient privilege, P's records will not be privileged.

Example 2: P brings a diversity case against D arising out of an auto accident that occurred in State X. The issue of whether P's medical records are privileged will be determined by reference to the privilege law of State X.

2. States: The states vary greatly on what privileges they recognize. Generally on the MBE, you won't have to make a guess about how state privilege law works, even if the case is a diversity case. The only exception is where a principle relating to privilege is almost universally accepted. For instance, the lawyer-client and psychotherapist-patient privileges cover only "confidential communications," so an MBE question might say that a third party is present without a good reason, and you'll be expected to know that even if state privilege law applies because this is a diversity case, the third person's presence causes the privilege to be lost.

II. THE ATTORNEY-CLIENT PRIVILEGE

A. Generally: The attorney-client privilege is basically that a client has the *right not to disclose* (and the *right to prevent his lawyer from disclosing*) *any confidential communication between the two of them relating to the professional relationship.* The key elements are:

1. **Client:** The "client" can be a *corporation* as well as an individual.

2. **Belongs to client:** The privilege *belongs to the client*, not to the lawyer or any third persons. The lawyer may assert it, but only if he is acting on behalf of the client in doing so.

3. **Professional relationship:** The privilege applies only to communications made for the purpose of facilitating the rendition of *professional legal services*.

4. **Confidential:** The privilege applies only to communications which are intended to be *"confidential."*

5. **Fact of employment or client's identity:** The fact that the lawyer-client relationship *exists*, and the *identity* of the client, are normally *not* privileged. Only the substance of the confidences exchanged between them is generally privileged (though there are a couple of exceptions).

6. **Physical evidence:** Normally, the privilege does not permit the lawyer to conceal *physical evidence* or documents given to him by the client; the lawyer may not only have to turn over the physical evidence but describe how and where he got it.

7. **Crime or fraud exception:** The privilege does not apply where the confidence relates to the commission of a *future crime or fraud*.

B. **Professional relationship:** The privilege applies only in the context of a professional lawyer-client relationship.

   1. **No retainer:** The required relationship can exist even though the client does *not pay a fee*.

      Example: Client receives a free initial consultation; the privilege applies even though, at the end of the consultation, either lawyer or client decides that the lawyer will not handle the case.

   2. **Non-legal advice:** But the mere fact that the person giving the advice is a lawyer is not enough — the relationship must involve the giving of legal advice. Thus, if the lawyer gives *business* advice, *friendly* advice, political advice, etc., the privilege does not apply.

C. **Confidential communications:** Only *"confidential"* communications are protected.

   1. **Client-to-lawyer:** Disclosures by the *client to the lawyer* are protected if they are intended to be confidential.

      a. **Lawyer's observation:** However, if the lawyer makes a physical *observation* that third parties could also have made, this will not be a confidential communication.

         Example: Lawyer observes scratch marks on Client's face, in a meeting that takes place right after Client's wife has been found stabbed to death. Since anyone could have made this observation, it is not privileged, and Lawyer can be forced to testify at Client's trial about the scratches.

   2. **Lawyer-to-client statements:** The privilege also applies to statements made *by the lawyer* to the client.

   3. **Presence of third person:** The *presence* of a *third person* when the communication takes place, or its later disclosure to such a person, may indicate that the communication was *never intended* to be *"confidential."* If so, the privilege will be deemed waived. But if the third party's presence is reasonably helpful to the conference, that presence will not destroy the confidentiality.

      Example 1: Client's friend attends the meeting in order to help supply facts and to cope with language difficulties; the friend's presence will not cause the privilege to be waived.

      Example 2: Client brings his brother to the meeting solely because he feels more comfortable having a family member with him when he has any meeting with a non-family member. The brother's presence will almost certainly be held to demonstrate that the meeting was not confidential, so that the privilege will be lost.

4. **Underlying facts:** It is only the *communication* that is privileged, not the underlying fact communicated.

D. **Physical evidence:** If the client turns over to the lawyer *physical evidence*, the lawyer may generally not conceal this evidence or refuse to answer questions about whether he has it, on attorney-client privilege grounds.

E. **Exceptions:** There are several situations where the privilege will be held not to apply even though the usual requirements are met:

1. **Crime or fraud:** Most important for the MBE, a communication relating to the carrying out of a future *crime or wrong* is not privileged.

   Example: Client says to Lawyer, "If X and I were to rob the First National Bank, and X were then to get caught and give a confession implicating me, could the police use this confession against me?" If the robbery is later committed, the prosecution may require Lawyer to testify about the statement in Client's trial, since even though Client was seeking legal services, he was doing so to seek assistance in committing a future crime.

2. **Death of client:** In general, the privilege *survives* the *death* of the client.

   a. **Exception for will contest:** But there is a key exception: if the suit is a *will contest* or other case in which the issue is who receives the deceased client's property, the privilege does *not* apply.

      Example: In a will contest, Son may call Lawyer to testify about Lawyer's conversations with Testator, in which Testator said that he wanted to provide for Son in his will.

3. **Attorney-client dispute:** The privilege does not apply to a *dispute between lawyer and client* concerning the services provided by lawyer.

   Examples: The privilege does not apply if Lawyer sues Client for a fee, or if Client sues Lawyer for malpractice.

III. PHYSICIAN-PATIENT PRIVILEGE

A. **No federal privilege:** Federal courts have *not* recognized a federal common-law *doctor-patient privilege*. So in a federal criminal case or a federal civil case involving a federal question rather than a diversity claim, there is *no doctor-patient privilege*, except for the special case of psychotherapists, discussed below.

   Example: D is charged with robbing a federal bank (a federal crime). The prosecution alleges that D, while wearing a mask and escaping after the robbery, was grazed on the forearm by a bullet fired by a pursuing police officer. The prosecution offers testimony by Doc, an E.R. physician who treated D two hours after the robbery for his arm wound, that "D told me that some cop incorrectly thought he was a robber and had fired at him and grazed his arm." Because there is no federal common-law doctor-patient privilege, Doc's testimony cannot be blocked by D on grounds of privilege (even though the testimony might well be privileged under statutes existing in most states).

1. **Psychotherapist-patient confidences:** But the Supreme Court has held that there *is* a federal common-law privilege for confidential communications between a licensed *psychotherapist* and her patient. [*Jaffe v. Redmond*]

a. **Confidentiality required:** As in the case of any attorney-client privilege, the psychotherapist-patient privilege will be *waived* if a *third person* not needed for the therapeutic purposes is present, since this will demonstrate that the communication was not "confidential."

IV. THE PRIVILEGE AGAINST SELF-INCRIMINATION

A. Constitutional basis: The U.S. Constitution creates a *privilege against self-incrimination*. The Fifth Amendment provides that "no person . . . shall be compelled in any criminal case to be a witness against himself...."

1. Applicable to states: This provision is binding not only on the federal judicial system but also on the *states*, by operation of the Fourteenth Amendment's Due Process Clause.

2. Two types: The privilege applies not only to criminal defendants, but also to any other person who is asked to give testimony that may incriminate him (e.g., witnesses in grand jury proceedings, congressional investigations, other people's criminal trials, etc.).

B. Requirements: The privilege applies only when four requirements are met: (1) it is asserted by an *individual*; (2) the communication sought is *testimonial*; (3) the communication is *compulsory*; and (4) the communication might *incriminate* the witness.

1. Individuals: The requirement that the privilege be individual and "personal" means that:

a. **Another's privilege:**   A person may not assert *another's* privilege.

Example: D is on trial for robbery. The prosecution puts on testimony by X, an unindicted co-conspirator, in which X says that he and D did the robbery together. D may not exclude this testimony by claiming that it violates X's privilege — since it is X who is testifying, only he may assert or waive the privilege.

b. **Business organization:**   *Business organizations* do *not* have the privilege. Thus, neither *corporations*, partnerships, nor labor unions may claim the privilege.

2. Testimonial: Only *"testimonial"* activity is covered. Thus, the suspect may be required to furnish a *blood sample, fingerprints, handwriting samples*, or even to speak so that his voice may be compared with a previously recorded conversation. Also, a suspect may be required to appear in a lineup for identification.

3. "Compulsory":   A communication must be *"compulsory."* The main importance of this requirement is that if a person *voluntarily* puts the information in *written form*, the document is not privileged. (But the writer may have a privilege against *producing* the document for the government.)

4. Incriminatory: The response must have a *tendency to incriminate* the person. Thus if there are procedural reasons why no prosecution can take place (e.g., the statute of limitations has run, or the witness has been given immunity), the privilege does not apply. The fact that answering the question might subject the witness to ridicule or civil liability is not enough.

C. Proceedings where applicable: The privilege applies not only where asserted by a defendant in a criminal trial, but also by any witness in *any kind of proceeding*. Thus it may be asserted by witnesses to a grand jury investigation, to another person's criminal trial, to a civil proceeding, to pre-trial discovery proceedings (e.g., W's deposition is being taken), or to questioning by the police.

D. Procedure for invoking:

1. Criminal defendant: When the assertion is made by the defendant in a criminal trial, he may invoke the privilege merely by *declining to testify*. In that event, he does not have to take the stand at all, and cannot even be questioned.

2. Non-defendant witness: But if the privilege is being claimed by a *witness* (i.e., someone other than the defendant in a criminal trial), the procedure is different: the witness must *take the stand*, be sworn, listen to the question, and then assert the privilege. In this event, it is the judge who decides whether the response might be incriminatory; but the person seeking the testimony bears an extremely heavy burden of proving that the response *could not possibly* incriminate W, a showing that can only rarely be made.

E. Waiver: A person who takes the stand and gives some testimony may be held to have *waived* the privilege with respect to further questions:

1. Criminal defendant: If a criminal defendant does take the stand, and testifies in his own defense, he has waived his privilege at least with respect to those questions that are *necessary for an effective cross-examination.*

> **Example:** In a murder trial, D testifies that he was not anywhere near the scene of the crime. The prosecution would certainly be entitled to ask D where he was, and D could not assert the privilege in refusing to answer.

F. Immunity: If W is given *immunity* from prosecution, he may not assert the privilege (since he has received the same benefit — freedom from having his testimony used against him — that the privilege is designed to provide).

1. "Transactional" vs. "use" immunity: There are two types of immunity: *"transactional"* and *"use."* Transactional protects the witness against any prosecution for the *transaction* about which he testifies. Use immunity is much narrower — it merely protects against the direct or indirect use of the *testimony* in a subsequent prosecution.

2. Use immunity sufficient: Use immunity is *sufficient* to nullify the witness's Fifth Amendment privilege. (But the prosecutor then bears a heavy burden of showing that she did not use the testimony, even indirectly, in preparing for the subsequent case.)

V. THE MARITAL PRIVILEGES

A. Generally: There are two distinct privileges protect the marital relationship: (1) the *adverse testimony* privilege; and (2) the *confidential communications* privilege. Federal courts applying "federal common law" under the FRE recognize *both privileges* to at least some extent.

B. Adverse testimony privilege: The *adverse testimony* privilege (sometimes called "spousal immunity") gives a spouse *complete* protection from having to testify against the other spouse.

1. Federal: In federal cases, the Supreme Court has ruled that the privilege *belongs only to the testifying spouse, not the party spouse.* Thus, the defendant in a federal criminal trial may not block his spouse's testimony; only the witness-spouse may assert or waive the right. [*Trammel v. U.S.*]

> **Example:** Herb is on trial in federal court in a case in which the prosecution is trying to show that Herb knifed V to death. Under the federal common law of privilege (applicable to any federal criminal case), the adverse testimony privilege enables Herb's wife Wanda to refuse to testify on behalf of the prosecution that the night of the killing, Herb came home with blood on his hands. But if Wanda is willing to testify against Herb to this effect, Herb cannot block her — the federal common-law adverse spousal testimony privilege belongs only to the testifying spouse.

C. Confidential communications: Federal common law also recognizes the *confidential communications* privilege. This privilege protects against the disclosure of confidential communications made by one spouse to the other during the marriage.

1. **Who holds:**   Under federal common law, *either spouse* may assert the privilege.

2. **"Communication" required:**   Only "communications" are privileged. So an "act" that is not intended to convey information is not covered.

    Example: H is on trial for murder. The confidential communications privilege allows either H or his wife W against W's being required to disclose that H confessed to W, "I shot V." But the privilege would not protect H against W's being required to describe (or against her choosing to describe) to the jury how she witnessed H shoot V, or how she saw blood on H's hands shortly after H is said to have stabbed V.

3. **Marital status:**   The parties to the communication must be married at the time of the communication. If so, the privilege applies even though they have *gotten divorced* by the time of the trial.

4. **Exceptions:**   Here are some common *exceptions* to the confidential communications privilege:

    a. **Crime against other spouse:**   Prosecution for crimes *committed by one spouse against the other*, or against the *children* of either;

    b. **Suit between spouses:**   Suits by *one spouse against the other* (e.g., a divorce suit);

    c. **Facilitating crime:**   Communications made for the purpose of *planning or committing a crime*.

    Example: H brings home loot from a robbery, and asks W to help him hide it. Since H is seeking W's help in committing an additional crime — possession of stolen goods — most courts would find the privilege inapplicable to H's request for assistance.

CHAPTER 8
REAL AND DEMONSTRATIVE EVIDENCE, INCLUDING WRITINGS

I. INTRODUCTION

A. **"Real" vs. "demonstrative" evidence:**   Keep in mind the distinction between "real" evidence and "demonstrative" evidence.

1. **"Real":**   *"Real"* evidence is a tangible object that *played some actual role* in the matter that gave rise to the litigation.

    Example: A knife used in a fatal stabbing is an item of real evidence.

2. **"Demonstrative":**   *"Demonstrative"* evidence is tangible evidence that merely *illustrates* a matter of importance in the litigation.

    Examples: Maps, diagrams, models, summaries, and other materials created especially for the litigation are demonstrative evidence. For instance, if the prosecution cannot find the actual knife used in stabbing, a newly-acquired knife believed to be similar to the one actually used may be presented as a model to help the jury understand.

3. **Significance of distinction:**   The foundation requirements needed to authenticate the two types of evidence are different. See below.

II. AUTHENTICATION

A. **Generally:** Every item of evidence other than testimony — writings, demonstrative evidence, and real evidence — must be *"authenticated"* before it is admitted. That is, the item must be shown to be *"genuine."* The Federal Rules have a simple, basic principle of authentication that applies to all such evidence: the proponent must come up with evidence *"sufficient to support a finding* that the matter in question is *what its proponent claims."* FRE 901(a). (FRE 901(b) then gives illustrations of acceptable methods of authentication for various types of evidence.)

1. **Real evidence:** If the object is *"real"* evidence, authentication usually means showing that the object is *the* object that was involved in the underlying event (e.g., the actual knife used in the stabbing).

2. **Demonstrative:** If the evidence is *demonstrative*, authentication usually means showing that the object *fairly represents or illustrates* what it is claimed to represent or illustrate.

   Example: In a murder case, the prosecution offers a diagram to show the position of all persons present at the time of the murder. Authentication of the diagram would consist of proof (probably in the form of a sponsoring witness's testimony) that would entitle the trier of fact to conclude that the diagram really does show the position of the parties at the time of the murder.

B. Methods of authentication:

1. **Real evidence:** For real evidence, authentication generally is done in one of two ways:

   a. **Distinctive characteristics:** If the item is *readily* or *uniquely* identifiable, it can be authenticated by showing that this is the case, and that the object is therefore the one that played the actual role. Thus FRE 901(b)(4) allows use of *"appearance,* contents, substance, internal patterns, or *other distinctive characteristics,* taken in conjunction with circumstances."

      Example: The prosecution in a murder case wants to introduce what it says is the knife used in the slaying of V. It offers testimony by Officer, who responded to the crime scene, who testifies as follows: "I found a pearl-handled knife next to V's body. I carved my initials, AB, into the handle. The knife you have just shown me is pearl-handled, has my carved initials in it, and looks like the knife I found at the murder scene, so it must be that knife." This testimony would be adequate to authenticate the knife, under 901(b)(4)'s "distinctive characteristics" standard, as being the knife found at the murder scene.

      Note: This "distinctive characteristics" method is an *alternative* to using a "chain of custody" authentication method, discussed immediately *infra*. In other words, even if the prosecution *can't* prove chain-of-custody, the item can be authenticated by showing its distinctive characteristics, as in the above Example.

   b. **Chain of custody:** If the item is not readily or unique identifiable, the item's *"chain of custody"* must be demonstrated. That is, every person who *handled or possessed the object* since it was first recognized as being relevant must explain what he did with it.

      Example: In a cocaine-distribution trial, each person who handled a bag of white powder taken from D must testify about how he got it, how he handled it during his custody, and whom he turned it over to, before the particular bag offered by the prosecution can be admitted.

2. **Demonstrative evidence:** If the evidence is demonstrative, authentication is done merely by showing that the object *fairly represents* some aspect of the case.

3. **Judge's role:** The judge does not have to decide whether the proffered item *is* what its proponent claims it to be (the jury does this). But the judge does have to decide whether there is *some evidence* from which a jury could *reasonably find* that the item is what it is claimed to be.

C. Authentication of writings and recordings: Special rules exist for authenticating *writings* and other recorded communications:

1. **Authorship:** Usually, authentication of a writing consists of showing *who its author is.*

2. **No presumption of authenticity:** A writing or other communication (just like any non-assertive evidence like a knife) carries *no presumption of authenticity.* Instead, the proponent bears the *burden* of making an affirmative showing that the writing or communication is what it appears to be and what the proponent claims it to be.

   a. **Signature:** Thus, a *writing's own statement* concerning its authorship (e.g., its *signature*) is *not* enough — the proponent must make some independent showing that the signature was made by the person who the proponent claims made it.

3. **Direct testimony:** One way to authenticate a writing or communication is by *direct testimony* that the document is what its proponent claims.

   Example: If the proponent wants to show that X really signed the document, he may produce W to testify that W saw X sign it.

4. **Distinctive characteristics:** A writing's *distinctive characteristics*, or the *circumstances* surrounding it, may suffice for authentication. See FRE 901(b)(4).

   Example: A diary that is introduced has these attributes: it contains the logo of D Corp.; its entries match testimony previously given by X (D Corp.'s employee); it was produced by D Corp. during discovery; and it is similar to other diaries previously authenticated. Taken together, these attributes suffice to authenticate the diary as having been kept by X on behalf of D Corp.

5. **Signature or handwriting:** A document's author can be established by showing that it was signed or written in the hand of a particular person. Even if no witness is available who saw the person do the signing or writing, the document may be authenticated by a witness who can identify the *signature or handwriting* as belonging to a particular person.

   a. **Expert:** If W, the person identifying the signature or handwriting, is a handwriting *expert*, he may base his testimony solely on handwriting specimens from X that he examined in *preparation for his trial testimony.* (But expert testimony on handwriting or signature-matching must meet the FRE 702 requirements for *scientific evidence*, designed to ensure that such evidence is scientifically reliable.)

   b. **Non-expert:** But if W, the authenticating witness, is *not* a handwriting expert, his testimony may *not* be based on comparisons and studies made directly for the litigation. See FRE 901(b)(2), allowing "nonexpert opinion as to the genuineness of handwriting, based upon *familiarity not acquired for purposes of the litigation.*"

   Example: Thus if W is not a handwriting expert, she may give testimony that X wrote the document in question if W has had occasion to see X's handwriting before the litigation began (e.g., because she has had correspondence with X). But W may *not* give such testimony based solely on her study of handwriting specimens from X in preparation for W's trial testimony.

   c. **Exemplars:** *Exemplars* (*specimens* prepared by the person claimed to have written the document in question) may be *shown to the jury*, which is then invited to *make its own comparison* between the exemplar and the questioned document, to determine whether both were by the same person. See FRE 901(b)(3), allowing "comparison by the trier of fact [i.e. the jury if it's a jury trial] ... with *specimens that have been authenticated.*"

6. **Reply letters and telegrams:** A *letter or telegram* can sometimes be authenticated by the circumstantial fact that it appears to be a *reply* to a prior communication, and the prior communication is proved.

> **Example:** P proves that he wrote a letter to D on Jan. 1; a letter purporting to have been written by D to P on Jan. 15, that alludes to the contents of the earlier P-D letter, is authenticated by these circumstantial facts as indeed being a D-P letter.

7. **Phone conversation:** When the contents of a *telephone conversation* are sought to be proved, the proponent must authenticate the conversation by *establishing the parties to it*.

   a. **Outgoing calls:** For *outgoing* calls (calls made *by* the sponsoring witness, W), the proponent can authenticate the call by showing that: (1) W made a call to the *number assigned by the phone company* to a particular person; and (2) the *circumstances* show that the person who talked on the other end was in fact the person the caller was trying to reach. FRE 901(b)(6).

      i. **Circumstances:** The "circumstances" showing that the person on the other end was the one the caller was trying to reach, include: (1) *self-identification* by the callee ("This is George you're speaking to"); or (2) the *caller's identification* of the callee's voice through prior familiarity.

      ii. **Call to business:** If the outgoing call is to a *business*, FRE 901(b)(6)(B) says that authentication can be made by showing that the call was made to the listed number for the business and that the conversation "related to *business* [of a sort that would be] *reasonably transacted over the telephone*."

   b. **Incoming calls:** Where the call is an *incoming* one (i.e., the sponsoring witness is the recipient), *self-authentication by the caller is not enough*. There must be some additional evidence that the caller is who he said he was.

> **Example:** W wants to testify that she received a call from X. It's not enough for W to testify, "I received a call from someone who said he was X." But if W adds, "I recognized the voice as belonging to X, from prior conversations with him," that *would* be enough to authenticate the call as having been from X.

8. **Ancient documents:** Under FRE 901(b)(8), a document or data compilation is automatically deemed authenticated as an *"ancient document"* if it: (1) is "in such condition as to create *no suspicion concerning its authenticity*"; (2) was in a place where it, if authentic, would likely be; and (3) has been in existence for *20 years or more*.

   a. **No guarantee of admissibility:** But keep in mind that a document that satisfies these requirements for the "ancient document" rule of authentication merely overcomes the authentication hurdle. The document still has to survive other obstacles (e.g., it must be non-hearsay or fall within some exception; but there is also an exception to the hearsay rule for ancient documents).

D. **Self-authentication:** A few types of documents are *"self-authenticating,"* because they are so likely to be what they seem that no testimony or other evidence of their genuineness need be produced.

1. **Federal Rules:** FRE 902 recognizes various types of documents as being self-authenticating. Here are the ones that are most likely to be tested on the MBE:

   (1) *official publications,* i.e., "books, pamphlets, or other publications purporting to be issued by public authority" (902(5));

   (2) *newspapers* or *periodicals* (902(6));

(3) *labels, signs,* tags, and other *"trade inscriptions"* that "purport[] to have been *affixed in the course of business* and indicat[e] *ownership, control or origin*" (902(7));

Example: A can of peas bearing the label "Green Giant Co." is self-authenticating as having been produced by Green Giant Co.

(4) *certified* copies of *public records* (e.g., a certified copy of a death certificate).

III. THE "BEST EVIDENCE RULE" FOR RECORDED COMMUNICATIONS

A. Generally:

1. **Text of rule:** The Best Evidence Rule (B.E.R.), as implemented in FRE 1002, provides that "To *prove the content of a writing, recording, or photograph*, the *original* writing, recording, or photograph is *required*[.]"

2. **Components:** The FRE version of the B.E.R. has three main components:

   a. **Original document:** The *original document* must be produced, rather than using a copy or oral testimony about the document.

   b. **Prove terms:** The Rule applies only where what is to be proved is the *terms* of a *writing, recording* or *photograph.*

   c. **Excuse:** The Rule *does not apply* if all originals are *unavailable* because they have been *lost or destroyed*, unless the proponent lost or destroyed them *"in bad faith."* FRE 1004(1).

3. **Not applicable to evidence generally:** The B.E.R. does *not apply to evidence generally*, only to writings (or equivalent photos or recorded communications). See *infra*, p. 91 for more about this point.

4. **Federal Rule:** The Federal Rules broadens the common-law B.E.R. in two major ways:

   a. **Broadened coverage:** Not just writings, but also *recordings* and *photographs* are covered by the FRE 1002, in contrast to the common-law rule, which covered writings only.

   Examples: An audio tape of a conversation, or a computer tape of data, would be covered under the federal approach, so that if these items are available, they must be introduced instead of using oral testimony to describe their contents.

   b. **Duplicate:** Unlike the common law, the federal rules allow a *duplicate* (e.g., a photocopy) in lieu of the original unless the opponent raises a genuine question about authenticity or it would be unfair in the circumstances to allow the duplicate. FRE 1003.

B. Communications covered:

1. **Writings:** *Writings* are, of course covered.

2. **Photographic evidence:** *Photographs* and X-rays are also covered by the Rule, if offered to prove the contents of the item.

   Example: P, to prove that she has been injured, wants to prove that her X-rays show a spinal injury. The X-rays themselves must be used if available, rather than a radiologist's testimony about what the X-rays show.

3. **Sound and video recordings:** Similarly, *sound recordings* and *video recordings* are covered. So if a party tries to prove the contents of a sound or audio recording, she must do so by presenting the actual recording rather than an oral or written account of what the recording contains.

4. **Other "real" evidence not covered:** But don't be mousetrapped into thinking that the FRE version of the B.E.R. applies to other types of "real" evidence beyond writings, photographs and recordings. The MBE examiners sometimes try to trick you into thinking that because a witness is referring to some item of physical, tangible evidence, the testimony is not allowed unless the physical item is produced — if the item is *not a writing, photograph or recording,* its "contents" (in the sense of its nature) *can* be described in testimony without any need for producing the item itself.

> **Example:** Murder prosecution, in which D is charged with shooting V with a 9 mm Glock Model 17 pistol with the initials "BC" carved into the handle. Officer, the investigating detective, testifies that he took a pistol from D's possession after accosting D standing over V's bleeding and soon-to-be-dead body. Officer then describes, in the above level of detail, the pistol he took. The prosecution (without explanation) does not produce the actual gun Officer claims to have taken from D. The B.E.R. does not apply — the gun is a not a writing, photograph or recording, so the B.E.R. does not require it to be produced. Therefore, Officer's testimony is admissible without qualification to prove that the pistol taken from D had these characteristics.

C. **Proving the contents:** The B.E.R. only applies where what is sought to be proved are the *"terms" or "contents" of the writing.*

1. **Existence, execution, etc.:** Thus if all that is proved is that a writing *exists*, was *executed*, or was *delivered*, the B.E.R. does not apply.

> **Example:** Prosecution of D for kidnapping. A prosecution witness, W, mentions that a ransom note was received but does not testify about the note's contents. Since this proof that the ransom note was delivered does not constitute proof of its terms, the note need not be produced in evidence. But if W goes on to give the details of what the note said, the note would have to be produced if available.

2. **Incidental record:** The fact that there happens to be a writing memorializing a transaction does not mean that the transaction can only be proved by the introduction of a writing. Here, the writing is treated as an *incidental by-product* of the transaction.

> **Example:** The earnings of a business can be proved by oral testimony, rather than by submitting the books and records, because those books and records are merely an incidental memorializing of the earnings.

a. **Transcript:** A person's prior *testimony* or *oral statement* can generally be proved by an oral account of a witness who heard the testimony or statement, even if a *transcript* exists. The transcript is merely an incidental by-product of the testimony/statement.

b. **Photos, recordings, etc.:** Similarly, if a *photograph*, X-ray, *audio recording*, *videotape*, diary entry, ledger entry, etc., has been made of an object or event, live testimony about the object or event will generally be *allowed* in lieu of introducing the photograph, etc. The MBE examiners like to test this point.

> **Example 1:** W may testify to seeing D shoot V, even though there happens to be a home movie showing the shooting. The movie is an incidental memorial of the event, so the event can be proved without the movie.

> **Example 2:** D is charged with making extortionate threats to V in a phone call by D to V. V happened to record the phone call, but does not bring the recording to court. V may testify about the contents of the call — the B.E.R. does not apply so as to require the call's contents to be proved by means of admitting the tape. That's because the "contents of the

recording" are not what's being proved; it's the contents of the *phone call* that are being proved, and the recording is just an incidental by-product of that call.

Example 3: P is a pawnbroker who is suing D for advances that P says he made to D over a period of months. P testifies to advancing D $500 cash on July 1. P acknowledges on cross that he kept a ledger of advances to all customers, and that he probably made an entry for this advance in the ledger. But he does not produce the ledger in evidence.

The B.E.R. does not require P to produce the ledger as a precondition to his testifying that he made the July 1 advance. P is not proving the "contents" of the ledger — he's proving the underlying loan, and the ledger is just an incidental memorandum of that alleged underlying transaction.

   c. **Contract:** But if a document truly *embodies* a transaction, the document comes within the B.E.R. and must be produced if available.

Example: If two parties to an agreement have signed a formal written *contract*, that contract must be produced at the litigation, even though the parties could have bound themselves orally to the same terms; the contract embodies their arrangement, rather than merely being an incidental by-product of it.

D. **Collateral writings:** The *"collateral writings"* exception to the B.E.R. means that a document which has only a *tangential connection* to the litigation need not be produced, even though its contents are being proved. See FRE 1004(4) (original need not be produced if the writing, recording, etc., is *"not closely related to a controlling issue"*).

Example: An issue in a case is the date on which D mailed a particular letter. D testifies that he mailed it in early November, and then says that he mailed it "on the same day I read in the *New York Times* that the New York Knicks had lost their home season opener the night before." D's testimony is acceptable, and the *New York Times* article need not be produced, because the document is collateral, i.e., not "closely related to a controlling issue."

E. **Duplicates:** The FRE make *photocopies* and other *duplicates* of business and public records admissible in most circumstances even if the original is available.

   1. **Federal:** Thus FRE 1003 says that a "duplicate" is *"admissible* to the same extent as an original unless: (1) a *genuine question is raised* as to the *authenticity* of the original or (2) in the circumstances it would be *unfair* to admit the duplicate in lieu of the original."

      a. **"Duplicate" defined:** FRE 1001(4) defines "duplicate" as "A counterpart produced by ... means of *photography*, including enlargements and miniatures, or by *mechanical or electronic re-recording*, or by chemical reproduction, or by other equivalent technique which *accurately reproduces the original*."

         i. **Illustrations:** So photocopies, carbon copies, images scanned into a computer and then printed out, copies of an original video or audio tape made by re-recording, etc., would all qualify as "duplicates" under the federal approach. But any copies produced *manually*, whether by typing or handwriting, are not "duplicates" and therefore may not be used if the original is available.

Example: P, a business, needs to prove that it sent a notice of claim to D. P's office manager, Wit, offers a photocopy she found in P's files of a notice of claim that is addressed to D and dated on the date P claims the original notice was sent. Wit testifies that it was the usual practice of P to make a photocopy of any letter or notice sent by it, and to put the copy in the appropriate file. The copy here will be admissible notwithstanding the B.E.R. — it's a "duplicate," but there's no genuine issue as to its authenticity, and it wouldn't be unfair to allow it to be admitted in lieu of the original (since if Wit is telling the truth the original is not in possession of D).

F. Excuses for non-production: FRE 1004 lists several scenarios in which non-production of the original will be *excused*, so that the proponent can use derivative evidence (e.g., a manual copy or oral testimony) instead of the original:

   1. Loss or destruction: All originals have been *lost or destroyed* (unless the loss or destruction is due to the proponent's "*bad faith*");

   2. Original not obtainable: *No original can be obtained* "by any available judicial process or procedure";

   3. Original in opponent's possession: At a time when an original was *under the control of the party against whom it is now being offered*, that party was *put on notice* that the contents would be a subject of proof at trial, and that party does not produce the original at the trial;

   4. Collateral matters: The item is "not closely related to a controlling issue" (see "Collateral writings," *supra*, p. 92).

G. Judge-jury allocation: The judge, not the jury, decides most questions relating to application of the B.E.R. Thus under FRE 1008, it is the judge who decides such questions as: (1) whether a particular item of evidence is an "original"; (2) whether the original has been lost or destroyed; and (3) whether the evidence relates to a "collateral matter."

IV. SUMMARIES OF VOLUMINOUS WRITINGS

A. Summaries generally: If original writings or other documents are so *voluminous* that they cannot conveniently be introduced into evidence and examined in court, the Federal Rules permit a *summary* to be introduced instead. See FRE 1006: "The contents of *voluminous writings, recordings, or photographs* which cannot *conveniently be examined in court* may be *presented in the form of a chart, summary, or calculation. The originals*, or *duplicates*, shall be *made available for examination or copying*, or both, by *other parties at reasonable time and place. The court may order that they be produced in court*."

   1. Sponsoring witness needed: The summary must be sponsored by a witness (usually an expert) who testifies that he has prepared or reviewed the underlying writings and the summary, and that the summary accurately reflects the underlying documents.

> **Example:** Lawyer has worked steadily on a case for Client over five-year period, with Client having agreed to pay a particular amount per hour worked. Lawyer keeps regular timesheets showing, for any day on which he has worked on the matter, how long he worked and what activities he performed on that day. There are hundreds of such timesheets. Lawyer has now brought suit against Client for non-payment, and does not offer into evidence the actual timesheets. Instead, in preparation for trial, Lawyer has used the timesheets to create a summary showing, for each week, how much time Lawyer spent on each of the activity types. Lawyer offers this summary in evidence, together with his testimony about how he prepared it.
>
> The summary is admissible under FRE 1006, since the hundreds of original timesheets are "voluminous" and not "convenient[] to examine[] in court." The summary is direct evidence of what the individual timesheets say. But Lawyer will have to make the original timesheets available for Client to examine, and the court may order that the originals be produced in court.

   2. Check for voluminousness: If summaries are used in your MBE fact pattern, check to make sure that: (1) the originals were *so "voluminous"* that they could not be conveniently examined in court; and (2) the *particular entries* that the proponent (the one who is trying to use the summary) is relying on are themselves voluminous.

> **Example:** P, a commission salesman, brings against suit against D, the company that employed him, claiming certain underpayments of commissions. There have been hundreds of transactions on which P was paid or due commissions, each shown by an entry on an invoice from D to the ultimate customer. P asserts that he was underpaid on 11 of these transactions.
>
> Even though there were hundreds of invoices showing P-D commissionable transactions, only the 11 invoices are material here. Therefore, P must offer the 11 individually into evidence, rather than a summary, chart or calculation of what the 11 show. That's because the 11 invoices actually at issue are not so "voluminous" that they can't be conveniently examined in court.

    a. **Absence of entries:** Also, testimony that one or more items *have not been found* in voluminous records, despite a diligent search by a person with access to the records, does *not* qualify under FRE 1006's summary-of-voluminous-records exception. So such testimony will have to come in under the exception in 803(7) for absence of regularly-kept records (*supra*, p. 63) or not at all.

> **Example:** P sues D, its customer, for non-payment of five particular bills out of hundreds that P sent D over the years. Wit, P's office manager, testifies that P keeps records of all payments received from any customer, and that Wit searched the records covering all transactions between P and D and could not find any indication in them that D paid the five bills in question. Wit's testimony is not admissible under FRE 1006 as a "summary of voluminous records," because it is not a summary of all the P-D records, merely the ones involving the five invoices in question (which are not sufficiently numerous). So her testimony will have to come in, if at all, via the FRE 803(7) hearsay exception for "absence of entry in records kept according to [the business-records exception]," not FRE 1006.

    3. **Originals need not be offered:** If a summary, chart or calculation qualifies under FRE 1006, it *becomes evidence* of the documents covered in it, and the originals *do not have to be offered in evidence* (though they may be so offered). So the summary, chart or calculation is an *evidentiary substitute* for the underlying records.

CHAPTER 9

OPINIONS, EXPERTS, AND SCIENTIFIC EVIDENCE

I. FIRST-HAND KNOWLEDGE AND LAY OPINIONS

A. **First-hand knowledge required:** An ordinary (*non-expert*) witness must normally limit her testimony to facts of which she has *first-hand knowledge*.

    1. **Distinguished from hearsay:** You must distinguish the "first-hand knowledge" requirement from the hearsay rule. If W's statement on its face makes it clear that W is merely repeating what someone else said, the objection is to hearsay; if W purports to be stating matters which he personally observed, but she is actually repeating statements by others, the objection is to lack of first-hand knowledge.

    2. **Experts:** The rule requiring first-hand knowledge does not apply to experts. (See below.)

B. **Lay opinions:**

1. **Traditional view:** The traditional view is that a non-expert witness must generally state only facts, not "*opinions*."

2. **Federal approach:** But the FRE view is that lay opinions will be sometimes be *allowed*. See FRE 701, allowing non-expert opinions or inferences that are "(a) *rationally based on the perception* of the witness and (b) helpful to a *clear understanding* of the witness's testimony or the determination of a fact in issue and (c) *not* based on scientific, technical, or other *specialized knowledge* within the scope of Rule 702 [dealing with expert testimony]."

   a. **Short-hand rendition:** One instance in which courts following the FRE recognize an exception to the rule against lay opinions is where the "opinion" is really a *"short-hand rendition."* That is, if the witness has perceived a number of small facts that cannot each be easily stated, she will be permitted to summarize the collective facts with a "short-hand" formulation. McC., p. 18.

      Examples: (1) The car "passed at high speed"; (2) X "looked like he was no more than thirty years old"; and (3) Z "looked like he was very worried." In each of these situations, it may be somewhat hard for W to articulate the precise underlying facts that have led him to the conclusion. Cf. Lilly, p. 108.

C. **Opinion on "ultimate issue":** Some older cases barred opinions on "*ultimate* issues." But FRE 704(a) *allows* opinions on ultimate issues, except where the mental state of a criminal defendant is concerned.

II. EXPERT WITNESSES

A. **Requirements for allowing:** FRE 702 imposes *five requirements* that *expert testimony* must meet in order to be admissible:

   [1] It must be the case that "scientific, technical, or other *specialized knowledge*" will "*assist the trier of fact to understand* the evidence or to determine a fact in issue";

   [2] The witness must be *"qualified"* as an expert by "*knowledge, skill, experience, training, or education*";

   [3] The testimony must be based upon *"sufficient facts or data"*;

   [4] The testimony must be the product of *"reliable principles and methods"*; and

   [5] The witness must have *applied* these principles and methods "*reliably* to the *facts of the case*."

Let's quickly review each of these five requirements.

1. **Specialized knowledge will be helpful:** It must be the case that "scientific, technical, or other *specialized knowledge*" will "*assist the trier of fact to understand* the evidence or to determine a fact in issue."

   a. **Ordinary evidence:** Therefore expert testimony will be most appropriate whether it involves the interpretation of facts of a sort that *lay persons are not usually called upon to evaluate*. So testimony about whether two bullets were fired from the same gun, or whether two DNA samples are from the same person, would be suitable for expert testimony, since lay persons usually don't have to make such determinations in ordinary life. By contrast, since juries and ordinary people are often called upon to evaluate the reliability of an eyewitness identification, expert testimony purporting to tell the jury why such I.D.s are often unreliable will often be rejected as not satisfying this requirement of "helpfulness."

2. **Qualifications:** Next, the expert must be *"qualified."* That is, he must have knowledge or skill in a particular area that distinguishes him from an ordinary person.

    a. **Source of expertise:** This expertise may come from either *education* or *experience.* So a special degree or formal credential is not required.

    b. **Need for sub-specialist:** Generally, a specialist in a particular field will be treated as an expert even though he is not specialist in the particular *sub-field* or branch of that field.

        Example: If a medical condition involves kidney failure, a general practitioner would probably be found a qualified expert, even though he is not a sub-specialist in nephrology.

3. **Based upon "sufficient facts or data":** The third requirement is that the testimony be *"based upon sufficient facts or data."* This requirement, plus the two that follow, reflect an attempt by the Rule drafters to *keep out unreliable testimony*, sometimes called "junk science." We explore this factor more in "Basis for expert's opinion," *infra*, p. 97.

4. **Product of "reliable principles and methods":** The fourth requirement in FRE 702 is that the testimony must be the *"product of reliable principles and methods."* In the case of "scientific" testimony, this requirement is essentially a requirement that the testimony be based on "good science."

        Example: Testimony based on astrology would be rejected, because the court would not be satisfied that it was based on "reliable principles and methods."

    a. **Applies to non-scientific testimony:** This requirement of reliable principles and methods applies not just to scientific testimony but to *other types of expert testimony based on technical knowledge.*

5. **Reliable application to the facts of case:** Finally, FRE 702 requires that the principles and methods referred to above be *"applied ... reliably to the facts of the case."* This is just common sense: the most reliable of "principles" and "methods" won't lead to useful testimony unless the witness shows that she is applying those principles and methods to the actual facts of the case.

        Example: Suppose that W, a prosecution DNA expert, offers to testify that under the principles of DNA comparison, a sample of blood purportedly found on the body of a murder victim, V, matched the blood of the defendant, D. If W (and other witnesses put on by the prosecution) cannot demonstrate that the sample tested by W was in fact found on V's body, W's testimony will be meaningless, and will be excluded.

B. **Illustration:** The following example illustrates an expert opinion that meets all the requirements of FRE 702 discussed above, and is thus admissible.

    Example of admissible expert opinion: P sues D for personal injuries suffered in an accident in which a car driven by D struck P's stationary car. P calls an eyewitness, who testifies that he saw D travelling at 70 mph at the moment D hit the brakes. D then offers the testimony of Wit, an experienced police accident investigator, who describes his extensive training and experience in examining high-speed car accidents. Wit explains that he examined skid marks left on the street by D's car at the time of the accident, and that such skid-mark evidence is typically relied upon by investigators trying to determine the speed at which an automobile was travelling at the moment the driver applied the brakes. Wit then states that it was his opinion that D was travelling no more than 45 mph at the moment he applied his brakes.

    Wit's opinion will be admissible, because it meets all the requirements of FRE 703. (1) Wit's testimony about D's speed prior to hitting the brakes will help the trier of fact to understand the evidence in the case (including whether D was speeding). (2) Wit is experienced and has received relevant training. (3) Wit's testimony is based on his examination of the physical evidence, and he has stipulated that these types of physical data are the ones examined in such matters. (4) There is no indication that Wit's methodology is not the product of reliable principles and methods. (5) Wit made his conclusion about D's speed after applying his training and experience to the physical evidence of the case. Having satisfied all five requirements, Wit's testimony, although it is an opinion and is not based on his personal knowledge from having viewed the accident, is proper and admissible.

C. Basis for expert's opinion: The expert's opinion may be based upon any of several sources of information, including: (1) the expert's *first-hand knowledge*; (2) the expert's observation of *prior witnesses* and other evidence at the trial itself; and (3) a hypothetical question asked by counsel to the expert.

    1. Inadmissible evidence: Under the FRE, the expert's opinion may be based on evidence that would otherwise be *inadmissible*. FRE 703 says that even inadmissible evidence may form the basis for the expert's opinion if that evidence is "of a type *reasonably relied upon by experts* in a particular field in forming opinions or inferences upon the subject[.]"

        Example: After an accident in which P is injured by a car owned by Owner and driven by Driver, P sues only Owner. Driver tells an accident investigator hired by P that the accident occurred when his brakes failed. The investigator writes a report, which is read by Expert, an accident analysis specialist. Expert gives testimony on behalf of P about the likely cause of the accident. Even if Driver's statement that "The brakes failed" is inadmissible hearsay, if experts in the field of accident analysis would rely on such hearsay statements, Expert's opinion may be based in part on this statement. Therefore, Expert may testify, "I believe the accident happened because the brakes failed."

        a. Evidence doesn't become substantively admissible: But don't make the mistake of thinking that because the expert has relied on otherwise-inadmissible data, that data thereby becomes substantively admissible in the case — it *doesn't*. And the MBE examiners like to try to trick you on this point.

            Example: On the facts of the above example, assume that Driver's statement "The brakes failed" would be inadmissible hearsay if offered by P against Owner. The fact that Expert was permitted to testify, and the fact that her testimony relied upon Driver's statement as being true, will not cause the underlying statement by Driver to become substantively admissible to prove that the brakes failed.

        b. Proponent and expert can't disclose: In fact, neither the *expert* nor the *proponent* of his testimony is even allowed to *disclose* to the jury any piece of inadmissible evidence on which the expert is relying, unless the court "determines that [the] *probative value* [of this inadmissible evidence] in assisting the jury to evaluate the expert's opinion *substantially outweighs* [its] *prejudicial* effect." FRE 703, final sentence. So in the above example, neither Expert nor P, who called her, will even be allowed to disclose to the jury that Expert is relying on Driver's statement about the brakes failing, unless the court "determines that [the] probative value [of this inadmissible evidence] in assisting the jury to evaluate the expert's opinion *substantially outweighs* [its] prejudicial effect."

    2. Disclosure of basis to jury: The Federal Rules *do not require that the expert disclose* during direct examination the *data and assumptions she is relying on*. FRE 705 says that "the expert may testify in terms of opinion or inference and give reasons therefor *without prior disclosure of the underlying facts or data, unless the court requires otherwise.*" But the rule goes on to say that "The expert may in any event be required to disclose the underlying facts or data *on cross-examination.*"

Example: P, while driving a car manufactured by D, is injured when the car runs off the road and strikes a telephone pole. In P's product liability suit against D, P calls a witness, Wit, who is properly qualified as an expert in the reconstruction of the type of accident in question. On direct, Wit testifies that it is his professional opinion that a manufacturing defect in the steering wheel caused the steering wheel to malfunction, leading to the accident. D's lawyer objects that the opinion should be stricken because Wit has failed during his direct testimony to set forth the underlying data on which he relied in forming his opinion.

The court will probably *overrule* the objection, because the data on which an expert relies need not be disclosed to the jury during the course of the expert's direct testimony. See FRE 705 ("The expert may testify in terms of opinion or inference and give reasons therefor without first testifying to the underlying facts or data, unless the court requires otherwise.") So the judge need not — and ordinarily will not — require the proponent to bring out the underlying data on direct examination of the expert. It will be up to the cross examiner (here, D's lawyer) to decide whether to require Wit to disclose the underlying data. (D's lawyer is entitled to insist on this in cross, by the provision of FRE 705 that says, "The expert may in any event be required to disclose the underlying facts or data on cross-examination.")

    a. Court has discretion: Observe, however, that the phrase "unless the court requires otherwise" in Rule 705 gives the court *discretion,* in a particular instance, to require that the expert disclose on direct her factual basis.

D. Court-appointed expert: The Federal Rules allow the appointment of an expert *by the court*, in which case each party may cross-examine the expert. FRE 706.

CHAPTER 10
BURDENS OF PROOF, PRESUMPTIONS, AND OTHER PROCEDURAL ISSUES

I. BURDENS OF PROOF

A. Two burdens: There are two distinct burdens of proof, the burden of *production* and the burden of *persuasion.*

    1. Burden of production: If P bears the burden of *production* with respect to issue A, P has the obligation to come forward with some evidence that A exists. This burden is sometimes also called the burden of "going forward."

        a. Consequence of failure to carry: If a party does not satisfy this burden of production, the court will decide the issue against him as a matter of law, and will not permit the jury to decide it.

    2. Burden of persuasion: If P has the burden of *persuasion* on issue A, this means that if at the close of the evidence the jury cannot decide whether A has been established with the relevant level of certainty (usually "preponderance of the evidence" in a civil case), the jury must find against P on issue A.

    3. One shifts, other does not: The burden of *production* as to issue A can, and often does, *shift* throughout the trial.

        Example: Suppose P has the burden of showing that D received notice of a fact. If P comes up with evidence that D received notice — e.g., P's own testimony that he told the fact to D — the burden will shift to D to come up with evidence that he did not receive notice.

a. **Burden of persuasion:** The burden of *persuasion*, by contrast, always remains on the party on whom it first rests. In civil cases, the plaintiff bears the burden of persuasion on most issues; in criminal cases, the prosecution bears the burden of persuasion (beyond a reasonable doubt) as to all elements of the crime.

II. PRESUMPTIONS

A. **Generally:** The term *"presumption"* refers to a relationship between a "basic" fact (B) and a "presumed" fact (P). When we say that fact P can be presumed from fact B, we mean that once B is established, P is established or at least rendered more likely.

B. **Effect of presumptions in federal civil cases:** In *civil* cases raising a *federal question* (i.e., non-diversity cases), the Federal Rules adopt the so-called *"bursting bubble"* view of the effect of a presumption on a case. Under FRE 301, in a federal-question civil case "a presumption imposes on the party against whom it is directed the *burden of going forward with evidence* to rebut or meet the presumption, but *does not shift* to such party the burden of proof in the sense of the *risk of nonpersuasion*, which *remains* throughout the trial upon the party on whom it was originally cast."

1. **How this works:** Under the FRE's bursting bubble approach, if B (the basic fact) is shown to exist, the burden of production — but *not* the burden of persuasion — will be shifted to the opponent of the presumption. In other words, once the opponent (the person burdened by the presumption) discharges his production burden by coming up with some evidence that the presumed fact does not exist, the presumption *disappears from the case*, and the jury decides the issue as if the presumption had never existed.

   Example: Assume that a court following the FRE recognizes a presumption that where a letter has been properly addressed and mailed (the basic fact) the letter will be presumed to have been received by the addressee (the presumed fact). Suppose that P is the beneficiary of this presumption, and that P starts out bearing the burden of proving that D received the letter. If P shows that the letter was properly addressed and mailed, under the FRE's bursting bubble approach D will now have to come up with some evidence that he never received the letter (and if he doesn't do this, the court will direct the jury to find that D received the letter). But once D comes up with some evidence of non-receipt (e.g., his testimony that he never received it), the presumption disappears from the case and need not be mentioned to the jury.

   a. **Instructions to jury:** Under the federal "bursting bubble" approach, the judge normally will *not mention* that the presumption exists (e.g., in the above example, she will not say, "The law presumes that a properly addressed and mailed envelope was received by the addressee unless there is evidence to the contrary"). But the judge has *discretion* to tell the jury that it *may* presume P if B is shown. And whether the judge so instructs the jury or not, the jury indeed has that discretion to find P if B is shown.

   Example: Same facts as the above example involving the presumption that a properly addressed and mailed letter was received by the addressee. Assume that P has the burden of showing that a particular notice was received by D. P testifies, "I properly addressed and mailed the notice to D on July 1." D testifies, "I never received any such notice." The judge has discretion whether to mention the existence of the presumption. The judge is therefore free to decline to mention the presumption, and to simply instruct the jury, "P has the burden of persuading you that he mailed a notice to D that D received." If the jury concludes that the notice was properly addressed and mailed, it has the right (but not the obligation) to find that it was timely received by D.

C. Effect of presumption in diversity cases: In federal *diversity* cases, the *presumption law of the state whose substantive law applies* also applies to determine the effect of a presumption.

> **Example:** Assume that State X's law applies to a federal diversity claim, and State X law says that once the beneficiary of a presumption proves the basic fact, the burden of persuasion as to the presumed fact shifts to the other party. Assume that P has the burden of proving that a particular notice was received by D, and that State X has a presumption that a properly-addressed and mailed letter was received. P testifies, "I properly addressed and mailed the notice to D." D testifies, "I never got it." The federal court must instruct the jury that if it believes the letter was properly addressed and mailed, D (not P) has the burden of persuading the jury that he never got the notice.

D. Effect in criminal cases: In criminal cases, *presumptions cannot shift the either the burden of production or the burden of persuasion on any element of the crime* — the burden is always on the prosecution to prove every element of the crime beyond a reasonable doubt, and the existence of a presumption cannot constitutionally make this burden easier for the prosecution.

III. JUDGE-JURY ALLOCATION

A. Issues of law: Issues of *law* are always to be *decided by the judge*, not the jury. Therefore, when the admission of a particular piece of evidence turns on an issue of law, it is up to the judge to decide whether the item should be admitted.

> **Example:** W refuses to disclose a statement she made to L, asserting the attorney-client privilege; L is a law school graduate but is not admitted to practice. It is the judge, not the jury, who will decide the legal issue of whether the privilege applies on these facts. FRE 104(a).

B. Issues of fact: If admissibility of evidence turns on an issue of *fact,* the division of labor between judge and jury depends on the nature of the objection:

1. Technical exclusionary rule: If an objection to admissibility is based on a *technical exclusionary rule* (e.g., hearsay), any factual question needed to decide that objection belongs *solely to the judge.* Thus the judge decides factual issues in connection with a *hearsay objection,* an objection based on *privilege,* whether a person qualifies as an *expert,* and most issues regarding the *Best Evidence Rule.* See FRE 104(a): "Preliminary questions concerning the qualification of a person to be a witness, the existence of a privilege, or the *admissibility of evidence* shall be determined by the court[.]"

> **Example 1:** In a civil case, P offers a letter, and D objects on the grounds that the letter is hearsay if used for the purpose P is proposing. It will be up to the judge, not the jury, to decide whether the letter is admissible.

> **Example 2:** In a car-accident case, P offers expert testimony by Wit, an accident investigator, that, based on the skid marks D's car left, D was travelling in excess of 65 mph at the moment he hit the brakes. The judge, not the jury, will decide whether Wit qualifies as an expert and whether his proposed testimony meets the expert-testimony requirements of the FRE.

a. Rules of evidence not binding: Under FRE 104(a), when the judge makes such a finding she is *not bound by the rules of evidence* except those regarding privileges.

> **Example:** In deciding whether V's out-of-court statement, "X shot me," qualifies as a "dying declaration" exception to the hearsay rule, the judge may consider other, inadmissible, hearsay declarations by V at about the same time that shed light on whether V knew he was dying.

i. Preponderance standard: The judge will normally decide such a preliminary factual issue by a *preponderance of the evidence* standard.

2. **Relevance:** If the objection is that the evidence is *irrelevant*, the judge's role may be more limited:

a. **Ordinary relevance problem:** Ordinarily, a relevance objection may be decided without any finding of fact — the judge merely has to decide whether, *assuming* the proffered fact is true, it makes some material fact more or less likely; this is purely a legal conclusion, so the judge handles it herself.

b. **Conditional relevance:** In some cases, the proffered evidence is logically relevant only if some other fact exists. If fact *B* is relevant only if fact *A* exists, *B* is *"conditionally relevant."* It is the jury that will decide whether fact *A* exists, but the judge decides *whether a reasonable jury could find that fact A (the preliminary fact) exists*. See FRE 104(a): "When the relevancy of evidence depends upon the fulfillment of a condition of fact, the court shall admit it upon, or subject to, the introduction of *evidence sufficient to support a finding* of the fulfillment of the condition." (The judge will conclude that there is evidence "sufficient to support a finding of the fulfillment of the condition" if and only if the judge concludes that a *reasonable jury could find* that the condition has been fulfilled.)

i. **Object offered in evidence:** On the MBE, the most common scenario in which this "conditional relevance" issue is tested is where one party offers a *document or other tangible item* into evidence. Assuming that the document or tangible item is only relevant if it is *"genuine"* — in the sense of being the very item that the proponent claims it is — a judge will allow the item into evidence only if she concludes that a reasonable jury could find that the item is what proponent claims it is.

Example: In a prosecution of D for kidnapping, the issue is whether D wrote the ransom note. The prosecution offers into evidence several handwritten documents that were unquestionably written by D. The prosecution then offers a handwritten document that it says is the ransom note. D's lawyer objects. You are asked whether and according to what standard the judge should allow the document into evidence.

The answer is that the judge should admit the document if and only if she concludes that *a reasonable jury could find that the document is the actual ransom note.* Notice that the judge does not have to make her *own* determination that, beyond a reasonable doubt, this document is the actual ransom note — all the judge has to conclude is that a reasonable jury could find, beyond a reasonable doubt, that the document is the actual ransom note. Notice that this is a problem of conditional relevance — the note is relevant to the case if and only if it is the "real" one, i.e., the one submitted to the victim's family.

ii. **Subject to connecting up:** The judge may allow the conditionally relevant fact into evidence prior to a showing of the preliminary fact; the conditionally relevant evidence is said to be admitted *"subject to connecting up."*

Example: In the above ransom-note example, suppose that at the time the prosecution offered the note in evidence, it had not yet presented all the proof it would ever present that the document was the very one submitted to the victim's family. A judge might conditionally admit the note, subject to its being "connected up" by means of later testimony by, say, the victim's family that the exhibit is indeed the ransom note they received.

C. **Limiting instructions:** If evidence is admitted that should properly be considered only on certain issues, the judge will on request give a *limiting instruction*, which tells the jury for what issues the evidence can and cannot be considered.

IV. APPEALS AND "HARMLESS ERROR"

A. "Harmless error": Appellate courts will only reverse if the error may have made a *difference to the outcome*. An error that is unlikely to have made a difference to the outcome is called *"harmless,"* and will not be grounds for reversal. See FRE 103 (error must affect a "substantial right" of a party).

    1. Standards for determining: The test for determining whether an error is "harmless" varies depending on the context:

        a. Constitutional criminal issue: In a criminal case in which evidence is admitted in violation of the defendant's *constitutional* rights, the appellate court will find the error non-harmless unless it is convinced "beyond a reasonable doubt" that the error was harmless.

        Example: A co-defendant's confession implicating D, given to the police while in custody, and admitted against D in violation of his Confrontation Clause rights, will almost never be found to be harmless beyond a reasonable doubt, and will thus generally be grounds for reversal.

        b. Other errors: But in civil cases, and in criminal cases involving non-constitutional errors, the error will be ignored as harmless unless the appellate court believes it *"more probable than not"* that the error affected the outcome.

B. Sufficiency of evidence: If the appellate court needs to decide whether the evidence was *sufficient* to support the findings of fact, the standard will depend on whether the case is civil or criminal:

    1. Civil: In civil cases, the sufficiency test mirrors the "preponderance of the evidence" standard used at the trial.

        Example: If P wins, the appellate court will ask, "Could a reasonable jury have concluded that P proved all elements of his case by a preponderance of the evidence?"

    2. Criminal: In a criminal case where D is appealing, the appellate court will ask, "Could a reasonable jury have found, beyond a reasonable doubt, that D committed all elements of the crime?"

CHAPTER 11

JUDICIAL NOTICE

I. JUDICIAL NOTICE GENERALLY

A. Function: Under the doctrine of *judicial notice*, the *judge* can accept a fact as true even though no evidence to prove it has been offered. In a civil jury case (but not a criminal case), if the judge takes judicial notice of a fact she will instruct the jury that it must find that fact; see *infra*, p. 104.

B. Three types: The doctrine of judicial notice has evolved to recognize three distinct types of judicial notice: (1) *"adjudicative"* facts; (2) *"legislative"* facts; and (3) *law*.

    1. Federal Rules: The only Federal Rule dealing with judicial notice, FRE 201, deals solely with notice of *adjudicative facts*, not legislative facts or law. Adjudicative facts are those facts which relate to the *particular event* under litigation.

        a. MBE tip: Notice of adjudicative facts is the only type of judicial notice that is likely to be tested on the MBE. Therefore, that's the only kind of notice you should worry about.

II. ADJUDICATIVE FACTS

A. General rule: FRE 201 treats as being an adjudicative fact any fact that is "beyond reasonable dispute" because it is either:

(1) *"generally known"* within the community; or

(2) "capable of accurate and ready *determination*" by the use of "sources whose *accuracy cannot reasonably be questioned.*"

1. "General knowledge": An instance of *"general knowledge"* in the community might be that a particular portion of Mission Street in San Francisco is a business district, or that traffic going towards Long Island beaches on Friday afternoon during the summertime is frequently very heavy.

    a. Judge's own knowledge: The fact that the *judge himself* knows a fact to be so does *not* entitle him to take judicial notice of it if it is not truly common knowledge.

2. Immediate verification: Some of the kinds of facts that are capable of *"immediate verification* by consulting sources of *indisputable accuracy"* include: (1) facts of *history and geography*; (2) *scientific principles*, and the validity of certain types of scientific *tests* (e.g., the general reliability of radar for speed detection); and (3) a court's own record of things that have happened in the same or other suits in that court.

    a. "Cannot reasonably be questioned" is tough standard: The "cannot reasonably be questioned" standard is a *tough* one. So, for instance, a witness's *recollection* of something that the witness remembers happened would normally not be such a fact.

    Example: At issue in a particular case filed in federal court for state X is whether Corp, a corporation, filed for bankruptcy last year in state Y federal court, located in a different region of the country. The proponent calls Clerk, a clerk of state X federal court, to testify that he remembers that Corp filed for bankruptcy in state Y federal court last year.

    Clerk may be generally reliable, but he is not, on this point anyway, a "source whose accuracy cannot reasonably be questioned." Therefore, Clerk's testimony does not permit the judge to take judicial notice of the fact that Corp filed for bankruptcy last year in state Y federal court.

    i. Newspaper account: Similarly, a newspaper or other *journalistic account* of an event will almost certainly not meet the "cannot reasonably be questioned" standard.

    Example: The issue is whether X was married on July 1, 1988. The proponent offers an article from a local newspaper dated July 2, 1988, which reads, "X and Y were married yesterday." The proponent is *not* entitled to have judicial notice taken of the July 1 marriage date based on the article, because a newspaper is not a "source[] whose accuracy cannot reasonably be questioned." For instance, the newspaper might well have made an editing or reporting mistake. (But the newspaper is self-authenticating under FRE 902(6), so it could be offered as *evidence* of the marriage date without a sponsoring witness [see *supra*, p. 89]; however, the article does not *conclusively establish* the wedding date, which it would, at least in a civil case, if judicial notice applied.)

B. Must take if requested, and may take without a request: MBE questions sometimes test the extent to which the trial judge has *discretion* about whether to take judicial notice. There are two principles that matter:

1. Mandatory notice: First, the judge *must* take judicial notice of any fact that meets the requirements, if "requested by a party and supplied with the required information." FRE

201(d). So the judge does not have discretion to refuse to take judicial notice if requested to do so by a party in a situation in which judicial notice is proper.

  2. **Discretionary notice:**   Second, the judge *may* take judicial notice on her *own*, without a request from a litigant. FRE 201(c).

C. **Instructions, and jury's right to disregard:** The MBE examiners like to ask you about the extent to which the jury is *bound* by the judge's finding that judicial notice applies, and about how the judge may or must *instruct* the jury about a judicially-noticed fact. Here are the rules given by FRE 201(g):

  1. **Civil case:**   In a *civil* case the court "shall instruct the jury to *accept as conclusive*" any judicially-noticed fact. So: (1) the court *must give* the instruction if the facts warrant taking judicial notice; and (2) the jury *must* treat the judicially-noticed fact as being established.

  2. **Criminal:**   But in a *criminal* case, "the court shall instruct the jury that it *may, but is not required to,* accept as conclusive any fact judicially noticed." So the jury has to be told that it's free to find the non-existence of the judicially-noticed fact. The reason for this rule is that if the jury were required to find the judicially-notice fact, this might impair D's constitutional right to a jury trial.

       Example: It becomes relevant whether there was still daylight present on 6:30 P.M. on the day in question. Assume that it can be determined from unimpeachable sources that the sun set at 5:15 P.M. on that day. In a civil case, the court would be required to instruct the jury that it must find that the sun had set that day at 5:15. In a criminal case, the court would be required to instruct the jury that it may, but need not, find that the sun set at 5:15.

    a. **On appeal:** This rule for criminal cases means that if the prosecution has failed at trial to ask for judicial notice of a fact, the *appeals court* may *not* take notice of that fact.

D. **When taken:** Most courts hold that judicial notice of an appropriate adjudicative fact may be taken *at any time* during the proceeding. Thus notice may be taken before trial, or even on appeal (except in criminal cases). (See FRE 201(f).)

MBE-STYLE QUESTIONS
ON EVIDENCE

EVIDENCE QUESTIONS

These questions are the Evidence questions from the Self-Assessment Test. They are presented here in approximately the order in which the main topic or theme of the question is treated in the substantive outline earlier in this book. Thus questions focusing on relevance come first, followed by questions on character evidence, etc.

1. In a civil action for breach of an oral contract, the defendant admits that there had been discussions, but denies that he ever entered into an agreement with the plaintiff.

   Which of the following standards of admissibility should be applied by the court to evidence proffered as relevant to prove whether a contract was formed?

   (A) Whether a reasonable juror would find the evidence determinative of whether the contract was or was not formed.

   (B) Whether the evidence has any tendency to make the fact of contract formation more or less probable than without the evidence.

   (C) Whether the evidence is sufficient to prove, absent contrary evidence, that the contract was or was not formed.

   (D) Whether the evidence makes it more likely than not that a contract was or was not formed.

   [Q7078]

2. A pedestrian died from injuries caused when a driver's car struck him. The executor of the pedestrian's estate sued the driver for wrongful death. At trial, the executor calls a nurse to testify that two days after the accident, the pedestrian said to the nurse, "The car that hit me ran the red light." Fifteen minutes thereafter, the pedestrian died.

   As a foundation for introducing evidence of the pedestrian's statement, the executor offers to the court a doctor's affidavit that the doctor was the intern on duty the day of the pedestrian's death and that several times that day the pedestrian had said that he knew he was about to die.

   Is the affidavit properly considered by the court in ruling on the admissibility of the pedestrian's statement?

   (A) No, because it is hearsay not within any exception.

   (B) No, because it is irrelevant since dying declarations cannot be used except in prosecutions for homicide.

   (C) Yes, because though hearsay, it is a statement of then-existing mental condition.

   (D) Yes, because the judge may consider hearsay in ruling on preliminary questions.

   [Q3147]

GO ON TO THE NEXT PAGE

3. A defendant is on trial for the murder of his father. The defendant's defense is that he shot his father accidentally. The prosecutor calls as a witness a police officer to testify that on two occasions in the year prior to this incident, he had been called to the defendant's home because of complaints of loud arguments between the defendant and his father, and had found it necessary to stop the defendant from beating his father.

The evidence is

(A) inadmissible, because it is improper character evidence.

(B) inadmissible, because the witness lacks firsthand knowledge of who started the quarrels.

(C) admissible to show that the defendant killed his father intentionally.

(D) admissible to show that the defendant is a violent person.

[Q3064]

4. At the defendant's murder trial, the defendant calls, as his first witness, a man to testify that the defendant has a reputation in their community as a peaceable and truthful person. The prosecutor objects on the ground that the witness's testimony would constitute improper character evidence. The court should

(A) admit the testimony as to peaceableness, but exclude the testimony as to truthfulness.

(B) admit the testimony as to truthfulness, but exclude the testimony as to peaceableness.

(C) admit the testimony as to both character traits.

(D) exclude the testimony as to both character traits.

[Q3164]

5. A state's code of civil procedure provides that no appeal may be prosecuted unless a notice of such appeal is mailed within twenty days after the entry of the final judgment which is being appealed. An appellee moves to dismiss an appeal on the ground that the notice of appeal was not timely served. At a hearing on the motion to dismiss, a secretary in the office of the appellant's attorney testifies that he personally enclosed the notice of appeal in a properly addressed envelope which he then sealed. He states further that he placed the envelope in a basket marked "outgoing mail" in the office conference room at 2 p.m. on the eighteenth day after the judgment appealed from was entered. He states that as a matter of office routine the "outgoing mail" basket is emptied and its contents taken to the post office every day at 4 p.m. by another employee, although he does not personally know whether it was done on that particular day. The testimony should be

(A) excluded, since evidence of past conduct is not relevant to what was done on any particular day.

(B) excluded, unless some evidence is offered that the envelope which was deposited in the basket was actually mailed that day.

(C) admitted, only if the office employee who usually mails the contents of the "outgoing mail" basket testifies to what is customarily done.

(D) admitted, to prove that the notice of appeal was actually mailed on that day.

[Q5087]

6. A drug enforcement agent had been informed that a person arriving from Europe on a particular airline flight, and answering to a particular description, would be carrying cocaine in his baggage. When the agent saw a man answering that description (the defendant), the agent stopped him and searched his bag. In it, he found a small brass statue with a false bottom. Upon removing the false bottom, the agent found one ounce of cocaine.

At the defendant's drug trial, he claimed that he had purchased the statue as a souvenir and was unaware that there was cocaine hidden it its base.

At trial the prosecution now offers to prove that the defendant was convicted fifteen years earlier of illegally importing cocaine by hiding it in the base of a brass statue. If the defendant's attorney objects, the court should rule that proof of the defendant's prior conviction is

(A) admissible, as evidence of habit.

(B) admissible, because it is evidence of a distinctive method of operation.

(C) inadmissible, because evidence of previous conduct by a defendant may not be used against him.

(D) inadmissible, because the prior conviction occurred more than ten years before the trial.

[Q5136]

7. A state statute provides that the owner of any motor vehicle operated on the public roads of the state is liable for damage resulting from the negligence of any person driving the vehicle with the owner's permission. A woman was injured when a vehicle operated by a priest struck her while she was walking across the street. At the scene of the accident, the priest apologized to the woman, saying, "I'm sorry. It isn't my car. I didn't know that the brakes were bad." The woman subsequently instituted an action against an accountant for her damages, asserting that the accountant owned the vehicle. She alleged that the accountant was negligent in permitting the vehicle to be driven by the priest while he (the accountant) knew that the brakes were in need of repair, and that he was also vicariously liable under the statute for the negligence of the priest. The accountant denied ownership of the vehicle. At the trial, the plaintiff offered testimony by a car mechanic that on the day after the accident the accountant hired him to completely overhaul the brakes. Upon objection by the accountant, the evidence is

(A) admissible, to show that the accountant was the owner of the vehicle.

(B) admissible, to show that the brakes were in need of repair on the day of the accident.

(C) inadmissible, because the condition of the vehicle on any day other than that of the accident is irrelevant to show its condition at the time the accident occurred.

(D) inadmissible, under a policy which encourages safety precautions.

[Q5072]

GO ON TO THE NEXT PAGE

8. In a personal injury case, the plaintiff sued a retail store for injuries she sustained from a fall in the store. The plaintiff alleged that the store negligently allowed its entryway to become slippery due to snow tracked in from the sidewalk. When the plaintiff threatened to sue, the store's manager said, "I know that there was slush on that marble entry, but I think your four-inch-high heels were the real cause of your fall. So let's agree that we'll pay your medical bills, and you release us from any claims you might have." The plaintiff refused the offer. At trial, the plaintiff seeks to testify to the manager's statement that "there was slush on that marble entry."

Is the statement about the slush on the floor admissible?

(A) No, because it is a statement made in the course of compromise negotiations.

(B) No, because the manager denied that the slippery condition was the cause of the plaintiff's fall.

(C) Yes, as an admission by an agent about a matter within the scope of his authority.

(D) Yes, because the rule excluding offers of compromise does not protect statements of fact made during compromise negotiations.

[Q7058]

9. A passenger is suing a defendant for injuries suffered in the crash of a small airplane, alleging that the defendant had owned the plane and negligently failed to have it properly maintained. The defendant has asserted in defense that he never owned the plane or had any responsibility to maintain it. At trial, the passenger calls a witness to testify that the witness had sold to the defendant a liability insurance policy on the plane. The testimony of the witness is

(A) inadmissible, because the policy itself is required under the original document rule.

(B) inadmissible, because of the rule against proof of insurance where insurance is not itself at issue.

(C) admissible to show that the defendant had little motivation to invest money in maintenance of the airplane.

(D) admissible as some evidence of the defendant's ownership of or responsibility for the airplane.

[Q3136]

10. Charged with forcible rape, the defendant relied on a defense of alibi. At the trial, the alleged victim testified that the defendant was the man who accosted her on the street, dragged her into the basement of an apartment building, and forced her to submit to sexual intercourse. During the case, the defendant's attorney offered the testimony of a woman who stated that she was familiar with the victim's reputation in the community and that the victim was thought of as a prostitute. The defendant's attorney also offered into evidence a certified court record indicating that the victim had been convicted of prostitution, a misdemeanor, two months prior to the alleged rape.

Upon proper objection by the prosecution to both the woman's testimony and the court record, which of the following should the court admit?

(A) The woman's testimony only.

(B) The court record only.

(C) The woman's testimony and the court record.

(D) Neither the woman's testimony nor the court record.

[Q5030]

11. In a civil trial for fraud arising from a real estate transaction, the defendant claimed not to have been involved in the transaction. The plaintiff called a witness to testify concerning the defendant's involvement in the fraudulent

scheme, but to the plaintiff's surprise the witness testified that the defendant was not involved, and denied making any statement to the contrary. The plaintiff now calls a second witness to testify that the first witness had stated, while the two were having a dinner conversation, that the defendant was involved in the fraudulent transaction.

Is the testimony of the second witness admissible?

(A) No, because a party cannot impeach the party's own witness.

(B) No, because it is hearsay not within any exception.

(C) Yes, but only to impeach the first witness.

(D) Yes, to impeach the first witness and to prove the defendant's involvement.

[Q7019]

12. In a civil trial arising from a car accident at an intersection, the plaintiff testified on direct that he came to a full stop at the intersection. On cross-examination, the defendant's lawyer asked whether the plaintiff claimed that he was exercising due care at the time, and the plaintiff replied that he was driving carefully. At a sidebar conference, the defendant's lawyer sought permission to ask the plaintiff about two prior intersection accidents in the last 12 months where he received traffic citations for failing to stop at stop signs. The plaintiff's lawyer objected.

Should the court allow defense counsel to ask the plaintiff about the two prior incidents?

(A) No, because improperly failing to stop on the recent occasions does not bear on the plaintiff's veracity and does not contradict his testimony in this case.

(B) No, because there is no indication that failing to stop on the recent occasions led to convictions.

(C) Yes, because improperly failing to stop on

the recent occasions bears on the plaintiff's credibility, since he claims to have stopped in this case.

(D) Yes, because improperly failing to stop on the recent occasions tends to contradict the plaintiff's claim that he was driving carefully at the time he collided with the defendant.

[Q7012]

13. At a defendant's trial for burglary, his friend supported the defendant's alibi that they were fishing together at the time of the crime. On cross-examination, the friend was asked whether his statement on a credit card application that he had worked for his present employer for the last five years was false. The friend denied that the statement was false.

The prosecutor then calls the manager of the company for which the friend works, to testify that although the friend had been first employed five years earlier and is now employed by the company, there had been a three-year period during which he had not been so employed. The testimony of the manager is

(A) admissible, in the judge's discretion, because the friend's credibility is a fact of major consequence to the case.

(B) admissible, as a matter of right, because the friend "opened the door" by his denial on cross-examination.

(C) inadmissible, because whether the friend lied in his application is a matter that cannot be proved by extrinsic evidence.

(D) inadmissible, because the misstatement by the friend could have been caused by a misunderstanding of the application form.

[Q3122]

14. The plaintiff sued the defendant for breach of a commercial contract in which the defendant had agreed to sell the plaintiff all of the plaintiff's requirements for widgets. The plaintiff called an expert witness to testify as to damages. The defendant seeks to show that the expert had provided false testimony as a witness in his own divorce proceedings.

This evidence should be

(A) admitted only if elicited from the expert on cross-examination.

(B) admitted only if the false testimony is established by clear and convincing extrinsic evidence.

(C) excluded, because it is impeachment on a collateral issue.

(D) excluded, because it is improper character evidence.

[Q3013]

15. The defendant was prosecuted for armed robbery. At trial, the defendant testified in his own behalf, denying that he had committed the robbery. On cross-examination, the prosecutor intends to ask the defendant whether he had been convicted of burglary six years earlier.

The question concerning the burglary conviction is

(A) proper if the court finds that the probative value for impeachment outweighs the prejudice to the defendant.

(B) proper, because the prosecutor is entitled to make this inquiry as a matter of right.

(C) improper, because burglary does not involve dishonesty or false statement.

(D) improper, because the conviction must be proved by court record, not by question on cross-examination.

[Q4044]

16. The plaintiff has sued the defendant for personal injuries arising out of an automobile accident. Which of the following would be ERROR?

(A) The judge allows the defendant's attorney to ask the defendant questions on cross-examination that go well beyond the scope of direct examination by the plaintiff, who has called the defendant as an adverse witness.

(B) The judge refuses to allow the defendant's attorney to cross-examine the defendant by leading questions.

(C) The judge allows cross-examination about the credibility of a witness even though no question relating to credibility has been asked on direct examination.

(D) The judge, despite the defendant's request for exclusion of witnesses, allows the plaintiff's eyewitness to remain in the courtroom after testifying, even though the eyewitness is expected to be recalled for further cross-examination.

[Q3153]

17. The plaintiff sued the defendant for illegal discrimination, claiming that the defendant fired him because of his race. At trial, the plaintiff called a witness, expecting him to testify that the defendant had admitted the racial motivation. Instead, the witness testified that the defendant said that he had fired the plaintiff because of his frequent absenteeism. While the witness is still on the stand, the plaintiff offers a properly authenticated secret tape recording he had made at a meeting with the witness in which the witness related the defendant's admissions of racial motivation.

The tape recording is

(A) admissible as evidence of the defendant's racial motivation and to impeach the witness's testimony.

(B) admissible only to impeach the witness's testimony.

(C) inadmissible, because it is hearsay not

within any exception.

(D) inadmissible, because a secret recording is an invasion of the witness's right of privacy under the U.S. Constitution.

[Q3026]

18. The plaintiff sued the defendant for personal injuries suffered in a train-automobile collision. The plaintiff called an eyewitness, who testified that the train was going 20 miles per hour. The defendant then offered the testimony of an experienced police accident investigator who described his extensive training and experience in examining high-speed accidents including ones involving trains. The investigator explained that he examined the physical evidence, including the types of damage inflicted on the metal structure of the car, and that such physical evidence is typically relied upon by investigators trying to determine the speed at which a collision occurred. The investigator then stated that it was his opinion that the train was going between 5 and 10 miles per hour at the moment of the collision.

This testimony by the investigator is

(A) improper, because there cannot be both lay and expert opinion on the same issue.

(B) improper, because the investigator is unable to establish the speed with a sufficient degree of scientific certainty.

(C) proper, because the investigator has demonstrated sufficient expertise to express an opinion on speed.

(D) proper, because the plaintiff first introduced opinion evidence as to speed.

[Q3117]

19. The plaintiff, who is executor of her late husband's estate, has sued the defendant for shooting the husband from ambush. The plaintiff offers to testify that the day before her husband was killed, he described to her a chance meeting with the defendant on the street in which the defendant said, "I'm going to blow your head off one of these days."

The witness's testimony concerning her husband's statement is

(A) admissible, to show the defendant's state of mind.

(B) admissible, because the defendant's statement is that of a party-opponent.

(C) inadmissible, because it is improper evidence of a prior bad act.

(D) inadmissible, because it is hearsay not within any exception.

[Q3045]

GO ON TO THE NEXT PAGE

20. In a personal injury action by the plaintiff against the defendant, the plaintiff claimed that the accident occurred because the defendant, who was operating a blue Ford sedan, was driving at an excessive rate of speed. At the trial, the plaintiff's attorney called a witness on the plaintiff's direct case. The witness testified that after hearing a broadcast on a police radio on the day of the accident, she looked out of her window and saw the defendant's blue Ford sedan strike the plaintiff's red convertible on Main Street. The witness said that she did not have a present recollection of what she had heard on the police radio, but that she made a written note of it immediately following the broadcast. The plaintiff's attorney showed her a piece of paper which had been marked for identification, and the witness said that she now remembered that she had heard a police dispatcher saying that officers were in pursuit of a blue Ford sedan which was traveling down Main Street at an excessive rate of speed.

If the defendant's attorney objects to the testimony of the witness regarding what she heard on the police radio, the court should hold that her testimony is

(A) inadmissible as hearsay, not within any exception.

(B) admissible as a sense impression.

(C) admissible as a past recollection recorded.

(D) admissible as present recollection refreshed.

[Q5068]

21. In an accident case, the defendant testified in his own behalf that he was going 30 m.p.h. On cross-examination, the plaintiff's counsel did not question the defendant with regard to his speed. Subsequently, the plaintiff's counsel calls a police officer to testify that, in his investigation following the accident, the defendant told him he was driving 40 m.p.h. The officer's testimony is

(A) admissible as a prior inconsistent statement.

(B) admissible as an admission.

(C) inadmissible, because it lacks a foundation.

(D) inadmissible, because it is hearsay not within any exception.

[Q4015]

22. A defendant was charged with aggravated assault. At trial, the victim testified that the defendant beat her savagely, but she was not asked about anything said during the incident. The prosecutor then called a witness to testify that when the beating stopped, the victim screamed: "I'm dying-don't let [the defendant] get away with it!"

Is the testimony of the witness concerning the victim's statement admissible?

(A) No, because it is hearsay not within any exception.

(B) No, because the victim was not asked about the statement.

(C) Yes, as a statement under belief of impending death, even though the victim did not die.

(D) Yes, as an excited utterance.

[Q7037]

23. A pastor was a well-known clergyman. A large daily newspaper printed an article by a journalist in its employ. The article accused the pastor of misusing church funds. The pastor commenced a defamation action against the newspaper. An issue in the case was whether the journalist, at the time he wrote the article, acted without malice in charging that the pastor had misused church funds. (For this purpose, it was relevant whether the journalist genuinely believed that the misuse had occurred.)

The newspaper's attorney called a bartender, who worked in a bar near the newspaper's office. The bartender stated that on the day after the journalist's article appeared in the newspaper, the journalist told him, "When I wrote that piece on the pastor, I believed every word of it." On objection by the pastor's attorney, the bartender's testimony should be

(A) admitted as evidence that the article was published without malice.

(B) admitted as a declaration of the journalist's state of mind.

(C) admitted as a self-serving declaration.

(D) excluded as hearsay not falling within any exception.

[Q5024]

24. The plaintiff was injured when the ladder on which she was standing collapsed without warning. Immediately following the accident, the plaintiff was taken to a hospital where she remained for approximately six hours. At the trial of the plaintiff's action against the manufacturer of the ladder, the plaintiff's attorney offered a properly authenticated record from the hospital. After examining the record, the defendant's attorney, outside the presence of the jury, moved to exclude a portion of the record which read: "History: Ladder collapsed. Patient fell." The motion to exclude that portion of the record should be

(A) granted, if, but only if, it can be excluded without causing any physical damage to the record.

(B) granted, because it has no bearing on the plaintiff's medical condition.

(C) denied, if the history was taken for the purpose of diagnosis or treatment.

(D) granted, since hospital personnel are not experts in determining the causes of accidents.

[Q5081]

25. At the defendant's trial for theft, a man, called as a witness by the prosecutor, testified to the

following: (1) that from his apartment window, he saw thieves across the street break the window of a jewelry store, take jewelry, and leave in a car; (2) that the witness's wife telephoned the police and relayed to them the license number of the thieves' car as the witness looked out the window with binoculars and read it to her; and (3) that the witness has no present memory of the number, but that immediately afterward he listened to a playback of the police tape recording giving the license number (which belongs to the defendant's car) and verified that she had relayed the number accurately.

Playing the tape recording for the jury would be

(A) proper, because it is recorded recollection.

(B) proper, because it is a public record or report.

(C) improper, because it is hearsay not within any exception.

(D) improper, because the witness's wife lacked first-hand knowledge of the license number.

[Q3040]

GO ON TO THE NEXT PAGE

26. A large daily newspaper printed an article by a reporter who worked for it, accusing a well-known local businessman of misusing corporate funds. The businessman commenced a defamation action against the newspaper. As a defense, the newspaper asserted the businessman's non-compliance with a state law that limited damages for defamation unless a demand for retraction is made.

The newspaper attorney offered the testimony of an editor employed by the paper. The editor testified that it was his job to note retraction demands in an office file, and that as a matter of company policy and practice all such demands were promptly reported to him for that purpose and promptly noted by him. He said that on the morning of trial, he had searched the file for notes of any retraction demand made by the businessman, and found none. If the newspaper's attorney offers the file in evidence, the businessman's objection should be

(A) sustained, since the absence of a notation cannot be used as evidence that an event did not occur.

(B) sustained, since the file is self-serving.

(C) overruled, if the file itself is admissible as a business record.

(D) overruled, since the editor used the file to refresh his recollection.

[Q5025]

27. The plaintiff was crossing the street on foot when she was struck by a delivery van owned by the defendant restaurant, and driven by a deliveryman who worked as an employee of the defendant and who was in the process of making a delivery. Following the accident, the deliveryman was charged with reckless driving and pleaded not guilty. At the trial on the charge of reckless driving, the deliveryman testified in his own defense. He stated that at the time of the accident, he had taken his eyes off the road to look for the address of the place to which he had to make his delivery, and that as a result he didn't see the plaintiff crossing the street.

The plaintiff subsequently brought an action against the restaurant under the theory of *respondeat superior* for personal injuries resulting from the deliveryman's negligence. At the trial of this action, the plaintiff proved that the deliveryman remained in the restaurant's employ until the deliveryman died from causes not related to the accident. The plaintiff then offered into evidence a transcript of the deliveryman's testimony at the reckless driving trial. Upon objection by the restaurant's attorney, the transcript should be

(A) admitted, under the prior testimony exception to the hearsay rule.

(B) admitted, under the past recollection recorded exception to the hearsay rule.

(C) admitted as a vicarious admission, under the public record exception to the hearsay rule.

(D) excluded as hearsay, not within any exception to the hearsay rule.

[Q5040]

28. In a civil trial for professional malpractice, the plaintiff sought to show that the defendant, an engineer, had designed the plaintiff's flour mill with inadequate power. The plaintiff called an expert witness who based his testimony solely on his own professional experience but also asserted, when asked, that the book Smith on Milling Systems was a reliable treatise in the field and consistent with his views. On cross-examination, the defendant asked the witness whether he and Smith were ever wrong. The witness answered, "Nobody's perfect." The defendant asked no further questions. The defendant called a second expert witness and asked, "Do you accept the Smith book as reliable?" The second witness said, "It once was, but it is now badly out of date." The plaintiff requested that the jury be allowed to

examine the book and judge for itself the book's reliability.

Should the court allow the jury to examine the book?

(A) No, because the jury may consider only passages read to it by counsel or witness.

(B) No, because the plaintiff's expert in testifying did not rely on the treatise but on his own experience.

(C) Yes, because an expert has testified that the treatise is reliable.

(D) Yes, because the jury is the judge of the weight and credibility to be accorded both written and oral evidence.

[Q7005]

29. The defendant is charged with the murder of the victim. The prosecutor introduced testimony of a police officer that the victim told a priest, administering the last rites, "I was stabbed by [the defendant]. Since I am dying, tell him I forgive him." Thereafter, the defendant's attorney offers the testimony of a witness that the day before, when the victim believed he would live, he stated that he had been stabbed by Jack (not the defendant), an old enemy. The testimony of this witness is

(A) admissible under an exception to the hearsay rule.

(B) admissible to impeach the dead declarant.

(C) inadmissible because it goes to the ultimate issue in the case.

(D) inadmissible because it is irrelevant to any substantive issue in the case.

[Q4022]

30. The defendant, a man, has been charged with murdering the victim. The defendant defends on the grounds that the murder was really committed by a particular woman, who has since died. The defendant offers a properly authenticated photocopy of a transcript of a deposition in a civil suit brought against the woman by the victim's family for the victim's death, in which the woman said, "Yes, I killed him because I hated him." The civil suit was brought because the woman was known to have quarreled with and disliked the victim. Upon proper objection by the prosecution, the statement should be

(A) admitted as a declaration against interest.

(B) admitted as former testimony by a person now unavailable.

(C) inadmissible as hearsay not within any exception.

(D) inadmissible, because the original rather than a photocopy must be offered.

[Q6001]

31. In a federal civil trial, the plaintiff wishes to establish that, in a state court, the defendant had been convicted of fraud, a fact that the defendant denies.

Which mode of proof of the conviction is LEAST likely to be permitted?

(A) A certified copy of the judgment of conviction, offered as a self-authenticating document.

(B) Testimony of the plaintiff, who was present at the time of the sentence.

(C) Testimony by a witness to whom the defendant made an oral admission that he had been convicted.

(D) Judicial notice of the conviction, based on the court's telephone call to the clerk of the state court, whom the judge knows personally.

[Q3167]

GO ON TO THE NEXT PAGE

32. At the trial of the case of *Smith v. Jones,* which of the following is LEAST likely to be admitted into evidence for the purpose of determining whether a certain letter was written by Jones?

   (A) A sample of Jones's signature, together with the testimony of a handwriting expert that the letter was signed by the same person who created the sample.

   (B) A sample of Jones's signature submitted to the jury together with the letter in question.

   (C) The testimony of a layperson who stated that he saw Jones sign the letter in question.

   (D) Testimony that the letterhead on the letter in question was Jones's.

   [Q5048]

33. A lawyer worked steadily on a case for a client over five-year period, with the billing agreed to be based on a particular amount per hour worked. The lawyer kept regular timesheets showing, for any day on which he worked on the matter, how long he worked and which of various activities (phone calls, letter-writing, etc.) he performed on that day. In the lawyer's suit against the client for non-payment, the lawyer did not offer into evidence the actual timesheets. Instead, in preparation for trial, the lawyer used the timesheets to create a summary showing, for each week, how much time the lawyer spent on each of the activity types. Then, at trial, the lawyer offered these weekly summaries, together with his testimony about how he had prepared them. If the client properly objects, the judge should hold that the summaries are

   (A) inadmissible for any purpose, because the underlying timesheets from which they were prepared were not offered into evidence.

   (B) inadmissible as substantive evidence, but usable as non-admitted materials to refresh the lawyer's present recollection.

   (C) admissible as substantive evidence of hours worked, if the underlying timesheets were made available to the client prior to trial.

   (D) admissible as substantive evidence only if the underlying timesheets were lost through no fault of the lawyer.

   [Q6002]

ANSWERS TO
EVIDENCE QUESTIONS

1. **B** This is the standard of relevance applied by the judge in determining admissibility under FRE 401. Under that rule, evidence is relevant if it has "any tendency to make the existence of any fact that is of consequence to the determination of the action more probable or less probable than it would be without the evidence."

    (A) is wrong because the test for admissibility is whether the judge believes that the evidence is probative, not whether a reasonable jury could believe it to be so. This is established by FRE 104(a).

    (C) is wrong because the judge determines admissibility and the jury determines sufficiency. It would be impossible for a party to build a case if every piece of evidence had to be sufficient to prove the point in dispute.

    (D) is wrong because the preponderance standard is applied by the jury to all of the evidence admitted. It is not applied by the court to determine whether a particular piece of evidence can be considered by the jury on the ultimate question. Thus, this answer confuses the standard of proof used by the jury with the standard of admissibility used by the judge.

    [Q7078]

2. **D** FRE 104(a) says that "Preliminary questions concerning ... the admissibility of evidence shall be determined by the court.... In making its determination it is *not bound by the rules of evidence* except those with respect to privileges." The pedestrian's statement to the nurse is admissible if, and only if, the statement qualified for the dying-declaration exception. That exception requires that the declarant knew or believed that he was about to die. The affidavit is relevant to that issue. It's true that the affidavit is hearsay (it's an out-of-court statement offered to prove the truth of the matter asserted, i.e., that the pedestrian really knew or believed he was dying). And this hearsay does not fall within any exception. But under 104(a), the judge may consider this inadmissible hearsay in making her preliminary ruling on the admissibility of the pedestrian's statement to the nurse.

    (A) is wrong because even though the affidavit is hearsay not within any exception, it may still be considered on the preliminary matter of the admissibility of the statement to the nurse. As described in Choice (D) above, the fact that the affidavit is hearsay not within any exception does not prevent the court from using it to resolve a preliminary question about the admissibility of other evidence.

    (B) is wrong because: (1) dying declarations are admissible in civil cases; and (2) the admissibility of the affidavit is irrelevant to whether it can be considered on the preliminary question here. First, FRE 804(b)(2) gives a hearsay exception for, "In a prosecution for homicide *or in a civil action or proceeding*, a statement made by a declarant while believing that the declarant's death was imminent, concerning the cause or circumstances of what the declarant believed to be impending death." So the proposition asserted in Choice (B) — that dying declarations can't be used except in homicide prosecutions —is simply incorrect as a matter of law. Furthermore, even if this statement of law were true, it would be irrelevant — as described in the discussion of Choice (D) above, the judge may consider inadmissible material in ruling on an evidentiary question.

    (C) is wrong because: (1) the affidavit is the "outer level" of a two-level hearsay statement, and that outer level doesn't qualify for the then-existing-state-of-mind exception; and (2) the affidavit's admissibility doesn't matter here anyway. First, notice that we have hearsay-within-hearsay. The "outer" level is the doctor's affidavit (a statement made out of court, repeating some other statement). The "inner" level is the pedestrian's statement to the doctor. Each must satisfy a hearsay exception. It's true that the inner statement arguably qualifies for the then-existing-state-of-mind exception (though even this is far from clear, since under FRE 803(3) "A statement of ... belief to prove the fact ... believed" does not qualify for the exception). But the *outer* statement is not a statement about *the declarant's* then-existing state of mind — for this purpose, the declarant is the doctor, and he's not summarizing his own then-existing state of mind (except insofar as he's making a statement of what he currently remembers the pedestrian to have said, which is inadmissible since FRE 803(3) denies the state-of-mind exception for "a statement of memory ... to prove the fact remembered"). Since one of the two levels is inadmissible hearsay, the entire statement-within-a-statement is inadmissible. Nonetheless, as described in Choice (D) above, the statement need not be admissible to be considered by the judge in making a preliminary admissibility ruling.

[Q3147]

3.   **C**   This answer is correct because the beatings would tend to prove that the killing was not accidental. Under FRE 404(b), "Evidence of other crimes, wrongs, or acts is not admissible to prove the character of a person in order to show action in conformity therewith." So if the prosecution were offering the prior beatings on the theory that "These beatings showed that the defendant had a violent character, making it more likely that he acted violently on this occasion," the evidence would be barred by the above-quoted portion of 404(b). However, FRE 404(b) goes on to say that such other-crimes-or-wrongs evidence "may, however, be admissible for other purposes, such as proof of motive, opportunity, intent, preparation, plan, knowledge, identity, or *absence of mistake or accident*..." Here, that's exactly what's happening: the defendant has claimed that the shooting was accidental, and the prosecution is offering the prior beatings to show "absence of mistake or accident." So the evidence is admissible.

(A) is wrong because the acts of violence here are not being offered as character evidence. It's true that if the evidence were offered as pure character evidence, to show that the defendant acted in conformity with his character (character for violence, say) on the present occasion, the evidence would be barred by FRE 404(b). But as described in the analysis of Choice (C), the evidence here is being offered to show "absence of mistake or accident," not to show "character," so it's admissible.

(B) is wrong, because the beatings show lack of accident regardless of who started the fights. The fact that the witness doesn't know first-hand who started the fights is irrelevant, if the mere existence of the fights would tend to show that the shooting on the present occasion was no mistake. For instance, even if the father started the two prior fights, the fact that the defendant responded by beating his father would make it at least somewhat less likely than it would otherwise be that the shooting now was an accident. So the evidence is relevant, and it's admissible (as described in Choice (C)) as tending to prove absence of accident.

(D) is wrong because evidence of a character for violence is not admissible under these circumstances. Under FRE 404(b), "Evidence of other crimes, wrongs, or acts is not admissible to prove the character of a person in order to show action in conformity therewith." So if the evidence of the prior beatings were really being offered to show that "the defendant has a character for violence, and is thus likely to have acted violently on the present occasion," the quoted sentence would apply to make the evidence inadmissible (not admissible, as this choice posits). However, "character for violence" is not what the prior-acts evidence is being offered for. Instead (as shown in the analysis of Choice (C)), it's being offered to show absence of accident, and that purpose is admissible under 404(b).

[Q3064]

4.   **A**   Only the testimony about peaceableness is a "pertinent trait" of the accused. FRE 404(a), after stating the general rule against character evidence to prove action in conformity therewith, gives an exception for "evidence of a pertinent trait of character offered by an accused[.]" Since peaceabil-

ity and truthfulness are each "traits of character," the evidence will be admissible if and only if it concerns a "pertinent" trait. What traits are "pertinent" depends on the nature of the crime charged and any defenses raised. Here, what's charged is a crime that involves violence, but not untruthfulness. Therefore, the accused's reputation for peaceableness involves a "pertinent" trait (one who is peaceable is less likely to have committed a crime involving violence). However, the accused's reputation for truthfulness would probably be held not to be pertinent (since one who is truthful is not less likely to have committed a murder than one who is untruthful). (Note, however, that if the defendant took the stand and the prosecution attacked his credibility, then the "reputation for truthfulness" testimony would become admissible because the defendant's truthfulness or untruthfulness would be in issue and thus a "pertinent" trait.)

To the extent that Choices (B), (C), and (D) each fail to admit the peaceableness testimony or admit the truthfulness testimony, it's wrong for the reasons described in the analysis of Choice (A).

[Q3164]

5. **D** Under FRE 406, evidence of an established business practice is admissible as circumstantial proof that it was followed on a particular day. So the proof here of the daily mailing practice is admissible to prove that the notice was mailed on the particular day in question.

(A) is wrong because when past conduct has a regularity amounting to a "routine practice of an organization," it is deemed relevant to the issue of whether the practice was followed on a particular day, and under FRE 406 is admissible on that issue.

(B) is wrong for the same reason Choice (D) is right: evidence of an established business practice is admissible as circumstantial proof that it was followed on a particular day, without the need to prove directly that the practice was following on the day in question.

(C) is wrong because FRE 406 says that the regular practice is admissible to prove that the practice was following on the particular occasion in question, "whether corroborated or not and regardless of the presence of eyewitnesses." So, any office employee who knows about the practice of his own knowledge may testify to it.

[Q5087]

6. **B** In general, evidence of a defendant's character or disposition is inadmissible for the purpose of proving that he acted in a particular way on a particular occasion. See FRE 404(a), first sentence. But 404(b) qualifies this rule by saying that "evidence of other crimes, wrongs, or acts ... may, however, be admissible for other purposes, such as ... absence of mistake or accident[.]" Since the defendant has claimed that he was "unaware that there was cocaine hidden in [the statue's] base," the fact that he was previously convicted of (knowingly) smuggling cocaine hidden in the base of another brass statue tends to prove absence of mistake or accident, and is thus admissible.

(A) is wrong because, although FRE 406 permits evidence of habit to be used as circumstantial evidence that on a particular occasion the defendant's conduct was consistent with his habit, such habit evidence requires a showing that the actor in question *consistently* acts in a particular way, and one prior experience is not sufficient to establish a habit.

(C) is wrong because, although evidence of a defendant's previous conduct is inadmissible if offered against him for some purposes, it may be admissible if offered against him for others. (C) is therefore overinclusive — for instance, it does not correctly reflect that the defendant's previous conduct here tends to prove absence of mistake, as discussed in Choice (B) above.

(D) is wrong because, although FRE 609(b) indeed says that evidence of a prior conviction is not usually admissible for the purpose of impeaching a witness if the conviction occurred more than ten years prior to the trial at which it is offered, the defendant's prior conviction is not being offered to impeach his credibility, but rather to establish absence of mistake.

[Q5136]

7. **A** FRE 407 seeks to encourage safety precautions by prohibiting evidence of subsequent remedial measures from being used for the purpose of showing fault or defect. Such evidence may be admissible for other purposes, however. Here, the accountant had denied ownership of the vehicle. Since it is unlikely that anyone other than the owner would arrange to have the brakes overhauled, the testimony of the mechanic is relevant to establish the accountant's ownership and should, therefore, be admitted.

(B) is wrong because of the above-stated policy of encouraging safety precautions.

(C) is wrong because the evidence is being used to establish that the accountant was the owner of the vehicle, not to establish the condition of the brakes on any particular day. (Also, the condition of the brakes on the day after the accident is relevant to show their probable condition on the day of the accident — FRE 407 keeps out this evidence if offered to show fault or defect not because it's irrelevant, but because allowing it would discourage the taking of socially-valuable remedial measures.)

(D) is wrong because the evidence is being offered to establish ownership, a purpose that is not forbidden by FRE 407's rule against the offering of remedial measures to show fault or defect.

[Q5072]

8. **A** FRE 408 excludes, when offered to prove liability for a disputed claim, evidence of "conduct or statements made in compromise negotiations regarding the claim[.]" Here, there is a disputed claim, and the manager's statement was made in an effort to settle that dispute. As such the entire statement is protected under Rule 408.

(B) is wrong because the fact that the statement denied that the slipperiness was the cause of the problem does not prevent the overall statement from falling within FRE 408's ban on "conduct or statements made in compromise negotiations regarding [a disputed] claim." Even though the manager's statement contained a large portion of self-serving "it's not our fault," the entire statement is inadmissible because uttered during the course of compromise negotiations.

(C) is wrong because, although the statement is true as far as it goes, it does not go far enough. The fact that the statement was an admission by an agent about a matter within the scope of his authority only means that the statement is not excluded as hearsay. There is another ground for exclusion, so the statement is inadmissible even though it satisfies the hearsay rule. FRE 408 excludes evidence of conduct or statements made in compromise negotiations, as further discussed in Choice (A) above.

(D) is wrong because FRE 408 protects not only offers of compromise, but also "conduct or statements made in the course of compromise negotiations regarding [a disputed] claim." The rationale is to allow the parties and counsel to speak freely during settlement negotiations, without having to worry that their statements will be used against them at trial. Here, there is a dispute, and the manager's statement was made in an attempt to settle that dispute. Therefore, the entire statement — including those portions consisting of statements of fact — would be excluded under FRE 408.

[Q7058]

9. **D** The FRE (like the common law) provide that evidence that a person carried or did not carry liability insurance is not admissible on the issue of whether that person acted negligently. (See FRE 411, first sent.) This rule bars such evidence when it is offered by a plaintiff to suggest that because the defendant was insured, the defendant was probably careless. However, the rule does not apply where the evidence is offered for some other purpose, "such as proof of agency, *ownership, or control* ..." (FRE 411, second sent.) That's what's happening here — the evidence is being used to show that because the defendant bought a liability policy on the plane, he had ownership or control of it.

(A) is wrong because the terms of the policy are not at issue, only the policy's existence. The Best Evidence Rule (B.E.R.) states that in proving the terms of a writing or a recording, where the terms are material, the original must be produced. Here, the B.E.R. would apply if the terms of the insurance policy were in question. But the terms are not in question here and are not material — Witness's testimony involves only the existence of the policy, not its terms, so the B.E.R. does not apply.

(B) is wrong because it misstates the rule. The rule against proof of liability insurance is not a general rule against "proof of insurance where insurance is not itself the issue" (as this choice asserts). Instead, the rule prohibits proof of a liability policy's existence when offered to prove negligence (and that rule applies here, as Choice (D) asserts).

(C) is wrong because such evidence is offered to suggest the defendant was probably careless. FRE 411, first sentence, says that "Evidence that a person was or was not insured against liability is not admissible upon the issue whether the person acted negligently or otherwise wrongfully." Since this choice suggests that an insured plane owner would be less likely to properly maintain the plane, it's a method of asserting the defendant's negligence, and thus flies squarely in the face of FRE 411.

[Q3136]

10. **D**   FRE 412, the federal "rape shield" provision, applicable to civil and criminal cases "involving alleged sexual misconduct," puts tight limits on evidence of an alleged victim's past sexual behavior and sexual predisposition. Except for a few narrow exceptions, evidence is inadmissible if offered either to "prove that any alleged victim engaged in other sexual behavior" or to "prove any alleged victim's sexual predisposition." Both the testimony and the court record here are evidence of the alleged victim's "other sexual behavior" and/or "sexual predisposition." Therefore, they're inadmissible under FRE 412 unless they fall within one of that rule's narrow exceptions. In criminal cases, the main exceptions are for (1) conduct with the defendant offered to support a defense of consent (covered in FRE 412(b)(1)(B)), and (2) conduct with others offered to show that the defendant was not the source of semen or the victim's injury (covered in FRE 412(b)(1)(A)). Since the defendant is relying on an alibi defense rather than on a consent defense, the first of these exceptions doesn't apply. Since the defendant is not offering the victim's history of prostitution to show that he was not the source of semen or of the victim's injuries, the second exception doesn't apply. So both pieces of evidence are excluded by FRE 412.

(A), (B) and (C) are each inconsistent with the above analysis and thus wrong.

[Q5030]

11. **C**   Prior statements that are inconsistent with a witness's present testimony impeach the witness's credibility because they tend to show that the witness's trial testimony is not believable. The prior inconsistent statement was not made under oath, and so does not fit the exemption to the hearsay rule provided by FRE 801(d)(1)(A). There is no other hearsay exception that is satisfied under the facts. Therefore, the statement is admissible only to impeach the witness and not for its truth.

(A) is wrong because, under FRE 607, "[t]he credibility of a witness may be attacked by any party, including the party calling the witness."

(B) is wrong because the prior statement of the witness is inadmissible hearsay under FRE 802 only if offered to prove that the defendant was involved in the transaction. It is not hearsay if offered to impeach the witness whose trial testimony is inconsistent with it. This is because, whether true or not, the statement is probative to show that the witness is not credible—he said one thing at trial and said something else previously.

(D) is wrong because the first part of the statement is correct but the second part is incorrect. The prior inconsistent statement was not made under oath, and so does not fit the exemption to the hearsay rule provided by FRE 801(d)(1)(A). There is no other hearsay exception that is satisfied under the facts. Therefore the statement is admissible only to impeach the witness and not for its truth. Using the statement to prove the defendant's involvement would violate FRE 802, the hearsay rule.

[Q7019]

12. **A**   Under FRE 608(b), a witness can be impeached with prior bad acts that bear upon truthfulness. Failing to stop at a stop sign has no bearing on truthfulness. As a general matter, a witness also can be impeached with evidence that contradicts a part of his testimony that bears on an important issue in dispute. However, in this case, the prior bad acts do not contradict the witness's testimony that he stopped on this occasion. Essentially, the defendant is trying to show that the plaintiff is a careless driver. Carelessness is a character trait, and evidence of a person's character is not admissible in a civil case to prove how that person acted on the occasion in question. FRE 404(a).

(B) is wrong because, under FRE 608(b), a witness can be impeached with bad acts that do not result in convictions. The reason that the prior acts here are inadmissible is not because there were no convictions, but rather because the acts have no bearing on veracity or contradiction of prior testimony.

(C) is wrong because it's factually incorrect. It's true that under FRE 608(b), a witness can be impeached with prior bad acts that bear upon truthfulness by demonstrating falsity, dishonesty, or the like; so if the prior acts bore on truthfulness, they could be used for impeachment here. But in this case, the plaintiff's prior acts may demonstrate carelessness, but they do not demonstrate dishonesty.

(D) is wrong, because the conclusion does not follow logically from the premise. A person can be acting carefully on one occasion and not another, so the prior acts are not contradictory of the plaintiff's testimony that he was careful in this instance, as this choice asserts. If the plaintiff testified that he had never run a stop sign, then the prior acts *would* contradict his testimony, and would be admissible.

[Q7012]

13. **C**   This choice is correct because the friend cannot be impeached on a collateral issue by extrinsic evidence. The manager's testimony is not relevant to any substantive issue in the case — it bears solely on the friend's credibility. Therefore, the matter is governed by FRE 608(b), which says in part that "Specific instances of the conduct of a witness, for the purpose of attacking or supporting the witness's credibility, other than conviction of crime as provided in Rule 609, may not be proved by extrinsic evidence." In other words, once a lawyer has completed cross-examination of a witness, he must be satisfied with whatever he could bring out on cross tending to show that the witness lied on a collateral matter (i.e., a matter not pertaining to the substantive issues in the case) — the lawyer may not introduce another witness, or document, to prove that the first witness lied. Here, the testimony of the manager is extrinsic evidence of specific conduct by the friend, offered for the purpose of attacking the friend's credibility. Therefore, it is barred by the just-quoted portion of 608(b).

(A) is wrong because there is no discretion to admit extrinsic evidence to impeach on a collateral issue. If the prosecutor had presented the friend with a document tending to show he had lied on his credit card application, *that* would be admissible in the judge's discretion, because the second sentence of Rule 608(b) says that "Specific instances of the conduct of a witness, for the purpose of attacking or supporting the witness's credibility ... may, however, in the discretion of the court, if probative of truthfulness or untruthfulness, be *inquired into on cross-examination* of the witness (1) concerning the witness's character for truthfulness or untruthfulness[.]" But since the testimony here is from witness 2 (the manager) about the credibility of witness 1 (the friend), it's extrinsic evidence governed by the first sentence of 608(b) (quoted in the discussion of Choice (C) above), not the sentence just quoted; therefore, the judge can't use her discretion to admit it.

(B) is wrong because, while the friend may have "opened the door" to being asked further questions about his application on cross, he did not (and could not) open the door to the use of extrinsic evidence to show he was lying. As the discussion of Choice (C) indicates, once a lawyer has completed cross-examination of a witness, he must be satisfied with whatever he could bring out on cross tending to show that the witness lied on a collateral matter (i.e., a matter not pertaining to the substantive issues in the case) — the lawyer may not introduce another witness, or document, to show that the first witness lied. So nothing the friend said could have "opened the door" to this type of extrinsic evidence.

(D) is wrong because whether the friend could have honestly misunderstood the form is irrelevant — the evidence is extrinsic evidence barred because it pertains to a collateral matter, as discussed in the analysis of Choice (C) above.

[Q3122]

14. **A** FRE 608(b) says that "Specific instances of the conduct of a witness, for the purpose of attacking or supporting the witness's credibility, other than conviction of crime as provided in rule 609, *may not be proved by extrinsic evidence.* They may, however, in the discretion of the court, if probative of truthfulness or untruthfulness, be *inquired into on cross-examination of the witness* (1) concerning the witness's character for truthfulness or untruthfulness..." The present use fits the second sentence of FRE 608(b): the giving of false testimony in a prior trial is obviously "probative of untruthfulness." And Choice's (A)'s limitation to matters "elicited from the expert on cross-examination" brings the situation into the second sentence (cross-examination) rather than the first sentence (extrinsic evidence).

(B) is wrong because, as described in Choice (A) above, the prior-bad-act evidence here can only be brought out on cross, making this choice wrong since it does not include this limitation. On the other hand, if the evidence *is* brought out on cross, it need not be supported by "clear and convincing" evidence. It's true that as a judge-made rule, the cross-examiner must have a "good-faith basis" for believing that the false-testimony episode actually occurred. But such a good-faith basis, not the possession of clear-and-convincing-evidence, is all that is required for introducing the topic on cross.

(C) is wrong because the defendant's testimony, though "collateral," would be admissible if elicited on cross-examination. If the evidence were being offered "extrinsically" (e.g., by testimony from a different witness who witnessed the false testimony), this choice would be correct — see the first sentence of FRE 608(b), quoted in the discussion of Choice (A) above. But the evidence would be allowed to be brought up ("elicited") on cross of the expert himself, even though it relates solely to credibility rather than to a substantive issue in the case (and thus concerns a "collateral matter").

(D) is wrong, because evidence of a prior bad act by the witness demonstrating the witness's poor character for truthfulness does not fall within the general ban on proof of character traits to show action-in-conformity-therewith-on-the-present-occasion. Instead, FRE 608(b) imposes specific rules governing when such evidence is admissible — as described in Choice (A), such prior-acts-of-lying evidence may be brought out only on cross of the witness whose veracity is in question, not by means of "extrinsic evidence." Therefore, Choice (D) is an incorrect statement of both the rule and the outcome.

[Q3013]

15. **A** Where the witness is an accused (a criminal defendant), FRE 609(a)(1) says that the court "shall" allow impeachment by proof of a less-than-10-year-old felony conviction, "if the court determines that the probative value of admitting this evidence outweighs its prejudicial effect to the accused."

Choice (A) exactly matches this standard. It's important to note that the conviction here was for burglary, a crime whose elements do not include "an act of dishonesty or false statement"; if the conviction *were* for such a dishonesty/false-statement crime (whether felony or misdemeanor), FRE 609(a)(2) says that it "shall" be admitted, without any provision for the trial judge to determine that its probative value outweighs its prejudicial effect to the accused.

(B) is wrong because it ignores the fact that (as described in the analysis of Choice (A) above), where the witness being impeached is a criminal defendant and the crime is not a crime of dishonesty/false-statement, the conviction is admissible only if the trial judge determines that its probative value outweighs its prejudicial effect to the accused. So on the facts here, admission is not "a matter of right" as this choice asserts.

(C) is wrong because the fact that the crime here (burglary) is not a crime of dishonesty or false statement doesn't prevent its use. Under FRE 609(a), any felony (crime punishable by at least one year in prison), or any felony or misdemeanor involving dishonesty or false statement, can be used to impeach a witness. Where the crime does not involve dishonesty, it's admissible only "if the court determines that the probative value of admitting this evidence outweighs its prejudicial effect to the accused." If it *does* involve dishonesty, admission is mandatory (with no balancing). So the fact that the crime here didn't involve dishonesty or false statement doesn't automatically block its admissibility, as this choice asserts.

(D) is wrong, because the conviction *can* be proven through intrinsic impeachment (i.e., on cross-examination of the witness being impeached). FRE 609(a) allows impeachment on these facts (as analyzed in the treatment of Choice (A) above), and that rule does not impose any requirement that the impeachment occur by means of the court record of the conviction. So impeachment by asking the witness, "Isn't it true that you were convicted ..." is proper.

[Q4044]

16. **D** FRE 615 says that "At the request of a party the court <u>shall</u> order witnesses excluded so that they cannot hear the testimony of other witnesses..." Although the eyewitness has already testified, the fact that he is expected to be re-called for further cross means that he's still to be treated as a witness who has not yet testified. By using the word "shall," the rule does not give the trial judge the discretion to allow the witness to remain. (The purpose of the sequestration rule is to prevent the witness from tailoring his testimony to that of other witnesses. This purpose would be thwarted by letting the eyewitness here be in the courtroom before his re-cross.)

(A) is wrong because the court has the discretion to permit inquiry into additional matters. FRE 611(b) says that as a general rule cross "should be limited to the subject matter of the direct examination and matters affecting the credibility of the witness." But that section goes on to say, "The court may, in the exercise of discretion, permit inquiry into additional matters as if on direct examination." The court's discretion would be especially proper in this case, since the defendant is effectively the direct examiner (because the plaintiff called the defendant as an adverse, or "hostile," witness).

(B) is wrong because leading questions are not proper on these facts. Here, if the defendant's lawyer is conducting "cross-examination" of the defendant, it must be because the plaintiff called the defendant as an adverse witness (which is, indeed, what Choice (A) specifies happened). In that scenario, this "cross" is to be treated by the court as if it were a direct exam, since the questioner is sympathetic to the witness. In that instance, the cross should not be allowed to make use of leading questions, any more than a standard direct exam may use leading questions. See FRE 611(c), stating the general rule that leading questions "should not be used on the direct examination of a witness except as may be necessary to develop the witness's testimony."

(C) is wrong because matters of credibility are within the scope of cross-examination. FRE 611(b), in defining the permissible scope of cross-examination, says that the cross may include, in addition to "the subject matter of the direct examination," "matters affecting the credibility of the witness." So the fact that credibility was not placed in issue in the direct does not bar it from being covered on cross.

[Q3153]

17. **B** The tape is admissible as a prior inconsistent statement offered to impeach the witness, but inadmissible substantively because of hearsay. First, let's consider the recording's admissibility for impeachment. FRE 613(b) implicitly allows use of extrinsic evidence to show that a witness has made a prior inconsistent statement. ("Extrinsic evidence of a prior inconsistent statement by a witness is not admissible unless the witness is afforded an opportunity to explain or deny the same and the opposite party is afforded an opportunity to interrogate the witness thereon, or the interests of justice otherwise require.") So here, once the witness said on the stand that the defendant had given a non-racial explanation for the firing, the witness's tape-recorded statement that the defendant had given a racial explanation was extrinsic evidence tending to show a prior inconsistent statement by the witness. Consequently, the statement was admissible for impeachment under FRE 613(b), since the witness was still on the stand (and thus had a chance to explain or deny the statement).

Now, let's consider substantive admissibility. Here, the tape recording is "hearsay within hearsay." The outer level is that the witness is making a recorded, and thus out-of-court, statement. The inner level is that the witness is repeating an admission made by the defendant. Here, the inner level is not inadmissible hearsay, because it falls within the exception for admissions introduced against the maker. See FRE 801(d)(2) (A statement is not hearsay if "The statement is offered against a party and is (A) the party's own statement...") But the outer level is hearsay that is not within any exception — the witness is making an out-of-court statement (the witness's words on the recording) offered to demonstrate the truth of the matter asserted (that the defendant made a certain admission to the witness). There is nothing in this statement ("The defendant told me he fired the plaintiff for racial reasons") that falls within any hearsay exception. Thus the statement can't come in for the substantive purpose of demonstrating that the defendant was racially motivated.

(A) is wrong because, as is described in the analysis of Choice (B), the recording is not admissible as "evidence of the defendant's racial motivation," which is a substantive (non-impeachment-of-the-witness) purpose.

(C) is wrong because, as is described in Choice (B), the statement is admissible for impeachment as a prior inconsistent statement of the witness.

(D) is wrong because no violation of the Constitution occurs when a person secretly records a conversation to which he is a party (and in any event, the witness was not a governmental actor, again preventing the recording from possibly being a constitutional violation).

[Q3026]

18. **C** FRE 702 imposes five requirements that expert testimony must meet in order to be admissible: (1) it must be the case that *scientific, technical, or other specialized knowledge* will *assist* the trier of fact to *understand the evidence or to determine a fact in issue*; (2) the witness must be qualified as an expert by *knowledge, skill, experience, training, or education*; (3) the testimony must be *based upon sufficient facts or data*; (4) the testimony must be the *product of reliable principles and methods*; and (5) the witness must have *applied these principles and methods reliably to the facts of the case*. The proposed testimony by the investigator meets these requirements: (1) The investigator's testimony about the speed of the train will help the trier of fact to understand the evidence in the case. (2) The facts state that the police accident investigator is experienced and has received training. (3) The investigator's testimony is based on his examination of the physical evidence, and he has stipulated that these types of physical data are the ones examined in such matters. (4) There is

no indication that the investigator's methodology is not the product of reliable principles and methods. (5) The investigator made his conclusion about the train's speed after applying his training and experience to the physical evidence of the case. Having satisfied all five requirements, the accident investigator's testimony is proper and admissible.

(A) is wrong because there is simply no principle that says that "there cannot be both lay and expert opinion on the same issue." (For instance, it is perfectly proper for one side to put on lay eyewitness opinion testimony about the approximate speed of the train, and for the other to put on expert scientific opinion on the same subject.)

(B) is wrong because there is no principle that scientific or other expert testimony must reach its conclusion with any particular degree of "scientific certainty." All that is required is that the conclusion be sufficiently "reliable." For the reasons discussed in Choice (C), this reliability standard is satisfied here. To the extent that this choice is referring to the fact that the investigator is testifying merely that the speed falls within a range, instead of giving a single number, the existence of a range does not pose a problem. (Indeed, use of a range is probably more, not less, reliable, since it's less likely to give a false impression of precision.)

(D) is wrong because the only requirements for expert testimony are those discussed in the analysis of Choice (C) above. There is no requirement that the other side have first introduced some sort of opinion evidence on the issue.

[Q3117]

19. **D** The plaintiff's testimony would be hearsay within hearsay, and the "outer level" is not within any exception. The FRE defines hearsay as "a statement, other than one made by the declarant while testifying at the trial or hearing, offered in evidence to prove the truth of the matter asserted." FRE 801(c). Anytime the evidence in question consists of an out-of-court statement by *A* repeating another out-of-court statement by *B*, you have to analyze *both* *A*'s statement and *B*'s statement — if *either* statement is hearsay not falling within any exception, the combined statement cannot come in.

Here, the "inner" level (the defendant's statement to the plaintiff's husband) is an admission being used against a party-opponent, so it falls within the admissions exception to the hearsay rule. But the "outer" level (the husband's statement to the plaintiff, "Here's what the defendant told me...") is hearsay not within any exception. First, notice that the statement ("The defendant told me he'd blow my head off one day") is being offered to prove the matter asserted: it's being offered to prove that the defendant indeed made the threat — if the defendant hadn't made the threat, the evidence would be of no probative value in the case. (The statement is also being offered for the additional not-really-hearsay inference that if the defendant made a threat to kill the husband by shooting, that's evidence tending to show that the fatal shooting of the husband by someone unknown was done by the defendant. But this "secondary" purpose doesn't detract from the fact that the primary purpose — to prove that the defendant made the threat — is a hearsay purpose.) Now, let's look at whether the husband's statement falls within any exception. It doesn't. For instance, it doesn't fall within the state-of-mind exception, because the husband wasn't saying, "I'm scared of the defendant because he threatened to kill me..." — it's offered for the pure purpose of showing that the defendant made the threat, and that purpose doesn't qualify for state-of-mind, excited-utterance, or any other exception.

(A) is wrong because the state-of-mind exception doesn't solve the problem that the husband's statement to the plaintiff is, separately, hearsay. It's true that the defendant's statement alone might well be admissible as evidence of the defendant's state of mind vis-á-vis the husband, under FRE 803(3) (covering declarant's "then existing state of mind, emotion, sensation, or physical condition"). But the problem (as further discussed in Choice (D) above) is that what's offered is what the husband said out of court that the defendant told him out of court. So if the husband's statement (the "outer" statement) is hearsay not within an exception, the fact that the defendant's statement (the "inner" statement) falls within a hearsay exception doesn't help. Here, the statement by the husband is hearsay not within any exception, as shown by the analysis in Choice (D). Therefore, the combined statements of the husband and the defendant can't come in.

(B) is wrong because the admissibility of statements made by, and offered against, a party-opponent doesn't solve the combined hearsay-on-hearsay problem present here. It's true that the defendant's statement, if made directly to the testifying witness (the plaintiff) could be repeated by her on the stand, since then it would be a statement made by a party opponent admitted against that opponent, a non-hearsay use under FRE 801(d)(2)(A). But the problem (as further discussed in Choice (D) above) is that what's offered is what the husband said out of court that the defendant told him out of court. So if the husband's statement (the "outer" statement) is hearsay not within an exception, the fact that the defendant's statement (the "inner" statement) is a non-hearsay admission doesn't help.

(C) is wrong because it mischaracterizes the evidence, and it also doesn't address the hearsay within hearsay issue. First, the answer choice characterizes the evidence incorrectly, as proof of a prior bad act, when it is being offered as a statement. Secondly, it does not address the pivotal issue: the hearsay problem presented by the husband's statement (the "outer" statement).

[Q3045]

20. **A** Hearsay is an out-of-court statement offered to prove the truth of the matter asserted in that statement. Since the statement by the dispatcher that a blue sedan was traveling at an excessive speed was made out of court, and since it was offered to prove that the defendant's blue sedan was traveling at an excessive speed, it is hearsay. No exception applies, as is analyzed below.

(B) is wrong because the "present sense impression" exception (given by FRE 803(1)), applies only to "A statement describing or explaining an event or condition *made while the declarant was perceiving the event or condition,* or immediately thereafter." The declarant would have to be the police dispatcher. But the dispatcher is extremely unlikely to have been perceiving the fact that "officers [are] in pursuit of a blue Ford sedan ... traveling ... at an excessive rate of speed" — rather, the dispatcher was almost certainly repeating information that the officers had themselves radioed to him, and he therefore did not have the requisite present sense impression.

(C) is wrong because the "past recollection recorded" exception (given by FRE 803(5)) allows a witness to read from a written record that satisfies various requirements. But here, the witness is not reading from the memorandum, she has instead used it to refresh her recollection, and that use does not qualify for the past recollection recorded exception.

(D) is wrong because the use here does not qualify for the present recollection refreshed doctrine. A witness may refresh her recollection while testifying by examining almost anything which will have that effect. She may then testify from her refreshed recollection, but *only if her testimony is otherwise admissible.* Since the statement to which the witness is attempting to testify is hearsay (the dispatcher's statement about the speed at which the officers were chasing the car), it is inadmissible, and is not made admissible by the fact that the witness properly refreshed her recollection by looking at a writing.

[Q5068]

21. **B** The plaintiff is offering the defendant's out-of-court statement to prove that the defendant was speeding. Since the statement is being offered to prove the truth of its assertion, the statement is hearsay. However, the statement will be admissible under the admission exclusion to the hearsay rule. FRE 801(d)(2)(A) gives a hearsay exclusion for a statement that is offered against a party and is "the party's own statement[.]" Since the statement was made by the defendant, and is being offered against the defendant, it meets the requirements of the just-quoted rule.

(A) is wrong because there is no basis on which to admit a prior inconsistent statement. The basic problem with the evidence here concerns hearsay, which is an out-of-court statement offered to prove the truth of its assertion. Here, if the defendant's out-of-court statement is offered to prove that the defendant was, in fact, speeding, the statement will have to be admissible *substantively* — that is, to prove that the defendant was, in fact, speeding. The out-of-court statement won't work as a substantively-admissible prior inconsistent statement, though, because although FRE 801(d)(1)(A) does give a hearsay exclusion for a prior statement of a testifying witness where the statement is "inconsistent with the declarant's testimony," that exclusion applies only where the prior statement was "given *under oath* subject to the penalty of perjury at a *trial, hearing or other proceeding, or in a deposition*." Since the defendant's prior statement during the officer's investigation was not made under oath or at a proceeding or deposition, it doesn't qualify. A second problem is that the defendant isn't the testifying witness.

Now, let's examine whether the statement can be used simply to *impeach* the defendant (in other words, call into question his truthfulness), rather than to prove substantively that the defendant really was speeding. Here, the plaintiff's counsel is trying to impeach the defendant by "extrinsic" evidence (i.e., evidence that doesn't come from the mouth of the impeached witness). But FRE 613(b) says that "Extrinsic evidence of a prior inconsistent statement by a witness is not admissible unless the witness is afforded an opportunity to explain or deny the same[.]" Since the plaintiff's counsel already had the defendant on cross and dismissed him without asking him about the prior statement, counsel has failed to comply with this rule, so the statement can't be used for impeachment except under the admission theory discussed in Choice (B).

(C) is wrong because the absence of a foundation doesn't matter here. That's because the statement is admissible as an admission by a party opponent under FRE 801(d)(2)(A), and admissions do not need any foundation to qualify under that Rule.

(D) is wrong because it fails to realize that the testimony will be admissible as an admission, for the reasons discussed in Choice (B) above.

[Q4015]

22. **D**   FRE 803(2) admits a hearsay statement that would otherwise be barred under Rule 802 where the statement "relat[es] to a startling event or condition made while the declarant was under the stress of excitement caused by the event or condition." In this case, the assault was a startling event, and the victim made the statement immediately after the beating, trying to identify the perpetrator. Thus, all the admissibility requirements of Rule 803(2), the excited utterance exception, are met.

(A) is wrong because, although the statement is hearsay, it is admissible under FRE 803(2), the excited utterance exception, as described in Choice (D) below.

(B) is wrong because the statement fits under the FRE 803(2)'s exception to the hearsay rule for excited utterances. Under the hearsay exceptions in Rule 803, there is no requirement that the declarant be made available to testify. In this case, the victim's statement would have been admissible even if she had not been available at trial. Nor is there any requirement that the declarant under an FRE 803 exception be asked about the hearsay statement.

(C) is wrong because, while the declarant does not have to die for a statement to be admissible as a dying declaration under FRE 804(b)(2), this statement fails to satisfy that exception for at least two reasons. First, the declarant has to be unavailable, as the dying declaration is one of the "declarant unavailable" exceptions of Rule 804. Here, the victim testified and so obviously is not unavailable. Second, a dying declaration is admissible only in homicide prosecutions and civil cases. This is a criminal case for aggravated assault.

[Q7037]

23. **D**   Hearsay is defined as an out-of-court statement offered to prove the truth of the matter asserted in

that statement. Since the newspaper can only be offering the journalist's statement "When I wrote the article, I believed it" in order to prove that when the journalist wrote the article, he believed in it, the statement is indeed being offered to prove the truth of the matter asserted therein. So it's hearsay, and it's not admissible unless some exception applies. No exception applies; most notably, the exception for state of mind (discussed in Choice (B) below) does not apply.

(A) is wrong because if the out-of-court statement by the journalist were admitted as evidence of with whether the article was published without malice, the statement would be being admitted to prove the truth of the matter asserted therein, and would thus be hearsay not falling within any exception.

(B) is wrong because the choice's reference to the admissibility of the declarant's "declaration of [his] state of mind" could only be a reference to FRE 803(3)'s exception for "A statement of the declarant's *then existing state of mind* ... but not including a *statement of memory or belief to prove the fact remembered or believed* unless it relates to the ... the declarant's will." Here, the journalist's statement was not about his present belief as of the moment of the statement, but rather about what he remembered his mental state to have been at the moment in the past when he wrote the article. So the statement falls within 803(3)'s inapplicability to "a statement of memory ... to prove the fact remembered." (The "fact remembered" was the journalist's prior mental state.) As the idea is often put, 803(3) does not cover "backward looking statements."

(C) is wrong because there is no rule allowing a party to put in a self-serving statement made by that party (or in this case, made by an employee that party). Indeed, one of the main purposes of the hearsay rule is to prevent a party from putting in statements made out of court by that party, for fear that these may be self-serving attempts to "manufacture evidence."

[Q5024]

24. **C** This is a multiple-level hearsay problem: the hospital record is an out-of-court statement (the "outer" level), and it contains another out-of-court statement, namely, the plaintiff's statement that she fell when the ladder collapsed (the "inner" level). Since the inner level is being offered for the truth of the matter asserted therein (that the plaintiff fell when the ladder collapsed), both levels must meet some exclusion to the hearsay rule. (See FRE 805, saying that "hearsay included within hearsay is not excluded ... if *each part* of the combined statements conforms with an exception to the hearsay rule[.]") Fortunately for the plaintiff, FRE 803(4) and (6), taken together, permit the introduction of both levels. First, FRE 803(6) grants an exception for a "record ... of conditions ... made at or near the time ... from information transmitted by, a person with knowledge, if kept in the course of a regularly conducted business activity, and if it was the regular practice of that business activity to make the ... record[.]" Here, the various facets of this rule are satisfied since: (a) the hospital regularly made such patient-intake records; (b) the record here was made at or near the time of the patient's fall; (c) the information was "transmitted by a person with knowledge" (the plaintiff); and (d) the particular record was "kept in the course of a regularly conducted business activity" (the running of the hospital).

Next, 803(4) gives a hearsay exception for the plaintiff's own statement, since that statement was "made for the purposes of medical diagnosis or treatment and describing medical history, or past or present symptoms . . . or the inception or general character of the cause or external source thereof insofar as reasonably pertinent to diagnosis or treatment." That is, the plaintiff was trying to get treatment, and was describing her present symptoms, as well as the "cause or external source" of those symptoms (the falling ladder). So each level of the hospital record is supported by its own hearsay exception.

(A) is wrong because there is no need to exclude the portion about the ladder, due to the availability of the two hearsay exceptions discussed above.

(B) is wrong because the sentence is admissible under the two hearsay exceptions discussed in Choice (C). It's true that 803(4)'s exception for "statements [made] for purposes of medical diagnosis or treatment" requires that the statement be "reasonably pertinent to diagnosis or treatment." But a terse statement about how an injury was caused — especially if not accompanied by any statements about fault — will generally satisfy the "reasonably pertinent" requirement, and the "ladder collapsed" statement here pretty clearly meets that requirement.

(D) is wrong because the statements in the record were not statements of opinion (and, indeed were not statements by the hospital personnel), so the fact that they were not made by experts in accident causation is irrelevant.

[Q5081]

25. **A** The events satisfy all the requirements of FRE 803(5)'s exception for recorded recollection (sometimes called "past recollection recorded"). These requirements are: (1) the memorandum must relate to something of which the witness once had first-hand knowledge; (2) the record must have been made by, or adopted by, the witness when the matter was fresh in the witness's memory; (3) there must currently be some impairment of the witness's memory of the events; and (4) there must be evidence that the record correctly reflects the witness's original knowledge. The tape satisfies all these elements: (1) the tape relates to something of which the witness once had first-hand knowledge, since the witness personally saw the events, including the license number; (2) the tape was made when the matter was fresh in the witness's memory, and although he didn't make it he adopted it by listening to the playback and verifying that his wife had relayed the license number correctly; (3) there is presently an impairment of the witness's memory, since he has said that he has no present memory of the license plate number; and (4) the witness's listening to it and concluding that it was accurately satisfies the requirement that the tape correctly reflects his original knowledge.

(B) is wrong because the witness is not a public official who had a duty to make the report. There is indeed an exception to the hearsay rule for public records and reports. This exception is codified in FRE 803(8), which allows the admission of "records, reports [or] statements ... of public offices or agencies" "setting forth ... (B) matters *observed pursuant to duty imposed by law* as to which matters there was a *duty to report*, excluding, however, in criminal cases matters observed by police officers and other law enforcement personnel[.]" But the public records exception does not apply in this case because the witness (the one who made the "observation") was not a public official, nor was the report he made to the police of the break-in part of an official duty. (And even if the witness *was* a police officer, the last clause quoted above starting with "excluding" would prevent the report from coming in against the defendant in the defendant's criminal trial.)

(C) is wrong because the tape recording of the call to the police falls within the past recollection recorded exception. (See the discussion of Choice (A) for why this is so.)

(D) is wrong because the witness's wife did not have to have first-hand knowledge of the license number in order for the recorded recollection exception to apply. It's true that the witness's wife was the one who "made" the recording (in the sense that she was the one who spoke the license number on to the tape). But the requirements of FRE 803(5)'s past recollection recorded exception do not require that witness be the one who physically made the record. All that 803(5) requires in this respect is that the record be one that is "made *or adopted* by the witness when the matter was fresh in the witness's memory," and that the witness have had first-hand knowledge. Here, when the witness immediately listened to the playback and pronounced the relayed number correct, the witness adopted the record; since he had the first-hand knowledge about the license number, the first-hand knowledge requirement is also satisfied.

[Q3040]

26. **C** FRE 803(7) gives a hearsay exception for "evidence that a matter is *not included in the ... records*

... kept in accordance with [the business records exception], to *prove the nonoccurrence or nonexistence of the matter*[.]" This exception applies perfectly here: the editor has kept a business record of all retraction demands received by the newspaper, and is submitting here evidence that no retraction demand from the businessman is included in that business record. So this can be used to show that no such retraction demand was received by the paper.

(A) is simply wrong as a matter of law: where a record is kept that satisfies the business records exception, absence of a notation *can* be used as evidence that an event did not occur, as further described in Choice (C) above.

(B) is wrong because the fact that evidence is self-serving is not, alone, sufficient to make it inadmissible.

(D) is wrong because, although almost anything may be used by a witness to refresh his recollection, the fact that a document was so used is not sufficient to permit its admission into evidence.

[Q5025]

27. **C** Since an employer is vicariously liable for the negligence of an employee committed within the scope of employment, statements tending to establish that the accident resulted from the deliveryman's negligence are relevant in the plaintiff's action against the restaurant. The evidence should, thus, be admitted unless excluded under the hearsay rule. Hearsay is an out-of-court statement offered to prove the truth of the matter asserted. These facts raise what is sometimes called a multiple-level hearsay problem (i.e., an out-of-court statement that contains another out-of-court statement). This is so because the deliveryman's testimony at the reckless driving trial was not made during the negligence trial and so is an "out-of-court" statement, and because the evidence of his statement is contained in a transcript which was also not made as part of the negligence trial and so is an "out-of-court" statement. In order for multiple-level hearsay to be admissible, each level must be separately admissible. (See FRE 805, saying that "hearsay included within hearsay is not excluded ... if *each part* of the combined statements conforms with an exception to the hearsay rule[.]")

The first level of hearsay is the testimony by the deliveryman at the reckless driving trial. But FRE 801(d)(2)(D)'s vicarious admission provision gives a hearsay exclusion for an agent's (including an employee's) statement concerning a matter within the scope of his employment, made while the agency (employment) relationship existed. (Note that under this provision — and in contrast to the common law — an agent's statement concerning a matter within the agency relationship qualifies, even if the principal, i.e., the employer, did not authorize the making of the statement.) The deliveryman's statement therefore qualifies as a vicarious admission, making it not hearsay.

The second level of hearsay is the transcript. Since it was made by a public official (the court reporter), regarding "matters observed pursuant to duty imposed by law as to which matters there was a duty to report" (that the deliveryman made the admission), the transcript qualifies as a public record or report under FRE 803(8)(B).

(A) is wrong because, under FRE 804(b)(1), prior testimony is admissible as an exception to the hearsay rule *only if the party against whom it is offered had an incentive and an opportunity to cross-examine* when the testimony was first given. Since the restaurant was not a party to the proceeding at which the deliveryman's testimony was given, the testimony does not qualify for admission under this exception.

(B) is wrong because the "past recollection recorded" exception (FRE 803(5)) applies only where (1) it concerns a matter about which a witness (the person on the stand) "once had knowledge but now has insufficient recollection"; and (2) the record was "made or adopted by the witness when the matter was fresh in the witness's memory[.]" Since the deliveryman never "made or adopted" the transcript, the only witness whose sponsorship of the record could possibly qualify was the court reporter who made the transcript. But the court reporter is not a "witness" here, and is not stating that his memory is now insufficient. (In any event, even if the past recollection recorded exception applied, it would only allow the transcript to be "read into evidence," not received as an exhibit as the restaurant is requesting.)

(D) is wrong because, while the facts do present a serious hearsay issue, the combination of the vicarious admission exclusion and the public records exception make the transcript admissible, as described in Choice (C) above.

[Q5040]

28. **A**   FRE 803(18), the learned treatise exception, provides that if the court finds a publication to be a reliable authority, then "statements" in it may be read into evidence, but that the publication may not be received as an exhibit (which is what would have to happen if the jury were to "examine the book" as the question asks). Thus, the jury is not allowed to bring learned treatises into the jury room — there is a concern that if juries were allowed unrestricted access to the whole publication, they might rely on parts of the publication that are not germane to the case. Moreover, the intent of the rule is that juries need to be guided through the pertinent parts of the publication by the testifying experts.

(B) is wrong because FRE 803(18), the learned treatise exception, allows statements from a treatise to be read into evidence where the treatise is "called to the attention of an expert witness" and is found to be reliable by the court. The rule does not require that an expert rely on the treatise. In this case, the publication was called to the attention of the defendant's expert.

(C) is wrong because it's not enough that one expert testifies that the treatise is reliable. FRE 803(18) allows statements from a treatise to be read into evidence when the treatise is *established as a reliable authority* by the testimony or admission of the witness or by other expert testimony or by judicial notice." In this case, one expert testified that the publication was reliable, but the other expert contests that assertion. The decision on reliability is for the court; it is not correct to say that the court should find the publication reliable simply because one expert has found it to be so. In addition, the rule allows "statements" from a learned treatise to be read into evidence, but does not allow the publication to be received as an exhibit (which would be required if the jury were to "examine the book" as the question asks).

(D) is wrong because, although the statement is true so far as it goes, it does not mean that the jury gets to consider any evidence that the parties wish to present. FRE 803(18), the learned treatise exception, requires the judge to determine that the publication is reliable before it can be considered by the jury. In addition, the rule allows "statements" from a learned treatise to be read into evidence, but does not allow the publication to be received as an exhibit (and since the question is asking whether the court should allow the jury to "examine the book," this should only happen if the book was received as an exhibit).

[Q7005]

29. **B**   The victim's statement about the defendant was hearsay, but was properly admitted under FRE 804(b)(2)'s "dying declaration" exception, because it was made by a person now unavailable to testify, believing he was about to die, concerning personal knowledge of the cause of death, and the statement is offered at either a criminal homicide trial or a civil wrongful death suit. Since that statement came in, his prior inconsistent statement (about Jack) can be used to impeach his credibility, since hearsay declarants *can* be impeached. Note that this impeaching evidence would not be admissible *substantively,* since it does not fulfill the requirements of 801(d)(1)(A)'s prior-inconsistent-statement hearsay exclusion — the prior inconsistent statement is only admissible substantively if the statement was made under oath, at a prior proceeding, subject to perjury, with the declarant now being the testifying witness; here, the victim's statement about Jack was not made under oath or at a proceeding.

(A) is wrong because the witness's testimony does not fit an exception to the hearsay rule; it's inadmissible hearsay. In particular, the statement does not fit the most obvious exception, the "dying declaration" exception to the hearsay rule, because the victim did not have an impending sense of death when he made the statement. FRE 804(b)(2). The rationale behind the exception is that no one wants to die with a lie on his lips; where a person thinks he's going to *live*, this is not applicable. (Also, the statement will not be admissible *substantively* as a prior inconsistent statement, for the reasons discussed in Choice (B) above.)

(C) is wrong because the FRE do not condition the admissibility of a statement on whether it addresses an "ultimate issue." See FRE 704(a).

(D) is wrong, because the testimony *is* relevant to a substantive issue in the case. A piece of evidence is logically relevant if it tends to prove or disprove a material fact. FRE 401. If the victim's prior statement about Jack is true, it will tend to prove that the victim was lying about the defendant's stabbing him, and thus make it less likely that the defendant is guilty of murder. As a result, it's *extremely* relevant!

[Q4022]

30. **A**   First, this is hearsay: the declarant's statement "I killed him" is being offered to show that she did indeed kill him. But FRE 804(b)(3) (one of the declarant-unavailable exceptions) gives a hearsay exception for a statement by a now-unavailable witness which "was at the time of its making so far contrary to the declarant's pecuniary or proprietary interest, or so far tended to subject the declarant to civil or criminal liability . . . that a reasonable person in the declarant's position would not have made the statement unless believing it to be true." The woman's statement in the deposition qualifies, since: (1) her subsequent death of course makes her unavailable; (2) the statement, viewed as of the time she made it, potentially subjected her to such civil and criminal liability that she would be unlikely to have made it unless she believed it was true. 804(b)(3) adds a further requirement, that a statement "tending to expose the declarant to criminal liability and offered to exculpate the accused is not admissible unless corroborating circumstances clearly indicate the trustworthiness of the statement." Here, the fact that the woman was known to have quarreled with and disliked the victim, and the fact that the victim's family chose to bring civil suit against the woman, supply the required corroborating circumstances to indicate the statement's trustworthiness.

(B) is wrong because, although there is indeed an exception for former testimony given under oath at a trial or other proceeding, the exception applies only if "the party against whom the testimony is now offered . . . had an opportunity and similar motive to develop the testimony by direct, cross, or redirect examination." See FRE 804(b)(1). Since the "party against whom the testimony is now offered" is the government, the statement could qualify only if the government had the opportunity and similar motive to "develop" (i.e., undermine) the woman's testimony in the earlier civil suit; since the prosecution was not part of that suit, this requirement was not satisfied.

(C) is wrong because, while the statement is indeed hearsay, the declaration-against-interest exception applies, as described in Choice (A) above.

(D) is wrong because, although the Best Evidence Rule does indeed sometimes require an original, FRE 1003 says that "a duplicate is admissible to the same extent as an original unless (1) a genuine issue is raised as to the authenticity of the original or (2) in the circumstances it would be unfair to admit to duplicate in lieu of the original." There is no indication on these facts that either of these problems is present.

[Q6001]

31. **D**   FRE 201(b) allows judicial notice of a fact that is "not subject to reasonable dispute" because it is either "(1) generally known within the territorial jurisdiction of the trial court" or "(2) capable of

accurate and ready determination by resort to *sources whose accuracy cannot reasonably be questioned.*" The fact here would be very unlikely to fall within category (1), since even the federal judge seems not to know it. So the only hope is category (2). The clerk of the state court might be a reasonably accurate source, but not a "source whose accuracy cannot reasonably be questioned." For instance, the clerk might be relying on a faulty memory, or might have some hidden motive to intentionally misstate the facts. In any event, the custom in most courts (including ones following FRE 201) is not to take judicial notice of the determinations of courts other than the court which is doing the noticing.

(A) is wrong, because a certified copy would be permitted under FRE 902(4). FRE 902 lists a number of categories of documents that are self-authenticating. One of these is 902(4)'s category of "certified copies of public records," defined to include "a copy of an official record or report ... certified as correct by the custodian or other person authorized to make the certification." A certified copy of a record of conviction would clearly fall within this definition.

(B) is wrong, because testimony of someone who heard the sentence be issued would be a good means of authentication. FRE 901(b) gives a number of illustrations of acceptable methods of authentication, i.e., of (in FRE 901(a)'s language) "evidence sufficient to support a finding that the matter in question is what its proponent claims." Since the claim is that there has been a conviction, authentication consists of evidence sufficient to find that the conviction really occurred. The first illustration given in FRE 901(b) is (1), "Testimony of witness with knowledge" — the text of (1) recognizes authentication by means of "testimony that a matter is what it is claimed to be." So here, the plaintiff's testimony, from his own personal knowledge, that a sentence of conviction was pronounced, will qualify.

(C) is wrong because the defendant's statement would be admissible as an admission. The testimony here is a classic admission by a party-opponent. Under FRE 801(d)(2), an out-of-court statement is admissible (as an exclusion to the hearsay rule) if it is "offered against a party and is (1) the party's own statement..." Since the "oral admission" by the defendant that he had been convicted is a statement by the defendant being offered against him, the testimony by the witness is admissible.

[Q3167]

32. **D** Under common law, self-identifying statements are not sufficient to establish the source of a writing. FRE 902 creates some exceptions to this rule, but letterheads are not among them.

(A) is wrong because an expert may state an opinion concerning the authorship of a particular writing based upon a comparison of the writing in question with an exemplar of the defendant's writing. See FRE 901(b)(2), giving as an illustration of proper authentication "comparison by ... expert witnesses with specimens which have been authenticated."

(B) is wrong because the trier of fact may form a conclusion about the authorship of a particular writing based upon its own comparison of that writing with an exemplar of the defendant's handwriting.

(C) is wrong because any person may testify to what he had seen, if what he has seen is relevant to the facts in issue.

[Q4058]

33. **C** FRE 1006 says that "the contents of voluminous writings, recordings or photographs which cannot conveniently be examined in court may be presented in the form of a chart, summary, or calculation." The individual timesheets here meet the "voluminous writings" standard, since they would be almost daily over a five-year timeframe, a stack that would be hard for the judge or jury to examine in court. FRE 1006 also says that "the originals, or duplicates, shall be made available for examination or copying, or both, by other parties at reasonable time and place." So the fact that the underlying timesheets were made available to the client prior to trial, as specified in this choice, is

a necessary condition for the summaries' admission under FRE 1006. By the way, the summaries: (1) become evidence (i.e., they're not just non-evidentiary testimonial aids); and (2) substitute for the underlying originals, which means that those originals must be independently admissible. Here, the underlying timesheets are hearsay, but they fall within FRE 803(6)'s business records exception.

(A) is wrong because the summary-of-voluminous-writings provision of FRE 1006 applies as described in Choice (C) above, and that provision does not require that the underlying writings being summarized be offered into evidence (although they may be).

(B) is wrong because, under FRE 1006, the summaries can come in as substantive evidence, as described in Choice (C) above.

(D) is wrong because the summaries can come in under FRE 1006 even if the underlying timesheets have not been lost. If you picked this choice, you may be thinking of FRE 1004(1), under which the B.E.R. can be satisfied by something other than the original writing or a duplicate thereof (e.g., a summary) if "all originals are lost or have been destroyed, unless the proponent lost or destroyed them in bad faith[.]" But FRE 1006 provides an independent means of getting summaries into evidence (one that does not depend on loss of originals), and that means 1006 is available here as discussed in Choice (C) above.

[Q6002]